C0-ATX-674

Studies in Housing

& Minority Groups

PUBLICATIONS OF THE

COMMISSION ON RACE AND HOUSING

Where Shall We Live? Report of the Commission on Race and Housing

Residence and Race: Final and Comprehensive Report to the Commission on Race and Housing by DAVIS MC ENTIRE

The Demand for Housing in Racially Mixed Areas: A Study of the Nature of Neighborhood Change by CHESTER RAPKIN and WILLIAM G. GRIGSBY

Privately Developed Interracial Housing: An Analysis of Experience by EUNICE and GEORGE GRIER

Property Values and Race: Studies in Seven Cities by LUIGI LAURENTI

Studies in Housing and Minority Groups edited by NATHAN GLAZER and DAVIS MC ENTIRE

Studies in Housing & Minority Groups

Edited by NATHAN GLAZER
AND DAVIS McENTIRE

With an Introduction by Nathan Glazer

SPECIAL RESEARCH REPORT
TO THE COMMISSION ON RACE
AND HOUSING

UNIVERSITY OF CALIFORNIA PRESS
BERKELEY AND LOS ANGELES 1960

Prepared under the direction of
DAVIS McENTIRE, *Research Director*
Commission on Race and Housing

UNIVERSITY OF CALIFORNIA PRESS
BERKELEY AND LOS ANGELES
CALIFORNIA
CAMBRIDGE UNIVERSITY PRESS
LONDON, ENGLAND

LIBRARY OF CONGRESS CATALOG CARD NUMBER: 59-13462
PRINTED IN THE UNITED STATES OF AMERICA

Foreword

Brought together in the present volume are the findings of seven local studies prepared for the Commission on Race and Housing in connection with a broader investigation of housing problems involving minority racial and ethnic groups. The present studies have been edited and prepared for publication by Nathan Glazer and Davis McEntire. Mr. Glazer has written an introduction summarizing the main conclusions which emerge from this group of studies considered together.

Where the members of minority racial and ethnic groups should live—whether in segregated communities or dispersed through the general housing supply—is a social problem of large and growing importance in American cities. To inquire into this problem was the purpose of the Commission on Race and Housing, formed in 1955. The Commission is an independent, private citizens' group, not a part of any other organization. Its work was made possible by a grant of $305,000 from the Fund for the Republic. The Fund's participation was limited to financial assistance, and it is not in any way otherwise responsible for the studies carried out for the Commission or for its conclusions.

The following persons have served on the Commission in their individual capacities and not as representing any organization or group:

Gordon W. Allport
Professor of Psychology, Harvard University, Cambridge, Massachusetts.

Elliott V. Bell

Chairman of the Executive Committee and Director, McGraw-Hill Publishing Company; Editor and Publisher, *Business Week,* New York.

Laird Bell

Attorney: Bell, Boyd, Marshall and Lloyd, Chicago.

Reverend John J. Cavanaugh, C.S.C.

Director, University of Notre Dame Foundation, Notre Dame, Indiana.

Henry Dreyfuss

Industrial Designer, South Pasadena, California, and New York.

Peter Grimm

Chairman of the Board and Director, William A. White and Sons, New York.

Col. Campbell C. Johnson

Assistant to the Director, Selective Service System, Washington, D. C.

Charles S. Johnson

President, Fisk University, Nashville, Tennessee. Deceased.

Charles Keller, Jr.

President, Keller Construction Corporation, New Orleans, Louisiana.

Clark Kerr

President, University of California, Berkeley.

Philip M. Klutznick

Chairman of the Board, American Community Builders, Inc., Park Forest, Illinois.

Henry R. Luce

Editor-in-Chief, *Time, Life, Fortune, Architectural Forum, House and Home,* and *Sports Illustrated,* New York.

Stanley Marcus

President, Neiman-Marcus, Dallas, Texas.

Harold C. McClellan

President, Old Colony Paint and Chemical Company, Los Angeles. Resigned following appointment as Assistant Secretary of Commerce in 1955.

Ward Melville

President, Melville Shoe Corporation, New York.

Francis T. P. Plimpton
Attorney: Debevoise, Plimpton and McLean, New York.
R. Stewart Rauch, Jr.
President, The Philadelphia Saving Fund Society, Philadelphia.
Robert R. Taylor
Secretary and Executive Director, Illinois Federal Savings and Loan Association, Chicago. Deceased.
John H. Wheeler
President, Mechanics and Farmers Bank, Durham, North Carolina.
Earl B. Schwulst, Chairman
President and Chairman of the Board, The Bowery Savings Bank, New York.

Professor Robert K. Merton of Columbia University, Professor Stuart W. Cook of New York University, and Dr. Robert C. Weaver, formerly State Rent Administrator of New York, served as research advisors to the Commission.

The central focus of research undertaken for the Commission was on the problem of inequality of housing opportunity connected with racial or ethnic distinctions, with emphasis on the situation of Negroes, Puerto Ricans, Mexican-Americans, and Orientals. The research was national in scope and endeavored to comprehend all major ramifications of a very complex problem —its causes, impacts and consequences, and directions of change. Some thirty special studies and research memoranda were prepared for the consideration of the Commission by the Research Director, his assistants, and coöperating social scientists in a dozen universities.

The Commission has previously published its own conclusions and recommendations in *Where Shall We Live?* (University of California Press, 1958). A comprehensive report of the findings of the entire study, by the Research Director, is pending publication. In addition, several of the particular inquiries which are of wide interest have been or will be published; the others are available in the library of the University of California, Berkeley.

In authorizing publication of research reports, including the present collection of studies, the Commission on Race and Housing believes that the research was conscientiously and competently carried out, in accordance with high scientific standards. However, the Commission assumes no responsibility for the accuracy of specific data in the various reports, nor does it necessarily endorse all of the interpretations and conclusions drawn by the authors. Persons desiring to know the position of the Commission are referred to its own report.

EARL B. SCHWULST, CHAIRMAN
Commission on Race and Housing

New York City

Contents

Tables

Maps

The Contributors

NATHAN GLAZER, sociologist and editor, is the author of *American Judaism* (Chicago, 1957), first presented as the Walgreen Lectures at the University of Chicago in 1955. He is co-author of *The Lonely Crowd* (Yale, 1950) and *Faces in the Crowd* (1952) and has published many articles on ethnic groups, prejudice, and social theory. He was a Guggenheim Foundation Fellow in 1954–1955 and is presently on the staff of the Schools and Mental Health Research Project of Bank Street College of Education, New York. Now a member of the faculty of Smith College, Mr. Glazer has taught previously at the University of California, Berkeley, and Bennington College. He was for nine years an associate editor of *Commentary*, has also been an editor of Doubleday Anchor Books, and is presently an editor for Random House-Modern Library.

DAVIS McENTIRE, economist and professor of Social Welfare at the University of California, Berkeley, directed the research for the Commission on Race and Housing and wrote the basic report, *Residence and Race* (California, 1960). He is the author of several monographs and articles on population, ethnic relations, and housing. He is a member of the U. S. Census Bureau's Technical Advisory Committee on the 1960 Housing Census and consultant to several local housing and redevelopment agencies. He was a Guggenheim Foundation Fellow in 1953–1954, studying international population movements. On invitation of the Universities of Rome and Padua, he was awarded a Fulbright grant for research and lecturing in Italy, 1959–1960.

ROBERT A. THOMPSON, as associate director of the Atlanta Urban League since 1942, has played a leading part in bringing about improvement of housing conditions for Negroes in Atlanta. In the organization and strategy of the Atlanta Negro community, described in the report of which he is co-author, Mr. Thompson was not primarily an observer but a central figure. Formerly, he was a member of the faculty at Atlanta

University, from which he holds a Master's degree in economics. He has published an essay, "Social Dynamics in Demographic Trends and the Housing of Minority Groups" in *Phylon,* and written several unpublished reports, among which are "Assets of Negro Savings and Loan Associations and Commercial Banks, 1949–1956" and "A Suggested Proposal for Redevelopment of the Atlanta University Area."

HYLAN G. LEWIS is a former managing editor of *Phylon* and professor of sociology at Atlanta University. At present, he is associate director of the Community Service Department, Unitarian Service Committee. He is the author of *Blackways of Kent* (North Carolina, 1955) and a half dozen journal articles on race relations in the United States and Africa. Dr. Lewis has been a Social Science Research Council Fellow, Rosenwald Foundation Fellow, and during his tenure at Atlanta received a faculty fellowship from The Fund for the Advancement of Education for study of developments in interdisciplinary research and training at three universities. He has served as consultant to the Southern Regional Council, The Fund for the Advancement of Education study of school desegregation ("Ashmore Project"), and the Volta River Project Preparatory Commission, Gold Coast, British West Africa. In 1958 he made a second trip to Africa (Nigeria and Ghana) in connection with a village development project of the Unitarian Service Committee.

JACK E. DODSON is chairman of the department of sociology at the University of Oklahoma. He holds the Ph.D. in sociology from the University of Texas (1955) and conducted the comparative study of minority housing in Houston and San Antonio while a member of the sociology faculty at Texas. He has also held teaching appointments at Southwestern at Memphis and the Texas College of Arts and Industries.

FOREST E. LAVIOLETTE is professor and head of the department of sociology at Tulane University, New Orleans. He is best known for his extensive studies on assimilation of the Japanese minority in the United States and Canada, having published two books and numerous articles on the subject. His books are *Americans of Japanese Ancestry: A Study of Assimilation in the American Community* (Toronto, 1946), and *Canadian Japanese and World War II* (Toronto, 1948). A book on the Coastal Indians of British Columbia is pending publication.

JOSEPH T. TAYLOR, formerly professor of sociology and chairman of the Division of Social Sciences at Dillard University, New Orleans, is now Director of Program Development at Flanner House, Indianapolis. He has published some half dozen articles on Negro life and race relations in the South. He has been a Rosenwald Fellow, a General Education Board Fellow, and field investigator for the Carnegie-Myrdal study of the Negro in America. In New Orleans he was prominent in community affairs, serving as president of the local chapter of the Louisiana Council on Human Relations, and a board member of the Metropolitan

Crime Commission, the New Orleans Council of Social Agencies, Urban League, and Family Service Society.

GILES A. HUBERT is professor of economics at Dillard University, New Orleans. He was formerly professor and head of the Department of Economics and Business Administration at Fisk University, senior agricultural economist in the Farm Security Administration, and for several years a Foreign Service officer. He has published articles in the *Journal of Negro Education*, the *Journal of Farm Economics*, and the *Southern Economic Journal*. Professor Hubert is a resident of Pontchartrain Park, described in the study of Negro housing in New Orleans.

ELIZABETH L. VIRRICK is a Hoover Research Fellow at the University of Miami. Her work for community betterment in the Miami area has received local and national recognition. She was the organizer and has been for more than ten years chairman of the Coconut Grove Citizens' Committee for Slum Clearance. She also organized the St. Alban's Day Nursery for working Negro mothers, and was one of the organizers of the Citizens' Housing and Planning Council of Dade County. Mrs. Virrick received the Woman of the Year award for Dade County in 1949. She was co-winner in 1957 of a national essay contest sponsored by the Foundation for Social Welfare on "How to Extend Voluntary Service in Social Welfare." Her prize-winning essay has been published in *Grass Roots in Private Welfare*.

MORRIS EAGLE is assistant research professor of psychology in the Graduate School of Arts and Science, New York University. He has taught at the City College of New York and Finch College and has been a postdoctoral fellow on a Ford Foundation grant in the Research Center for Mental Health, New York University.

HARRY H. L. KITANO is assistant professor of social welfare in the University of California, Los Angeles. Formerly, he was a social worker in the International Institute of San Francisco and psychiatric social worker in the San Francisco public schools. He holds a Master's degree in social welfare and a Ph.D. in education from the University of California, Berkeley.

ALBERT J. MAYER is associate professor of sociology at Wayne State University, Detroit, and director of the Detroit Area Traffic Study, a metropolitan research organization associated with Wayne. He is a member of the Michigan Governor's Study Commission on Metropolitan Problems, the Detroit Regional Planning Commission, and the Research Committee of the Detroit Metropolitan Area. He is author of *Man's Capacity to Reproduce*, co-author of *When Labor Votes* and *Medical Public Relations*, and many journal articles. He is a resident of the racial transitional neighborhood which is the subject of his present study.

NATHAN GLAZER

Introduction

The seven studies in this volume form a small part of the research undertaken at the instance of the Commission on Race and Housing and under the direction of Davis McEntire into the housing of minority groups in the United States. The major findings and recommendations of the Commission have already been published in its report, *Where Shall We Live?* (University of California Press, 1958). The main body of the research on which these findings are based is to appear in the volume *Residence and Race,* by Davis McEntire. Other special researches undertaken for the Commission have been published or will remain in unpublished but accessible form in the library of the University of California in Berkeley. The studies were financed by a grant from The Fund for the Republic, Inc., to the Commission on Race and Housing.

Where in this extensive body of research do the following studies fit? And what contribution can they make to our understanding of the housing of American minority groups?

Generally, the studies collected in this book deal with special, local situations and try to suggest the wide range of factors which explain the outcome in terms of housing for different minority groups in different cities. As against the other research undertakings (though in order to emphasize whatever special virtues these studies may have we exaggerate the contrast), these studies deal with the special, rather than the general; with local forces, rather than national forces; with groups in their local peculiarities, rather than with groups in their large, general characteristics.

Residence and Race analyzes census data covering the entire United States, or all of urban America, or the major metropolitan centers in which minority groups play an important role. It considers the major forces that affect the housing industry: government, financial institutions, builders, real estate brokers, special agencies devoted to the problems of minority groups. Out of this, a large national picture emerges. It is a complicated picture, and one whose complexity is in no way slighted in *Residence and Race* and *Where Shall We Live?*. It is in general a picture of deprivation in housing for the Negro, the Mexican, the Oriental, and the Puerto Rican groups, a deprivation that may be traced to poverty, to prejudice and discrimination, and to the special social characteristics of the groups in question. This national picture is not a uniform one. It varies from region to region, from city to city, from group to group.

In the studies in this volume, each of which deals with the problem of a single group in a single setting, or contrasts two individual settings, we are inevitably led to focus on a somewhat different facet of the problem: not on its general character, which has already been so fully explored, but on its variations. In these studies, our attention is immediately drawn to the fact that a somewhat different picture emerges in each city, and for each underprivileged group. So whereas the main body of the research concentrated on the national problem in all its complexity, the studies collected here bring to our attention the wide range of *variation* characteristic of this problem as we move from city to city and from group to group.

It leads us to concentrate on one other aspect of the problem, too. Since these studies concentrate on individual cities, we see the whole range of forces that affect minority housing in its individual, local forms, and we see the interplay of these forces, and their outcome, in a somewhat more detailed fashion than might be observed from the national picture. Consequently we are led to consider the matter of *process:* just how forces interact to produce an outcome which, despite its great variations, is almost uniformly bad for the minority groups.

To review briefly the field that is covered: The first study describes housing for Negroes in Atlanta and Birmingham, contrasts the two situations, and considers what makes for the contrast. The second selects two other cities for contrast: San Antonio and Houston, Texas; the section on San Antonio discusses the housing of Negroes and Mexicans, the section on Houston limits itself to the study of the Negro group. The third study considers the housing of Negroes in New Orleans; the fourth the housing of Negroes in Miami. The fifth study leaves the South, and the Negroes, and describes the housing of the Puerto Rican group in New York. The sixth deals with the Japanese in the Bay Area (San Francisco and Berkeley). The last study shifts the focus from the general housing problem of some group in some city to a narrower one: it considers a single case of Negro "invasion" in a middle-class area in Detroit.

This is a wide range of variation indeed, illustrating the entire range of possibilities from extreme to relatively mild deprivation. Our approach here will be to consider what factors are associated with the varying degrees of prejudice, such as to suggest to us how, by either presently ongoing processes or common action, the situation of the most deprived groups might be improved.

We might, to begin with, summarize the highly varied situations revealed in these studies by the use of two relatively simple and crude variables: the prejudice directed against a group, and the economic power of a group. Each of these variables alone, if large enough, is sufficient by itself to consign a group to poor housing. Thus, it would appear there is somewhat less prejudice against Mexicans in this country than against Negroes. Professor Dodson reports that in San Antonio the well-to-do and assimilated Mexican may live almost anywhere and is not subject to a formal Jim Crow system; the Negro does not have as wide an area in which he can live and is subject to formal rules of discrimination. On the other hand, the Negro has a somewhat higher income than the Mexican. The outcome in San Antonio is that the Negro has somewhat better housing than the Mexican—a higher degree of prejudice is here overcome by greater economic capacity. If we next consider the situation of Puerto Ricans in New York, we see a situation in which prejudice is probably lower than that faced by either Negroes or Mexicans in the South and Southwest. Economic power—and here we must compare it with that of prevailing high incomes and high rents in New York—is low. The outcome in terms of housing is poor.

The Japanese are in the most favored situation of the groups discussed. Economically, they are hardly inferior to the white group; prejudice against them has been sharply reduced (indeed, in certain limited situations—that of Japanese girls seeking office work, for example—the former prejudice may now have turned into a small degree of favoritism). Their housing is best of all.

No one, we are sure, will be deceived into thinking our understanding of the variations we deal with is much advanced by our consideration of these two variables in the crude form in which they have been presented. Other factors outside them are also relevant: the two large variables themselves have other determinants, and both are interrelated. Our aim here is not to give a complete picture of the determinants of prejudice and economic power—both enormous tasks—but to point to certain analytic distinctions which the consideration of these two variables suggest and which, while not totally unfamiliar, do not, it seems to us, yet play the role in the discussion of this problem that they should, and that the studies in this volume bring out with some clarity.

First: *Prejudice in its pure form—that is to say, as unreasoning and inflexible antipathy—rarely plays a decisive role in the determination of the housing of minority groups.* It is in the South that the role of prejudice may be seen perhaps in its sharpest form. And yet even here every action of discrimination —and there is discriminatory behavior by builders, renters, lenders, government, and other groups—is based on economic factors in the situation somewhat independent of prejudice, as comes out clearly in our five southern studies. In the North the relatively small role of pure prejudice is even more striking. Negroes are highly segregated and have poor housing. But the decisive factors in this poor housing is Negro economic weakness and white middle-class fears of the deterioration of neighborhoods on Negro entry. In lower-class areas of northern cities, it is not atypical for nonwhite and white groups to live together, and for nonwhites and whites to compete for housing on roughly the same basis. Nor is there necessarily a pattern of flight of whites from such areas. Now if we were to assert that it was largely prejudice alone that prevented whites and nonwhites from living together, we would have to say that the white residents of lower-class areas are less prejudiced than the white residents of middle-class areas—which is not at all the case.

The difference, of course, is that the white residents of middle-class areas are paying for certain values that the white residents of lower-class areas do not possess. Various institutional forces protect these values—real estate brokers, financial institutions, homeowners' associations, and the like. The values of a middle-class neighborhood include such things as quiet, protection from violence, cleanliness, and good schools—none of which exist in the slums, where there is consequently nothing to protect against the presumed impact of nonwhite invasion. These values are generally seen as threatened by the entry of *any* lower-income group. Their low economic position will require crowding; this will increase noise and complicate garbage collection; responsibility for the care of the house will be diffused with greater subdivision and will in any case become more difficult because of heavier use; the number of crimes will increase; and the school will face the problem of an influx of more poorly educated, and perhaps less disciplined and educable elements.

All these are real consequences of neighborhood change: we are all aware of them; and consequently the attack on prejudice as such is often only partly relevant to a solution to the problem —better housing for minority groups. There are situations—Professor Mayer describes one in Detroit—where a group that displays relatively little prejudice will react to Negroes moving into a neighborhood in very much the way a group characterized by a high degree of prejudice would act: simply because of the fear of real consequences of the change from middle-class white to less unequivocally middle-class Negro occupancy.

Second: *A rise in the economic capacity of a group is an extremely powerful force in improving its housing, even though it may have little effect on the degree of segregation and on prejudice against it.* There are few large-scale examples of a group that contains large numbers of well-to-do and prosperous people who are poorly housed. Birmingham, as described in the study by Thompson, Lewis, and McEntire in this volume, is possibly the only example. Birmingham is also located in one of the two or three states in the Union which have been consistently most extreme in their treatment of the Negro and most resistant to modern forces, whether economic or political, which have tended to improve the Negro's position. When prejudice is at a maximum, even a great degree of economic power will be helpless. (By contrast, as we will see in our fifth point, when prejudice is replaced by a positive concern for a group, this may overcome the effects of the group's economic weakness.) The case of the Negro in Birmingham shows a certain measure of prosperity compared with other cities, but one which has been ineffective in improving housing for Negroes in any large degree in Birmingham. On the other hand, it seems clear that in less frozen situations—New Orleans, Houston, Atlanta, Miami—Negro housing has to some degree reflected Negro purchasing power.

In certain ways, the North presents more problems for upper-income Negroes than the South, for here the problem is not only to get good housing—and if Atlanta can supply a Negro market for extensive Negro subdivisions, unquestionably this can also be done in northern cities—but to get good, *unsegregated* housing.

Here we return to our first point: the middle class, including the Negro middle class, looks for more than housing. It looks for neighborhoods. Certainly one of the marks of status for a middle-class neighborhood in which Negroes live is the presence of whites. But this is more important than simply a mark of status—it is also a sign of better neighborhood facilities.

This problem of maintaining a neighborhood in "mixed" form after middle-class Negroes begin to move in is discussed in some detail in Professor Mayer's paper. It is different from the problem of simply "getting housing." And here we deal with another generalization.

Third: *The differences between different nonwhite groups, and between nonwhite and various white groups, are large, and these differences affect the capacity of each group to maintain a middle-class neighborhood.* In the previous section we have said that Negro housing in certain southern cities has reflected differences in Negro purchasing power. The difference has not been directly proportional to the purchasing power. But now we must consider differences in the *quality* of the purchasing power of different groups which have apparently been taken into account by builders and lenders, as we can see from almost every report in this volume, and that are not reflected in gross income statistics.

To begin with, it turns out that at the same income level non-whites will spend less for housing than whites. (*Residence and Race*, chapter viii.) The same income, we also know, will have somewhat different home-buying power, depending on whether it comes from the main earner or from the main earner supplemented by other earners, from a fixed salary or from more variable wages, and so on. So as against total income, we must also consider the "quality" of income in terms of home-buying or renting power. Not only is Negro income lower than white income; its quality is also poorer at the same levels. So crude figures will show an economic power for Negroes that the analysis of given situations will probably not support.

But these differences in use of income and quality of income (how many earners, from what sources, how dependable, and so on) are only the most obvious of the differences between groups. Another important difference is the proportion of the group made up of middle-class and lower-class families, and the actual or potential supply of middle-class or lower-class families. For example, the decline of anti-Japanese prejudice is in part because the entire Japanese group is by now of middle-class or approaching middle-class status. If there were only a few middle-class Japanese, and if there were a host of lower-class Japanese forced to live under crowded conditions, etc., there would be a fear—whether legitimate or not may for the moment be disregarded—by the white middle-class homeowners that the moving in of the middle-class element precluded the moving in of lower-class elements. There is one simple way in which the high rents may be overcome by people desperate for housing; i.e., by subdivision and crowding. White homeowners are guaranteed against this outcome in the case of the Japanese by the fact that there is no large supply of lower-class Japanese remaining in this country, and they know there cannot be many owing to the strict immigration laws which prevent their entry.

The matter is quite otherwise in the case of Negroes, and, in New York, of Puerto Ricans. The supply of lower-class and relatively impoverished members of the groups is for all practical purposes unlimited, owing to the large numbers of poor Negroes in the rural South, and poor Puerto Ricans on the island.

However, is it not simple prejudice to discriminate against middle-class members of this group because lower-class members do have a downward effect on residential areas? Again, this is not a complete statement of the case, for just as the quality of the same gross income differs in home-purchasing and renting power, the quality of the same degree of middle-class status (though hardly as simply measurable as gross income!) will also differ from group to group. The recency of such status will affect behavior: for example, it may lead to less satisfactory school attitudes; it leads, as Professor Mayer points out in his Detroit study, and as may be observed in new Atlanta subdivisions, to a different age distribution in which the well-to-do in such groups will tend to be older and to be childless or have very few children. This again affects the character of a neighborhood. If there were very large middle-class groups among the Negroes and Puerto Ricans, such that an unself-conscious middle-class culture could be created, we would be in a position to see just what the power of prejudice in the North was in restricting the housing of such groups.

In order to make clearer this point of the difference in the qualities of the middle class in different groups, it might be pointed out that the various lower classes differ greatly in certain respects that are critical for neighborhoods. Thus, lower-class Negroes in northern cities have high crime rates. Other lower-class groups against whom prejudice has been fairly strong in the past—Chinese, Jews, and Japanese—had lower crime rates. These certainly reflected differences of what we may call "culture." Again, discriminatory behavior on the basis of such differences, insofar as they are relevant to affecting the qualities of neighborhoods, would exist even in the absence of prejudice.

Fourth: *The dynamic elements in the situation, in addition to prejudice, are economic capacity—kinds of jobs and income—and middle-class characteristics, as revealed in attitudes toward education, crime, neighborhood facilities, and the like.* These are *dynamic* elements in the situation, for a group that gravitates into occupations of high status and high income, and that accompanies this movement with the existence or development of "middle-class" attitudes, will tend to weaken prejudice against it, and to acquire a share in the housing market equivalent to its economic power. Now prejudice will *affect* its capacity to get good jobs and earn high incomes; prejudice too will *affect* its acquisition of middle-class traits. We deal with an interrelated system. But to say that all three dynamic factors (to limit ourselves for the moment to economic capacity, middle-class traits, and prejudice) are interrelated is not to say that the only strategic place necessarily to attack the interrelated system is at the point of prejudice. Thus, even in the presence of prejudice some economic advancement and some middle-class traits may exist (consider the Japanese, as described in Professor Kitano's paper); these may then ultimately serve to weaken prejudice. Certainly the movement may proceed in the opposite way: the weakening of prejudice may improve the economic capacity of the group. But an attack at all points, to the extent that the forces of society and the group itself permit, would seem wisest.

A corollary of this statement—and one which I believe to be true—is that housing is not dynamic as an element in improving the general position of groups in society: it is not dynamic in the same way that provision of sustenance is not dynamic, though both are equally necessary. One can see—as one possibility which would support this view—government measures in the form of low-rent housing, easy credit, and the like that might raise the level of housing for nonwhite groups to that of white groups of the same income. This might not affect, however, either prejudice or economic capacity or middle-class attitudes—it is these that are dynamic elements in the situation. These, of course, may be influenced by many social measures, and yet good housing is one of those that is not likely to have any "multiplier effect." While poor housing can defeat efforts to rise in the social scale, by the steady drain on personal and emotional resources created by crowding, dirt, noise, and the like, good housing is by itself not sufficient to start any such movement. Here I believe we understand the matter better than certain naïve reformers of the 1930's who attributed large dynamic effects to slums or to good housing.

Fifth: *Even though differences in the economic and social qualities of groups play a dynamic role in affecting their housing, a reduction of prejudice and discrimination will by itself be sufficient to improve greatly the housing of nonwhite groups.* This is almost a tautology: yet we have so strongly emphasized the power of certain social developments to affect the over-all and housing position of a group that we must point out again that tolerance may balance out even great weaknesses in economic capacity, and even weaknesses in capacity to maintain good neighborhoods. Thus, in these studies we see the importance of differences in prejudiced attitudes in affecting housing for the Negroes in various southern cities. In Houston and New Orleans, liberal-minded builders—and in both cases, the liberal-mindedness was related to the fact that some of the builders were Jewish—led to better housing for Negroes than market forces alone might have provided. Then again, changes in government regulations on mortgages, positive efforts to see that government money made available to the housing industry went to benefit all groups, helped provide housing for Negroes when their economic power alone was insufficient. Certainly the lack of prejudice and discrimination, and more important, the introduction of positive measures to balance the weakness of many generations of impoverishment and depressed social conditions, will by itself do much to improve the housing conditions of Negroes.

Sixth: *It is likely that color alone, serving as an almost unmistakable cue to behavior, plays a dynamic role in the situation. And for this reason real changes in the character of the Negro group are likely to have less effect on their housing than real changes in the character of the Mexican or Puerto Rican group.*

It is the unfortunate fate of the Negroes that they may be unmistakably identified, and that what we might call "assimilation" to American middle-class ways of life, which is proceeding rapidly among them as their income rises, as they achieve better occupational positions, and as more of them come to the North and West, does not make it any less difficult to identify them as Negroes. The opposite is true of European ethnic groups; middle-class Italians and Jews are not particularly identifiable as Italian or Jewish, because their identifiability originally rested on cultural traits much more heavily than on physical traits. The Mexicans and Puerto Ricans fall somewhere between the position of the Italians and Jews and the Negroes. As they become middle-class, it becomes harder to identify them unambiguously.

These differences in identifiability will inevitably have consequences for the fate of these groups as they rise in the social scale. A middle-class Puerto Rican or Mexican neighborhood will not be unambiguously definable as such; a middle-class Negro neighborhood will be so definable. Thus previous settlers in such a neighborhood (assuming such a neighborhood is being created by a process of ethnic succession) will have a much clearer symbol to react to in the case of Negroes than if the newcomers are Mexican or Puerto Rican.

The issue is not identifiability alone: Orientals may also be unambiguously defined. *Color* alone plays a role in the American system of prejudice, as Warner and Srole pointed out in *The Social Systems of American Ethnic Groups.* Groups are ranged according to the degrees of their darkness. (This is not to say at all that color is the *exclusive* determinant of prejudice, for groups are also ranged according to poverty and social characteristics.) The Oriental groups do not fall into this color range, and although prejudice against them in the past has been intense, it has been based on economic competition, on certain social characteristics of these groups, and on their relationship to foreign states. The more fundamental color prejudice did not develop against them.

And again—to clarify this point—we do not mean to suggest that there is necessarily any primal reaction to dark-skinnedness among white Americans. The color reaction is clearly linked to the experience of two hundred years of slavery. This has left deep traces in the American mind, as well as, of course, in the Negro mind, that a hundred years of freedom have been insufficient to eradicate. Insofar as a group participates in the traits characteristic of the Negroes, it suffers. This explains, I think, the rapid change in attitudes toward Orientals—they had not been part of the experience of slavery, which has marked whites almost as deeply as Negroes, nor did they physically share their traits.

We cannot understand prejudice merely as a rationale of economic exploitation—which it is—or merely as a reaction to real and unpleasant characteristics—which it also is; it is also a deep reaction to physical characteristics, which themselves have developed important and wide-ranging symbolic overtones as the result of a painful history.

In view of all the immediate work laid out for us it may seem far-fetched to consider the implications of a social situation in which Mexicans, Puerto Ricans, and Negroes show roughly the same social constitution as the rest of us. However, in the case of the Negroes such large middle-class groups are already developing. They will change greatly the whole character of anti-Negro prejudice in America. But—and this is the point of this last observation—the Negroes will still be a long way from taking up the status in American society of assimilated European ethnic groups. The Mexicans and Puerto Ricans, because of their physical characteristics, will find it easier to achieve this status.

The studies in this volume were planned and carried out in consultation with Davis McEntire. To fit them into a single volume, the authors' original reports have been substantially abridged by the editors, with a necessary minimum of rewriting for continuity. In condensed form for publication the studies were reviewed and approved by the respective authors, who are responsible for the facts and interpretations in them. June Harvey of the Commission staff prepared the index.

The present writer is alone responsible for this introduction, which has tried to draw out from the several studies implications they have suggested to him as to the significance of the variations among groups and local situations, and as to the nature of some of the processes affecting the housing of racial and quasi-racial groups in America.

ROBERT A. THOMPSON, HYLAN LEWIS
AND DAVIS MCENTIRE

I

Atlanta and Birmingham
A Comparative Study in Negro Housing

Those acquainted with the South know that there is no one "South," but many and diverse "Souths." The status of the Negro, the opportunities open to him, and the social and economic progress he has made are not everywhere the same. This is nowhere more apparent than in housing; and nowhere, perhaps, is the difference in what he has been able to accomplish more striking than when we compare Atlanta, Georgia, and Birmingham, Alabama. The two cities are strikingly different in history and character; their Negro populations, for this reason and others, are also different; and what Negroes have been able to achieve in housing in these two cities illustrates the broad range of diversity that we may find in two not very distant metropolises in the Deep South.

This study is based on field observation, interviews, and experience, as placed against the background afforded by available statistics, and supported by documentation from private and public agencies and the press. It points to the various influences, from the most general—such as the nature of the economy and social climate of each community—to the most specific—such as the role of key organizations and individuals—that seem to have been most influential in determining the housing picture in each community that we see today.

ATLANTA

The Setting

Favored by a strategic location that permits direct transportation to all sections of the country, Atlanta has established itself solidly as the leading commercial city of the Southeast. No other city of the region surpasses it in population or the value and diversity of its products and functions. It is the most cosmopolitan of southeastern cities and, with its varied and broad-based economy, among the most economically stable and balanced in the United States.

In 1950, it ranked twenty-third among the cities of the nation in population, with just under half a million, but eighteenth in postal receipts, fourteenth in bank clearances, and ninth in air passenger arrivals and departures. More than three thousand national concerns have Atlanta factories, sales offices, and warehouses; and some fifty-five federal agencies, employing over fourteen thousand persons, are located there.

Since the 1890's, Atlanta has shown a consistently strong and highly self-conscious orientation toward change and progress. Despite the recurrent stress upon the "Southern way of life," and the ubiquitousness of regional symbols and myths, it is less parochial in outlook than most cities of the region and any other of Georgia. The Negro, too, shares in the dominant tone created by an emphasis on change, the expectation of continued growth, and the pride in past achievements. For the Negro in Atlanta also has substantial achievements to his credit: six institutions of higher learning for Negroes are located there, making Atlanta a leading Negro intellectual center; the most successful group of Negro financial institutions is found there; and some of the most striking advances toward an important political role for Negroes in the South have been made there. There has also been extensive coöperation with whites in various spheres, and the Negro thus feels himself, in large measure, a part of Atlanta.

The participation of the Negroes in local politics has been particularly significant and has provided an important lever for improving housing facilities and gaining access to land sites. In 1946, 24,137 Negroes were on the registration books and eligible to vote in Atlanta elections, as compared to 56,854 whites. One of the objectives of extending the city limits in 1952 was to add a large number of white voters, and thus reduce the significance of the Negro vote. However, in 1953, Rufus E. Clement, president of Atlanta University, was elected a member of the Atlanta Board of Education, defeating his white opponent by a margin of 10,000 votes, many of them from whites. In the same election, two Negroes were elected members of the city Democratic Executive Committee. For the first time since 1870, Atlanta had elected Negroes to municipal offices. One writer has summed up the effects of Negro political activity as follows:

> Through the efforts of Negro leaders, the Negro voters have been educated on the issues of the day. Before casting their votes they have studied and have been told of the merits and demerits of each candidate. This wise policy has resulted in a friendly administration being elected in 1949 and in 1953, both in county and city. Negro policemen have been hired. Police brutality has been reduced to a minimum. Race-baiting groups such as the Klan and the Columbians have been suppressed. City officials have been more courteous and sensitive to the demands of Negroes. Courtroom decorum has improved. In city planning the city fathers began looking at the needs of all citizens regardless of color. . . . Better streets, lights, sewers, water, and sidewalks have made Negro neighborhoods attractive. In addition, modern school buildings have been erected to accommodate the growing Negro population.[1]

Whites and Negroes in Atlanta's Growth

In 1955, Atlanta had a population of 492,000 and its Standard Metropolitan Area, as defined by the Bureau of the Census, a population of 814,000. Twenty-three percent of the population of the Atlanta Standard Metropolitan Area was Negro, but the proportion has been dropping steadily since 1890 (see table 1). In recent years, there has been very heavy white in-migration, only slight Negro in-migration. Between 1950 and 1955, in-migration accounted for less than 10 percent of the growth of the Negro population, as compared with nearly 60 percent of the growth of the white population. Since 1940, almost all of the growth of white population has taken place outside the city of Atlanta, which is typical for the growth pattern of many American cities

[1] Clarence A. Bacote, "The Negro in Atlanta Politics," *Phylon*, Fourth Quarter, 1955, pp. 349–350.

in this period of great suburban housing developments. The Negro population's growth, however, is concentrated within the city and its adjacent areas. While the proportion of Negroes in the metropolitan area declined between 1940 and 1950, the proportion within the city rose, as we may see from table 2. In 1950, as we may see from table 3, only two-fifths of the whites in the metropolitan area lived within the city, whereas almost three-quarters of the Negroes did.

TABLE 1

POPULATION OF ATLANTA STANDARD METROPOLITAN AREA, BY COLOR, 1880 TO 1955

Year	Population			Percent increase		Nonwhite as percent of total population
	Total	White	Nonwhite	White	Nonwhite	
1880	100,613	64,552	36,061	...	...	35.8
1890	139,453	87,118	52,335	35.0	45.1	37.5
1900	179,420	115,528	63,982	32.6	22.1	35.6
1910	252,124	173,938	78,186	50.6	22.4	31.0
1920	325,688	234,257	91,431	34.7	16.9	28.1
1930	440,906	317,296	123,610	35.4	35.2	28.0
1940	518,100	374,706	143,394	18.1	16.0	27.7
1950	671,797	505,981	165,816	35.0	15.6	24.7
1955	813,632	627,546	186,086	24.0	12.2	22.9

SOURCE: Metropolitan Planning Commission, *Population · Housing* (Atlanta, April, 1955).

TABLE 2

PERCENT OF POPULATION NONWHITE AND PERCENT INCREASE OF POPULATION BY COLOR AND GEOGRAPHIC AREA, METROPOLITAN ATLANTA, 1940 AND 1950

Geographic area	Percent of population nonwhite		Percent increase, 1940–1950		
	1940	1950	Total	White	Nonwhite
Standard Metropolitan Area	27.7	24.7	29.7	35.0	15.6
City of Atlanta	34.6	36.6	9.6	6.2	16.1
Adjacent tracted areas ..	18.0	13.2	66.3	76.0	22.0
All other areas	18.0	12.8	43.1	52.2	1.7

SOURCE: U. S. Bureau of the Census, *Sixteenth Census of the U. S., 1940* and *U. S. Census of Population: 1950*.

TABLE 3

NUMBER AND PERCENT DISTRIBUTION OF POPULATION BY COLOR AND GEOGRAPHIC AREA, METROPOLITAN ATLANTA, 1940 AND 1950

Geographic area	Total		White		Nonwhite	
	Number	Percent	Number	Percent	Number	Percent
1940						
Standard Metropolitan Area	518,100	100.0	374,706	100.0	143,394	100.0
City of Atlanta	302,288	58.3	197,686	52.8	104,602	72.9
Adjacent tracted areas	136,160	26.3	111,702	29.8	24,458	17.1
All other areas	79,652	15.4	65,318	17.4	14,334	10.0
1950						
Standard Metropolitan Area	671,797	100.0	505,981	100.0	165,816	100.0
City of Atlanta	331,314	49.3	209,898	41.5	121,416	73.2
Adjacent tracted areas	226,467	33.7	196,638	38.9	29,829	18.0
All other areas	114,016	17.0	99,445	19.6	14,571	8.8

SOURCE: U. S. Bureau of the Census, *Sixteenth Census of the U. S., 1940* and *U. S. Census of Population: 1950.*

We may sum up the Negro's economic circumstances by saying he fares much worse than the whites, but much better than he did. The one-fourth of the population that was Negro in 1950 received less than one-eighth of the income of the area; but the average cash income of Negro families was nevertheless four times as great in 1949 as it was in the mid-1930's.

The Negro Sections of Atlanta

Railroads made Atlanta. They had a decisive effect on early street patterns and the location of residential units. Their effect was undoubtedly more decisive on residential sites for Negroes. "Across the tracks" and "down by the railroad" were quite accurate designations of the early settlements of Negroes, and retain validity today for more Negroes than whites. Many of the early Negro residents were railroad workers who settled close to their places of work: the land blighted by railroads and their attendant nuisance features was cheap and undesirable for resi-

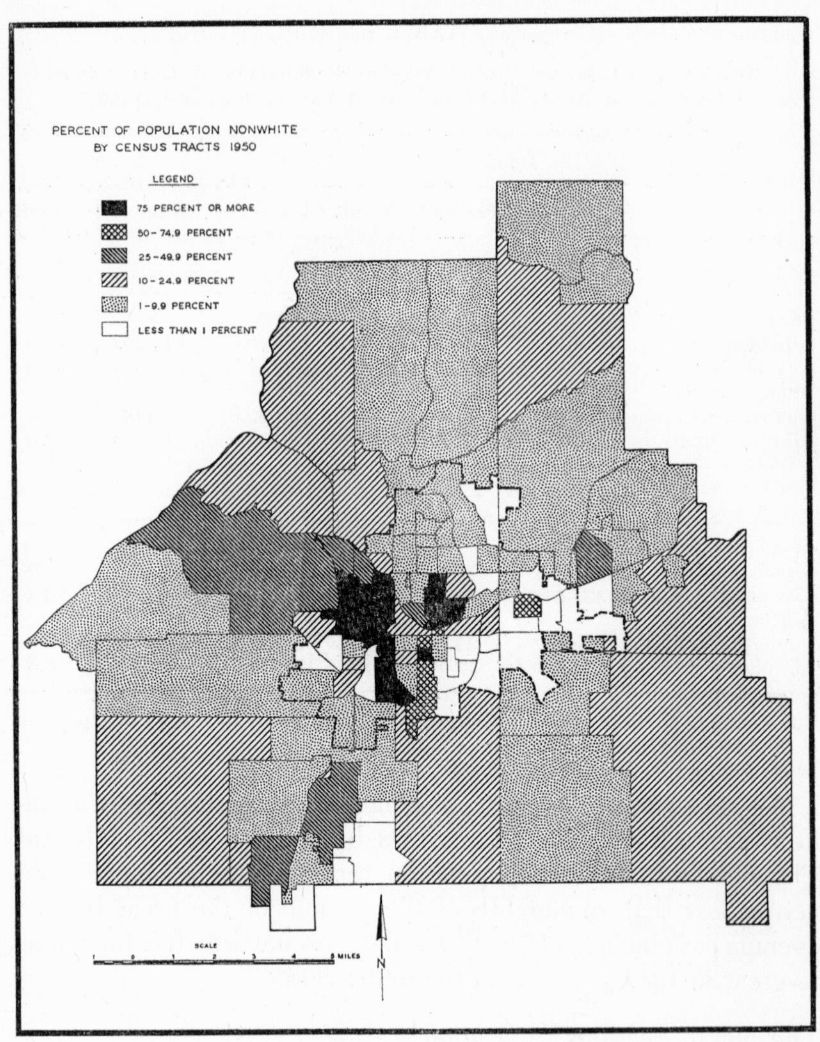

Map. 1. City of Atlanta and adjacent areas, percent of population nonwhite by census tracts, 1950.

dential purposes, and thus it was more available to low-income Negroes; and railroad lines often served as barriers, marking off or pocketing residential enclaves.

The earliest Negro settlements were near the central railroad stations and in the southeast. Just before and for a considerable period after World War I, the predominant movement was eastward. Barriers such as railroad lines and white residential districts to the east and south slowed up or stopped expansion in this direction. When subsequent moves to expand northward were slowed up by white resistance, the mounting pressure for more and better housing turned the movement westward. The story since 1940 has been featured by the enlargement of the west side community and, since 1946, by the development of new residential areas in the west outside the old city limits.

The early movement of Negroes to the West Side was in large measure due to the efforts of Heman E. Perry, an energetic and imaginative promoter, who in the 1920's laid the groundwork for much of the business activity and spirit of enterprise that marks the Atlanta Negro community today. Perry took option on West Side land and sold a portion of it to the city for a site for Booker T. Washington High School, the first—and still the largest —for Negroes in Atlanta. He expected that people would move to the high school area and took options on properties over a wide area. His companies handled the real estate operations, the building of homes, and the financing. A contemporary comments: "Perry wanted to get hold of the West Side before Negroes were fenced in by whites. He was twenty-five years ahead of his time."

In 1931, a newspaper account described the results of Perry's pioneering efforts up to that time:

> Heman E. Perry . . . started a home building program in First Ward on the West Side. . . . The plot contained originally 211 acres. In it have been built about 511 homes costing from $3,000 to $15,000, the average home costing from $3,000 to $8,000. About 10 percent of the homes are brick. About 90 percent of the streets in the section are paved. . . .
>
> Not only did Negroes move from the southeast section of Atlanta (Auburn Avenue section) to the west division, but prominent Negroes from other cities in Georgia, and from other states moved to Atlanta and built fine brick homes in the division. . . .[2]

By 1940, nearly 40 percent of the Atlanta Negro population lived in the West Side area. From 1930 on, while the trend for whites was to the outskirts of the city, the trend for Negroes was to the West Side within the city. At this time, further ex-

[2] Floyd J. Calvin; "Heman Perry Started Atlanta on Its Home Building Program," *Pittsburgh Courier*, October 31, 1931, cited in Charles S. Johnson, *Negro Housing*, Report of the Committee on Negro Housing of The President's Conference on Home Building and Home Ownership (Washington, D. C., 1932), p. 237).

pansion westward was balked by the predominantly middle-class white community of Mozley Park.

The West Side included both good and bad housing. The Atlanta University district was one of these areas of mixed quality, including housing that ranged from the row of Atlanta University faculty houses on Beckwith Street [3] to the notorious "Beaverslide" slums which were later demolished to make way for the first public housing project for Negroes in the United States, University Homes.[4]

During the same period, before World War II, in northeastern Atlanta the Negro population was seeking to move to the north and the east, where there were several areas that were marginal or in transition. In some of these, racial tension developed. In this same general area was Auburn Avenue, for many years the center of much of the business, recreational, and organizational life of the Atlanta Negro community. Much collective sentiment and pride is attached to Auburn Avenue—"Sweet Auburn"—as a symbol of accomplishment; in fact, however, the street and its institutions were in the midst of blight and decay.

The main features of housing for Negroes in Atlanta up to the end of World War II (and to a large extent, at present) were the poor quality of most dwelling units, prevalence of crowding, and containment of a growing population within limited space. In the main, the Negro population had overflowed the maximum possible use of existing facilities with the result that colored families had been forced to seek housing in fringe areas of white occupancy. Racial friction developed between white and colored residents, with sporadic violent outbursts.

Public Housing for Negroes, 1934–1956

The public housing program that began in the mid-1930's was

[3] This strip of about two blocks with less than a dozen houses, until the recent expansion of the Negro community and the increase in quality housing, was referred to as "Ph.D. Row." Until the mid-1940's, these blocks of Beckwith Street, a section of Boulevard in northeast Atlanta, and Hunter Road practically exhausted the list of premium, prestige areas.

[4] See later section, "Public Housing for Negroes." It might be noted here that this and subsequent public housing projects built for Negroes in the prewar period involved the clearing of slums in existing Negro neighborhoods and had the effect of anchoring or fixing populations in these areas. The projects that were built after the war were placed on open land outside the congested central areas of the city, thus establishing new communities or augmenting small concentrations.

among the more important prewar developments affecting housing for Negroes in Atlanta.[5] The public housing program authorized under the National Recovery Act of 1933 began in Atlanta with the construction of University Homes for Negroes in a slum section near Atlanta University. From 1934 to the present, the Atlanta Housing Authority, in coöperation with the Public Housing Administration, has built projects with a total of 7,494 dwelling units of which 4,955 are occupied by Negroes.[6]

The federal Public Housing Administration's "racial equity formula," based on the racial composition of families in substandard housing, would require allocation of 54 percent of Atlanta units to Negroes. Actually, Negroes have received two-thirds of all public housing units built in the Atlanta area since 1934. If a currently programmed 1,000-unit project is built and occupied according to present plans, the Negro proportion will rise to over 70 percent. This has been caused by the larger volume of applications from Negro families and their lower move-out rate as compared with white families. The bulk of units for Negroes has been placed in the western section in established Negro communities or in recently annexed areas earmarked for Negro expansion. No units were placed in the disputed northeast section. Thus, public housing in Atlanta has served to guide and concentrate the distribution of Negro population.

Public housing for whites has also been used, in at least one instance, to serve the purpose of Negro containment. In the early 1950's, when Negro expansion on the West Side in and around Mozley Park was threatening white residential and business sections to the south and west, efforts were made to stop the Negro advance. The "answer" eventually arrived at by city officials was the erection of Joel Chandler Harris Homes for whites—a 510-unit public housing project.[7] This was erected at a site chosen as a dividing line despite the protests of Negro leaders.

---

[5] This section draws heavily upon an unpublished study by Hubert M. Jackson, Racial Relations Officer, Public Housing Administration, Atlanta, Georgia: "Public Housing in the 'Atlanta Story.' "

[6] An additional 545 units for Negroes are located in the metropolitan area outside the city of Atlanta.

[7] Unofficial reports are that many of these units are "going begging" because of a lack of applications. Negroes say wryly: "It won't be long before it will be ours. It will serve them right."

The Problem of Expansion

Thus contained, the problem set for the Negro community just after the war was where and how to expand. And the Atlanta community gave an amazing demonstration of organizational, political, and financial ability in greatly expanding the supply of housing available to Negroes, even within the rigid frame of segregation. The story begins in late 1946, when the pressure for good housing for Negroes had been accentuated by the general housing shortage, the return of Negro veterans, a rising Negro population, and new political and economic strength producing a new concept of what was desirable and possible. At this time, the Atlanta Urban League, which played the crucial role of catalyst—and more—throughout this whole development, called a meeting of representatives of business, social agencies, and government to discuss measures to provide housing for Negroes. The group met in the office of W. H. Aiken, a Negro contractor. A Temporary Coordinating Committee on Housing (TCCH), with Aiken as chairman, was set up. The committee first concerned itself with the task of discovering the number of housing units needed by Negroes in Atlanta and arrived at a figure of 4,500 for Negro veterans alone.

The TCCH then set up two agencies to push a housing program: a land committee, headed by T. M. Alexander, a leading real estate broker, "to investigate further the possibilities of getting outlet areas for Negro expansion"; and a corporation committee, chaired by J. P. Whittaker of the (Negro) Atlanta Mutual Building and Loan Association, to study the feasibility of forming a corporation which would, in turn, build on the sites obtained by the land committee. Representatives of two other leading Atlanta Negro financial institutions, the Atlanta Life Insurance Company and the Citizens Trust Company, also sat on this committee. A third committee was appointed to work closely with county planning officials, the Atlanta Chamber of Commerce, and others interested in housing for Negroes.

In May, 1947, the land committee enlarged its membership to include representatives from the Community Planning Council, the Empire Real Estate Board, and the Land Planning and Racial Relations sections of the local Federal Housing Administration office. This committee—which in its expanded form became the Atlanta Housing Council—then took an important step: it issued a report locating six areas in which it felt the Negro population could and should expand. In each of these areas some Negroes were living, and land, much of it owned by Negroes, was available for good residential quarters. As the report said:

> It is recognized that the above areas cannot legally be designated as areas for expansion of Negro housing. However, in order to provide adequate housing in complete self-contained neighborhoods, to raise the standard of living for the minority group, to permit subsistence gardening, and to make possible the reclamation of the present blighted areas, all properly guided for accomplishment by private enterprise, it is hoped that business and civic groups alike will recognize and endorse the above recommended areas as being in fact, if not by law, the proper areas in which Negroes may build and live without racial or economic conflict to strive with all of us for a more prosperous and more democratic community.

This report would have remained only an expression of what was desirable had it not been followed up by action. Fortunately, the Atlanta Negro community had capable and resourceful individuals and institutions to back up this approach to its housing problems. The Atlanta Housing Council conducted a careful land-ownership analysis of the area called "Expansion Area No. 1," and in January, 1948, two members of the corporation committee, acting independently, authorized the representative of the Atlanta Urban League to offer to purchase a large tract of land in the area from its Negro owners. An offer was made, but refused by the property owners. An alternate proposal was then made that the property owners themselves form a corporation and build low-cost homes for Negroes. This proposal was accepted and two property owners formed a corporation known as Chenault, Inc., in May, 1948. Two adjacent property owners were also persuaded to build homes on their properties.

The property owners decided to name the project "The Fair Haven Subdivision" and requested the Atlanta Urban League to serve as sponsor of the project. At this point, the Atlanta Urban League began functioning as the coördinating agency between the FHA and property owners, and assumed responsibility for getting an engineer and exploring possible sources of funds for financing the project. It was successful in interesting the Life

Insurance Company of Georgia, owned by whites, which agreed to finance the entire project of 153 single-family homes. The director of the company's mortgage department stated that he wanted all arrangements to be handled by Negroes who, he felt, could get the best results. The company appointed the J. R. Wilson Realty Company (Negro) as its official representative for preparing applications to FHA and collecting the monthly payments. This was a significant "first."

A second important project in which the Atlanta Urban League played an instrumental role was "High Point Apartments," developed by Housing, Inc. Option was taken from the Methodist Church in late 1949 on a tract of land earlier marked for Negro expansion. Immediately, several problems confronted the developers: getting the proposed express highway shifted; getting the land rezoned for apartment-house use by the Fulton County Commissioners; submitting an application to FHA in time for processing before expiration of Section 608 of Title VI (March 1, 1950); and overcoming the objections of adjacent white residents who did not want Negroes living on this property. The developers hastened to solve these problems as quickly as possible. It was alleged by Housing, Inc., that the express highway had been shifted from its original position onto the property proposed for the project at the instance of white real estate developers. When local efforts to restore the highway project to its original position failed, a delegation went to Washington, D. C., to seek assistance from the federal Bureau of Public Roads.

County officials responded favorably to the proposal for rezoning the land. The County Planning Commission, after a public hearing in January, 1950, recommended that the land be rezoned for apartments, and the county commissioners finally accepted the Planning Commission's recommendation. The chief obstacle to the rezoning was the active and vocal opposition of white citizens from nearby Lakewood Heights. They objected to any further Negro occupancy in this South Atlanta area, which had always been a major Negro residential center, and in which Negroes owned significant amounts of both developed and undeveloped property. Probably the most important device in getting approval for the project was the creation of a buffer zone. Twenty-seven acres of land were cut off from the project acreage and designated for industrial development, separating the white and Negro communities.

Another hurdle arose when the FHA State Director refused to accept the developers' application for the stated reasons that the rents ($40 to $70) were too high for Negroes, a multistory building with efficiency apartments was not suited to the Negro market, and the project was too ambitious because it included a community center, auditorium, and playgrounds in addition to 384 efficiency apartments.

Again a delegation proceeded to Washington, D. C., this time to discuss the project with officials of the HHFA and the FHA. The delegation represented to the HHFA Administrator, Mr. Raymond Foley, and FHA officers that local FHA action was not based on any analysis of the Negro market in Atlanta, and that while about five thousand Section 608 units had been built for white Atlantans, only twenty-four had been built for Negroes.[8]

The trip to Washington evidently produced results, since the FHA rescinded its unfavorable decision and agreed to issue mortgage insurance on a 452-unit project. Final approval was given on the last day Section 608 was in force.

The fourth and last problem was met head-on when the County Commissioners convened February 1, 1950. A hundred or more white residents appeared in opposition to the proposed rezoning of the area for apartments. But the County Commissioners voted to approve the project unanimously.

The Role of City Planning

While members of the Negro community and their supporters in various agencies proceeded to extend the area of Negro residence in Atlanta, the Metropolitan Planning Commission was engaged in preparing a plan for Atlanta's expansion. No representative of the Negro community was a member of the policy-making or technical staff of the commission, but the technical staff did keep in touch with leaders and groups in the Negro community. In 1952, the commission issued a major planning document, *Up Ahead,* to guide Atlanta's growth. This document accepted and elaborated the idea of Negro expansion areas de-

[8] Actually, at this time, an application by Aiken involving 209 units was being processed. It was later approved at the same time Highpoint was approved, February 28, 1950.

veloped by the TCCH. (At the time, the Negro community was upset by a proposal of much less importance, that of redeveloping its beloved Auburn Avenue, the Negro business center; it protested strongly, and Auburn Avenue was saved, but as the Negro community is more and more heavily concentrated in the new areas to the west, the avenue has lost some of its importance, and even its value as a symbol might well be replaced by newer business development to the west.)

The concept of "Negro area" had, of course, no more legal or moral validity when the Planning Commission proposed it than when the TCCH first spoke of it; but if the commission had been ostrich-like about the facts of color and housing and proposed or planned residential sites in a neutral manner, the chances are that the already restricted Negro population would have been even more disadvantaged in competing for desirable and needed sites. In addition, by 1952, the commission's proposals were tacit acceptance of what the Negro community was already accomplishing on its own; but the approval was important politically and in terms of getting the support of public opinion for what the Negro community was doing.

Of course, the Planning Commission was not wholly motivated by concern for the welfare of Negroes. Its specific proposals and arguments (its concern for natural boundary lines, for example) made it clear that preservation and rationalization of the system of residential segregation was a major goal. Nevertheless, there was recognition in the commission's recommendations of the legitimate needs of Negroes for living space. On this elementary level, white and Negro leadership could and did coöperate. By 1955, all six areas named by the TCCH in 1946 as expansion areas, and four of those named in *Up Ahead,* had been occupied or "nailed down" by Negroes.

The Conflict over Expansion—the Case of Mozley Park

The areas for Negro expansion were generally open and not yet built upon. But almost everywhere there were some whites already settled. While the Negro movement took place with the blessing of officialdom, there was, nevertheless, tension and conflict. A Klan-like group calling itself "The Columbians" was active during the period of greatest tension; bombings, burnings, and other forms of coercion were used to keep Negroes from moving in. The local newspapers, the *Constitution* and the *Journal*, condemned and fought the Columbians and helped discredit the group. The support of opinion leadership thus aided the Negro movement.

Of the postwar tension areas, perhaps the most crucial for Negroes and whites was Mozley Park. The expansion into the Mozley Park area took place after Negroes had occupied new expansion areas beyond. The section is named after the city park located there, which was itself one of the main bones of contention in the struggle to keep Negroes out of the area. In addition to houses, Negroes wanted the park and the school adjoining it; many of the whites were even more determined to keep Negroes out of the park and the school than they were to prevent them from buying the houses. The significance of the park as a symbol can perhaps be seen in the fact that even after the transition of the section from a white to a Negro neighborhood was conceded, some die-hard whites were proposing that the park be destroyed and converted into a housing development.

What happened in the transition of the Mozley Park section is significant not only because it illustrates some of the problems which arise when Negroes move into a "restricted" area in Atlanta, but because it has had a continuing effect on the thinking and the activities of buyers, sellers, builders, financing agents, and city officials involved in similar situations in other parts of Atlanta.

The Mozley Park area is located in the northwest and southwest sections of Atlanta, about three miles from the downtown business district. During the westward expansion inaugurated by the Negro entrepreneur Heman Perry in the 1920's, Negroes had purchased land extending to and beyond the boundaries of the white community. In 1937, a Negro physician acquired three lots in Mozley Park, secured a building permit, and hired a contractor, but when the building crew appeared, there were threats from the whites in the neighborhood, and the owner gave up his plans to build. About a year later, when a Negro businessman was building on another lot, a group of whites, some of them wearing hoods, warned him that there must be no encroachment into the Mozley Park area lying just beyond his house.

In the period immediately following Word War II, Aiken and other Negro contractors began building homes on the West Side, in the direction of Mozley Park. In an effort to fix Westview Drive (a principal street) as the southern limit of Negro expansion, the white residents did not allow Negro builders to build within one hundred yards of Westview Drive; the paving of streets feeding from the new Negro developments into Westview Drive stopped one hundred yards short of that thoroughfare. This was the situation in 1948 when the son of a Negro publisher, a veteran who had returned to Atlanta from overseas in 1946, despairing of finding adequate housing for his growing family, finally decided to build a home on the two lots he had inherited on Mozley Place.

As soon as the whites in the neighborhood learned, early in 1948, that the Negro owner had secured a permit to build on Mozley Place, some of them attempted to have the building permit revoked. They were told at City Hall that nothing could be done. Direct efforts to halt the erection of the house began with phone calls to the young veteran by the minister of one of the large churches in the area. The young man was unmoved by his pleas and arguments that he build elsewhere, or at least turn his house around so it did not face Mozley Place, which residents were trying to keep all white. Other efforts to dissuade him were equally ineffective, and while there were vague proposals made that he sell his property to his white neighbors, no specific offers were made. But in the meantime, white residents became interested in selling—perhaps because in a meeting with his neighbors, the Negro veteran asserted that Negroes would pay much more for these lots than the whites thought they were worth. A Negro real estate broker arranged for sales of three houses, and just before the veteran completed his house, one of the Negro owners, a minister, moved in. He was greeted by a mob of 200, and after a brief period, he sold and moved again.

The Negro broker who had arranged these sales was now charged with misrepresentation before the Georgia Real Estate Commission, for a Negro couple to which he had sold one of the houses had asserted, in an effort to break the contract, that he had led them to understand the entire block in which they bought was going over to Negroes, and they would have peaceful possession. The Superior Court had already ruled that the contract was binding. But the Real Estate Commission nevertheless revoked the broker's license. (It was restored ten months later.)

The Negro veteran occupied his house without incident in February, 1949, by which time the other three houses that had been sold were in white hands again. However, this was only a temporary setback. Some residents had been impressed by the fact that one of the three homes sold had been built for $3,700 and had been sold for over $9,000 to the Negro buyer. They approached Negro brokers, who refused to sell their houses when the owners said they could not insure peaceful possession. But other brokers were willing to handle these properties, using various techniques. Thus, a broker might refuse to take a house unless every other house on the block was listed, making possible complete transition from white to Negro occupancy. Sales were also arranged with the understanding that the white seller would continue to occupy the house until conditions permitted the Negro to move in.

Financing always raises special problems for Negroes, and in the Mozley Park transition the white residents persuaded at least one bank to refuse loans to Negroes wishing to buy in the area. But the Negroes could turn to their own institutions. Just prior to this time, Citizens Trust Company had begun taking an interest in housing loans, partly as a result of information that FHA was liberalizing its policies in regard to commitments on behalf of minority group borrowers. Negroes wishing to build in the Mozley Park area and elsewhere often found themselves able to qualify for permanent insured loans but could not find money for the general construction loans without which their FHA or VA commitments were useless. Tentatively, Citizens Trust Company entered this field, working in conjunction with downtown mortgage firms. In 1951 Citizens Trust effected an agreement with two Negro insurance companies which provided additional mortgage money sources for Negroes. Some of these loans made possible the "breaking" of the Mozley Park bottleneck.

The city government had generally attempted to protect the Negro citizens—as well as whites who were selling—from violence or mob action, and this decision to maintain law and order, rather than the previous residential pattern, was of the greatest importance in limiting the effectiveness of the "radical" element. But the city had to take a more than neutral role: the Negroes needed and wanted the park and the elementary school and this required positive action. (Both the park and the school were turned over to Negroes in 1954.) There came into existence, to guide this complex transition, an unofficial biracial group, known as the "Mayor's Committee," which attempted to iron out problems as they arose and to make the transition as peaceful as possible. (It was taken for granted in the work of the committee that a district must be all-white or all-Negro.) It is typical of Atlanta that there should be such organized negotiations between the white and Negro communities.

A major, concrete outcome of the committee's work was an agreement by the Empire Real Estate Board, an organization of Negro real estate brokers and agents, to coöperate in halting the southwestward movement of Negroes at a certain boundary, namely, the north side of Westview Drive. The language of the agreement, adopted in September, 1952, follows:

> . . . that a copy of all listings held by its members would be turned over to Mr. Farris, a representative of the Mayor in this instance, and Councilman for the area, and who will then be encumbered with the responsibility of contacting, or having contacted, the owners of said property and of asking them to withdraw their property from the market; whereupon, the brokers agreed they would take down their signs and refuse, for the time being, to accept any further listings from the south side of Westview Drive. While this Board is not setting up any property boundary line or zoning area for Negro expansion, in the spirit of good will and public relations, in coöperation with the people of West End, this agreement is being made for the time being. The Board is requesting that all white brokers as well as the residents of that area be contacted and requested to make the same commitment which is being required of our Board; otherwise, the agreement will be without effectiveness and will impose upon the Empire Real Estate Board an unfair penalty in the operation of their business.

In establising a limit to the southwestward movement, the agreement tacitly recognized the "allocation" of Mozley Park to Negroes. Today, the entire Mozley Park area of some 737 homes is occupied by Negroes—most of them drawn from the middle- and lower-income groups (and some few of them freed from lower-class status by the fact that their former homes in the blighted areas stood in the way of industrial development and were sold at prices which enabled them to purchase homes in the Mozley Park section). Meanwhile, certain agents and brokers have begun to regret their agreement to check the Negro movement at Westview Drive.

In talking with persons who had been involved in the Mozley Park transition in one way or another, the authors asked for expression of opinion as to factors which facilitated or hindered the movement of Negroes into the Mozley Park area. From the answers given, and from study of news reports, memoranda, and records, the authors venture to put forward the following judgments. The transition to Negro occupancy was facilitated by:

1. The Supreme Court decisions invalidating racial zoning and enforcement of racial restrictive covenants.
2. The fact that Negroes were already living in neighborhoods adjoining the Mozley Park area and that certain Negroes already owned land located within the "restricted" section.
3. The fact that white leaders and citizens found the "logical" transition of a formerly all-white community into an all-Negro community much less distasteful than the prospect of a racially "mixed" neighborhood.
4. The availability of some financing from Negro sources.
5. The fact that some white property owners in the area discovered that Negroes would pay higher prices for houses and land than could be secured in the general market.
6. The readiness of certain white leaders to concede the "core" of the Mozley Park area to Negroes in return for time and a "coöperative" attitude on the part of Negroes, making possible the establishment of new and more rigid "buffers" and boundaries.
7. The "property depreciation myth" which made white owners anxious to sell before the expected drop in property values.
8. The relaxation of FHA and VA policies in regard to minority groups, which facilitated the making of loans to Negroes desiring to build homes in the area.
9. The willingness of Negro real estate brokers and agents to "pioneer" in neighborhoods which were still predominantly white.

10. The existence of a group of Negro Atlantans with business knowledge, experience, and financial resources. This group would include bankers, real estate brokers, other businessmen, Urban League officials, builders and contractors, and certain educators.

11. The relative calmness and common sense of a large proportion of the Negroes and whites involved in the transition; a thoughtful climate reduced the effectiveness, during this period, of radical anti-Negro elements.

12. The acuteness of Negroes' need for housing, which made some of them willing to move into the area even in the face of hostility and threats.

13. The existence of suitable, even better, housing elsewhere for the white population of Mozley Park. Many of the former residents of the area were able to purchase better housing and still realize a profit on the exchange.

14. The significance of the Negro vote as a factor to be reckoned with by political leaders; and the recognition of their power by Negroes themselves.

Hindering the smooth transition were:

1. Various fears of whites: of a racially "mixed" neighborhood, of economic loss, and the generalized "if we let them in here, there's no telling where they'll stop."

2. The deep-rooted acceptance, by many whites—and Negroes—of the semiofficial and "understood" boundaries and "buffers" separating Negro and white neighborhoods.

3. The efforts of the West End Business Men's Association and of other organizations to keep Negroes out.

4. The revocation of the license of the Negro broker whose operations had taken him into the controversial section during the early stages of the transition.

5. Pressures upon whites in the area who were disposed to sell or to accept Negro neighbors.

6. The unwillingness of the city government to take any firm position in support of the Negro home-buyers.

7. The reluctance of financial institutions (other than those Negro-controlled) to make mortgage loans to Negro buyers and home-builders in the area.

8. The uncoördinated and perhaps unwise behavior of certain

of the real estate brokers and agents operating in the controversial area.

9. A certain amount of division in the Negro community in regard to the wisdom of moving into the Mozley Park area.

During the years when westward expansion was still being hampered by the white resistance in the Mozley Park area, Negroes were already bypassing and encircling the area through new housing developments on vacant land. From 1946 through 1949, four new subdivisions with a total of nearly 600 houses were built for sale to Negroes on the West Side. The largest of these was the Fair Haven development, previously described, located northwest of Mozley Park and started in 1949. Whites living in the vicinity moved out in the summer of 1949. Also erected in the same area, in 1950, was a 95-unit "608" rental apartment development. Efforts had been made to insure a better quality of housing in Fair Haven by having the section zoned for single-family residences only. These efforts failed, however, and the rental project was approved and completed, one of the results being that apartments renting for $39 to $44 per month were located just across the street from two new homes costing approximately $40,000.

The role of local transit companies in maintaining segregated housing patterns in the South may be seen in the part played by the Atlanta Transit System during this period. The simplest and most efficient transit route for Negroes living in the Fair Haven section would have been provided by extending an existing route past the contested Mozley Park area. This would have provided convenient transportation for any Negroes moving into the Mozley Park area. However, in spite of repeated requests, the Atlanta Transit System refused to provide such service, and Negroes who lived in Fair Haven were compelled to walk long distances. Service to the new Negro areas in the west was not provided until 1954–1955.

Meanwhile, the large amount of land owned by Negroes in the northwest section beyond the city limits and new purchases rendered impossible any further attempt to confine the Negro population to the central city and its immediate fringes. Negroes continued to buy land beyond the city limits. Western Land, Inc., a corporation formed for the purpose indicated, bought 85 acres on Fairburn Road. The Chennault family purchased 126 acres, including a 20-acre lake. Dr. J. B. Harris purchased 52 acres of land in the southwest section. The latter purchase played a key role in the "negotiated" transition of Collier Heights, a white residential area, to Negro occupancy. The National Development Company (Negro) had been negotiating for a tract of undeveloped land beyond the Collier Heights settlement. It was known that whites in the southwest section were displeased with the fact that a Negro owned land in the area. As a result of some rather complex negotiations, one of the owners was persuaded to put the fifty-two acres he owned in trust to his wife for a specified period of time, thus "freezing" it against residential use for Negroes. In return, the undeveloped tract beyond Collier Heights was made available to the National Development Company, and it was possible to begin negotiations for the white homes in the Collier Heights section, now "in the middle." Negro financing agencies and brokers handled the matter with some skill, acquired from their experience in Mozley Park. White homeowners were called together and told that the land beyond them had been purchased and was to be developed; agreements were reached that the homes of whites wishing to move would be purchased at adequate but not exorbitant prices; real estate brokers and agents were asked to refrain from sprinkling the neighborhood with signs, and every attempt was made to effect the transition quietly and without the intemperance and hostility which had marked the change-over in the Mozley Park area. In the main, the efforts to accomplish a peaceful transition were successful. Some 300 homes were transferred from white to Negro ownership during 1954 and 1955.

Gains and Losses, 1945–1956

In this section we wish to draw up a balance sheet of Negro housing in Atlanta in the postwar period. Between 1945 and 1956, an estimated 10,550 units were added to the housing supply available to Negroes. Mortgage money in excess of $70,000,000 was involved. Four out of five of these newly acquired units were new houses; approximately half of all the units were owner-occupied and half renter-occupied.

This maintained a tendency evident during the 1940's for a strong shift among the Negro population to homeownership. Between 1940 and 1950, homeownership among whites in the metropolitan area increased 106 percent, among Negroes, 117 percent. The proportion of whites who are homeowners is still, of course, greater than the proportion of home-owning Negroes, but the gap narrows as we proceed outward from the city into the outlying areas, as table 4 shows.

TABLE 4

PERCENT OF DWELLING UNITS OWNER-OCCUPIED, BY COLOR AND GEOGRAPHIC AREA, METROPOLITAN ATLANTA, 1950

Geographic area	White	Nonwhite
Standard Metropolitan Area	56.7	29.1
City of Atlanta	47.6	24.4
Adjacent tracted areas	64.8	44.6
Other areas	61.0	40.4

Of the more than five thousand newly acquired rental units, the recently built public housing projects, Perry Homes and Carver Homes, accounted for nearly two thousand and considerably more than one-half of the mortgage money (table 5). There was approximately an equal number of government-insured units ("608's") and nongovernment-insured units, but the ratio of

TABLE 5

TYPE AND TENURE OF DWELLING UNITS NEWLY ACQUIRED BY NONWHITES, AND MORTGAGE INVESTMENT, METROPOLITAN ATLANTA, 1945–1956

Kind of housing	Number of units	Estimated mortgage investment
Total	10,550	$70,446,600
Owner-occupied	5,120	39,614,800
New homes in subdivisions	2,180	16,983,800
New individually built homes	1,270	10,976,000
Used homes	1,670	11,655,000
Renter-occupied	5,430	30,831,800
New government-insured apartments	1,540	8,275,000
apartments		
New nongovernment-insured	1,560	3,941,200
Used apartments	340	615,600
New public housing	1,990	18,000,000

mortgage money involved was more than two to one, reflecting the poor quality of the noninsured new rental housing. About 6 percent of the total rental units made available were used units. Many of these were in apartment buildings turned over in the fringe Boulevard area in northeast Atlanta.

Thirty-seven percent of all newly acquired housing was located in the old city of Atlanta, including four in five of the used houses, but only one in four of the new houses. Table 6 gives the number of units and geographic distribution of the newly acquired housing, and table 7 gives the percent distribution by geographic area. The fact that the new nongovernment-insured rental units are generally of poorer quality, more speculative, and built for low-income groups is reflected in the 83 percent of these units located in the old city.

TABLE 6

NEWLY ACQUIRED NONWHITE OWNER- AND RENTER-OCCUPIED DWELLING UNITS BY AREA, METROPOLITAN ATLANTA, 1945–1956

Type of housing and tenure	Geographic area			
	Total	Old city[a]	Annexed area[a]	Outside central city
Total	10,550	3,920	5,950	680
New housing	8,540	2,290	5,570	680
Used housing	2,010	1,630	380	...
Owner-occupied	5,120	1,710	3,050	360
New homes in subdivisions	2,180	350	1,530	300
New individually built homes	1,270	80	1,130	60
Used homes	1,670	1,290	380	...
Renter-occupied	5,430	2,210	2,900	320
New government-insured apartments	1,540	570	750	220
New nongovernment-insured apartments[b]	1,560	1,300	150	110
Used apartments	340	340	...	...
New public housing	1,990	...	1,990	...

[a] The old city contained 34 square miles; after the extension of city limits in January, 1952, the total became 117 square miles.

[b] Many of these are of cinder block construction with a minimum of "extras." They are often but latter-day versions of the older "shotgun" houses and are frequently erected on small lots in old areas that are blighted and unattractive. Characteristically, these are rented by the week. They are known as good investments with the initial outlay being returned quickly and with a minimum of maintenance and upkeep required.

TABLE 7

PERCENT DISTRIBUTION OF NEWLY ACQUIRED NONWHITE OWNER- AND RENTER-OCCUPIED DWELLING UNITS BY AREA, METROPOLITAN ATLANTA, 1945–1956

Type of housing and tenure	Geographic area			
	Total	Old city	Annexed area	Outside central city
Total	100.0	37.1	56.4	6.5
New housing	100.0	26.8	65.2	8.0
Used housing	100.0	80.9	19.1	...
Owner-occupied	100.0	33.4	59.6	7.0
New homes in subdivisions	100.0	16.0	70.3	13.7
New individually built homes	100.0	6.2	89.1	4.7
Used homes	100.0	77.0	23.0	...
Renter-occupied	100.0	40.6	53.4	6.0
New government-insured apartments	100.0	37.0	49.0	14.0
New nongovernment-insured apartments	100.0	83.0	10.1	6.9
Used apartments	100.0	100.0	...	...
New public housing	100.0	...	100.0	...

It is important to note, because it is indicative of a policy change that has helped to "nail down" expansion areas, that the public housing recently built for Negroes is located outside the old city in newly annexed areas. Nearly two-thirds of the "608" units were also built outside the old city.

The westward trend of the Negro population is emphasized when we consider the figures by geographic sections of the city. The western section (northwest and southwest combined) was the location of nine out of ten of the newly acquired owner-occupied units, nearly three-fourths of the "608" units, and slightly more than 40 percent of the new rental units built without government mortgage insurance.

Twenty-nine subdivisions for homeowners, representing total estimated mortgages of approximately $17,000,000, have been built since 1945. At least, 2,180 units are represented. Prices vary from $4,000 in the Bennett subdivision built in 1947 to those in the recently developed Crestwood Forest where the range is $12,000 to $30,000. The Atlanta Urban League was involved at some stage in the development of seventeen of the twenty-nine projects. Negro operators were importantly involved as developers, contractors, and financiers in practically all of these ventures. Negro real estate brokers were involved in twenty-five of the twenty-nine. Financing was furnished by institutions controlled by Negroes or by Negroes in coöperation with white credit institutions in most cases. Information concerning sources of land, capital, and building has been compiled for nineteen home-owner developments, including the larger ones, representing about four-fifths of all units. These data are presented in table 8.

TABLE 8

Sources of Land, Capital, and Construction, by Color, for Nineteen Owner-occupied Subdivisions for Negro Occupancy, Metropolitan Atlanta, 1945–1956

Name of subdivision	Land				Capital furnished by			Built by		
	Owned by		Bought by							
	White	Negro	White	Negro	White	Negro	White and Negro	White	Negro	White and Negro
Ashby Street	x			x			x		x	
Andrews		x		x			x		x	
Crestwood Forest	x		x				x			x
Bennett	x				x			x		
Fair Haven	x						x			x
Florida Plains	x			x			x		x	
Joyland Park	x				x			x		
Fountain Drive		x		x			x			x
Norwood		x	x				x	x		
Old Marietta Road	x		x			x		x		
Parsons Village		x	x		x			x		
Porter Drive-Leathers Circle		x					x		x	
Richardson Road		x					x		x	
Rose Gardens	x						x	x		
Simpson Road		x				x			x	
Thomasville		x	x		x			x		
Urban Villa	x			x			x		x	
Simpson Heights		x					x		x	
Woodlawn	x			x			x		x	
Total	10	9	5	6	4	2	13	7	9	3

From 1947 through 1950, a total of 153 rental projects, of which eleven were for Negroes, were constructed in Georgia with FHA mortgage insurance to the amount of $126,889,000. Altogether 18,184 apartment units were involved. Ninety-six of these projects, with 12,463 units, were built in metropolitan Atlanta, for the most part beyond the old city limits. The nonwhite veteran outside of Atlanta received no "608" rental apartments, all of those for Negroes in Georgia being constructed in metropolitan Atlanta. The provisions of Section 608 were much slower in being utilized for Negro than for white housing in Atlanta. Prior to 1950, only two small projects (40 units) had been built under this section for Negroes, although 58 projects with more than 7,600 units had been constructed for white Atlantans. Of the eleven "608" projects eventually built for Negroes, nine were built in 1950. Four of these were developed by Negro builders.

The postwar housing story was not entirely one of housing gains. There were losses, too, owing to slum clearance projects, the condemning of land for expressways and other public uses, and the like. In the suburban town of Buckhead, for example, some 400 Negro families lived in a section known as "Bagley Park." The white residents had long been interested in acquiring this land for a park, and in 1947 the Fulton County Commissioners formally determined a public park for white use should be developed there.

Urban redevelopment is still in its early stages in Atlanta, but it will eventually displace several thousand Negro families. Three areas have been officially designated for redevelopment planning, and these contained 9,500 families in 1950, 70 percent of whom are Negro.

Large numbers of Negroes are also being displaced by the alley and rear dwelling clearance program.[9] In the Atlanta of 1900, many servants lived in rear or alley dwellings behind private residences. Many of the residential sections became business areas but the alleys continued to be occupied by Negroes. A 1954 survey found a total of 1,181 rear or alley dwellings in the city. It is the existence of these units that accounts in part for the fact that Negroes are still widely dispersed throughout the city. The elimination of such units will not only result in the diminution of the number of dwelling units available to Negroes, but will also reduce or eliminate Negroes as a population factor in certain areas of the city.

In November, 1954, the Aldermanic Council voted to launch

[9] Much of the material in the next few paragraphs is drawn from Charles L. Sanders, "A Study of the Relocation of Rear and Alley Tenants in Atlanta," (unpublished Master's thesis in Social Work, Atlanta University, 1956).

a five-year alley slum clearance program. The program specified demolition of the dwellings within six months of receipt of notice to demolish, but the city did not provide any plan or machinery for relocation of the alley dwellers. The program actually began on January 1, 1955, with the expectation that it would take about two years to clear the first group of 447 units declared to be below all minimum standards for human habitation.

Some of the displaced are eligible for public housing. But households with large families have found it particularly difficult to move because of the unavailability or cost of adequate housing. The median monthly income of families in the first group of alley dwellings scheduled for demolition was reported to be $127, while the families paid a median rent of $18 per month. Adequate housing for larger Negro families is very scarce in Atlanta and what is available rents for as much as $70 to $80 per month, a cost completely beyond the means of these low-income families. Many of these people are recipients of public assistance or small pensions. Many of the persons to be relocated are aged. Their relocation presents acute problems both because of their financial status and because of the unavailability of adequate housing for the Negro aged in Atlanta.

Financing Homes for Negroes

The availability and the cost of land and money are the crucial factors affecting the supply and quality of housing for Negroes in the Atlanta market. The impressive increase after 1945 in both new and used housing makes it evident that some significant changes had occurred in the flow of money into housing for Negroes. This is not to suggest that there were not and still are not racial differentials in the flow of money or credit and in the costs to the clients—developers, builders, homeowners, or occupants. The changes that occurred can be ascribed to the general increase in family income among Negroes which made their demand more effective and also made them more acceptable to financial institutions; the entrance into the housing market for Negroes of new, energetic, and resourceful entrepreneurs, both white and Negro, who recognized untapped possibilities and new opportunities; the liberalization and expansion of credit services by old and large credit organizations in Atlanta; the leveling off of demand in the market for whites and the consequent exploration of the market for Negroes as an outlet for idle capital, equipment, and labor; and—strategically significant—the existence in the community of three financial institutions controlled by Negroes, the expansion of their services, and the increasing sophistication of their agents and clients in the intricacies of housing finance.

A *Fortune* writer reporting on advances in housing in the Atlanta community since World War II, concluded:

> The whole credit for this—moral as well as monetary—belongs to both Negroes and whites. Atlanta's Negroes and whites have long shown intelligent capacity to work together, notably on housing problems. But common sense and good will have mattered less than a cruder force: Negro purchasing power and credit standing. Negroes, who today can get loans from any Atlanta bank, owe thanks to the Auburn Avenue financial institutions, which, by their own fine records, shattered the myth that the Negro is financially irresponsible. As L. D. Milton, . . . the president of Citizens Trust Company, says: "Our role has been to set up pilot institutions. We have been economic *interpreters* of Negro life addressing a white financial community. We have simply given the needed proofs. This institution can say, 'It is a lie if you say the Negro is a bad bank risk.' The Mutual can say, 'It is a lie to say that the Negro is a bad mortgage risk.' The Atlanta Life can say, 'It is a lie to say that the Negro is a bad insurance risk.' And in downtown Atlanta—as white bank presidents have abandoned segregated lines before their cashiers' windows, department store clerks have generally come to address Negroes politely . . . —the decisive factor has not been the white citizenry's quickened sense of charity or propriety. As the men along Auburn Avenue often murmur wryly, 'Dollars, you see, are not segregated.'" [10]

The Atlanta Life Insurance Company, the Citizens Trust Company, and the Mutual Federal Savings and Loan Association had combined assets in excess of $57,300,000 on December 31, 1955, and had invested nearly $14,000,000 or 24.4 per cent of their total combined assets, in first mortgage loans.

The Atlanta Life Insurance Company, with assets of over $39,000,000 in 1955, is the largest nonwhite financial institution in Atlanta. The company operates in eleven states, including five northern and border states. It has made $3,700,000 in mortgage

---

[10] Emmett John Hughes, "The Negro's New Economic Life," *Fortune*, September, 1956, p. 251. (Copyright 1956 by Time, Inc.; reprinted by special permission.)

loans—9.4 percent of total assets—on both residential and other types of real property.[11] Many of Atlanta's better homes, including the Magnolia Terrace Apartments of 44 one-bedroom apartments, with an FHA mortgage of $160,000, have been financed by the Atlanta Life Insurance Company.

The Citizens Trust Company and the Mutual Federal Savings and Loan Association operate primarily in metroplitan Atlanta; it may be assumed that practically all of their $10,275,000 in first mortgage loans is invested in Atlanta. Mutual has invested $9,175,-000, or 85 percent of its total assets, in residential property in metropolitan Atlanta.[12] These two Atlanta lending institutions have made more loans to nonwhites than all nine of the white savings and loan associations in Birmingham, which had loaned Birmingham Negroes about seven million dollars of their seventy-four million invested in first mortgages.

Although nonwhite Atlantans have been fortunate in having three financially sound and well-run lending institutions to draw upon for first mortgage loans, some local white savings and loan associations and life insurance companies have also financed houses and apartments for Negroes in Atlanta. During World War II, the Atlanta Federal Savings and Loan Association (largest of its kind in the city) advanced $1,625,000 to W. H. Aiken to build 250 FHA homes and 50 duplexes; it has also financed many homes for Negroes in all sections of the city since 1945. Other white financial institutions have also helped finance decent homes for Negroes. The Life Insurance Company of Georgia financed many of the 233 homes in the Fair Haven subdivision, sponsored by the Atlanta Urban League in 1948. The availability of so-called "white" and "nonwhite" money—although all of it is green—to the nonwhite homeseeker by both local and outside financial institutions tends to substantiate the contention of the former state director of FHA, the late R. E. Matheson, that the nonwhite homeowner is a very good risk.

At the end of 1955, there were fifteen federal savings and loan

---

[11] The Institute of Life Insurance Companies reported in the *Life Insurance Fact Book for 1950* that 21.7 percent of assets of all insurance companies was invested in "mortgage loans." Atlanta Life would appear, therefore, to have a considerably smaller proportion of its investments in mortgages than is characteristic of life insurance companies in general.

[12] This concern has also made a few loans to white owners.

associations in Atlanta. These institutions had combined assets of $348,700,000, of which 85.5 percent was invested in first mortgage loans. Of the total $295,000,000 invested by these institutions in first mortgages, 81 percent was in conventional loans. Only 4 percent of the funds on loan were insured by FHA, and 15 percent had been loaned under VA guarantees. Only two of the institutions invested in FHA loans to any significant extent; nine of the fifteen carried no FHA loans at all.

The extent to which nonwhites have been able to obtain loans from these institutions or from lending institutions outside of the South is not precisely known. However, Negro builders and the members of the Empire Real Estate Board indicate that Atlanta Federal, Fulton County Federal, Standard Federal, and First Federal have been most coöperative in making loans on both new and existing housing for nonwhites. Nonwhite homeowners and renters have shared in obtaining loans from many of the white savings and loan associations largely because of the persistence of members of the Empire Real Estate Board, Negro contractors, and a few white speculative builders. Great credit for searching out and stimulating sources of mortgage financing should be given to the Negro real estate brokers.

Outside mortgage money helped (on some occasions) in Atlanta. A local Negro contractor found funds outside of the South to construct rental dwelling units. With the assurance of a permanent commitment, it was relatively easy for W. H. Aiken, Atlanta's largest Negro contractor, to secure construction loans from local savings and loan associations at the prevailing short-term rates. For example, Mr. Aiken was able to obtain $1,863,000 from three financial institutions in New York to build the four-story apartment house of 129 one-bedroom and efficiency units known as Waluhaje Apartments. The white developers of the 452-unit Highpoint Apartments obtained $2,504,000 from a financial institution in New York. All of these units were insured by the FHA between 1945 and 1950.

As late as 1948, the general opinion among Atlanta Negroes active in housing was that the FHA discriminated against Negro borrowers. At about this time, local FHA officials indicated informally that a more liberal policy with respect to commitments for minority group housing was to be inaugurated. With the

FHA becoming more coöperative, it became easier to interest outside institutions, through their local correspondents, in projects for Negroes.

The difficulty Negroes had in getting construction loans was aggravated to a degree by the fact that Citizens Trust Company did not enter this field until about 1951. Since 1952, Citizens Trust Company has had a mortgage loan department.

During the latter part of 1955 and 1956 the growing tightness of the mortgage money market greatly slowed the Negro housing advance in Atlanta and virtually put an end to further construction of rental units for nonwhites. There is no gainsaying the fact that the southern Negro, while not barred from sources of housing finance, is rarely, if ever, in the class of preferred borrowers (Negro institutions excepted). The interworking of racial discrimination and changes in the money market is summed up succinctly by one Negro real estate broker, with over forty years of experience, in the remark that "when money gets tight, the southern white man gets a little and the Negro gets none."

One of the codevelopers of Highpoint Apartments wrote in May, 1956, that

> presently I have been contemplating several Negro apartment developments, either on my own behalf or for clients. We find the mortgage market impossible. In the first place, the general interest rates are so high that such loans as are available for apartments must be at rates which are economically unsound when you consider that such building must compete with developments erected at times when interest rates were lower. . . . There is a reluctance on the part of financial institutions to enter the Negro housing field. This is an unjustified position, but that fact makes it no less burdensome to the Negro community and to the builders who wish to develop such projects.

Most informants report that the scarcity and high cost of land are prime obstacles to building more houses. As a rule of thumb, it is said that no developer should pay more than five hundred dollars per unit for undeveloped land, since curbing, paving, sewer lines, and the like will add up to another thousand dollars. If he pays a thousand dollars or more—as many have been doing recently—the chances are very large that he will be overextended. Whether the negotiator is the individual home builder or the developer, the owner has to pay a premium price and is likely to have corners cut on such things as landscaping.

Most savings and loan associations will lend 50 to 60 percent of the cost of a new house, but this too frequently is not enough to permit the typical client to build, because not many prospective homeowners have the difference. This fact, coupled with the built-in added costs because of land prices, explains in part the frequency of second mortgages.[13] Second mortgages reflect at once inflated prices, limited income, and the strong desire to own one's home.

The scarcity of better land sites also contributes to costs in another way. Frequently—and before 1948, usually—higher-priced homes were built or improvements were made on homes in neighborhoods where the bulk of other houses were significantly lower in price or in poorer condition. This built-in economic obsolescence meant that the owner suffered potential loss because it was unlikely that he could get out of the house what he had put in it—even immediately after construction.

There has been significant expansion of the Negro community and marked improvement over-all in the housing available; but on the whole the housing opportunities and alternatives available are still far from equivalent to those available for whites. The poorer competitive position of the Negro homeseeker, as well as the developer and builder as they seek land and apply capital, information, and technical skill, means that housing gains have been obtained at premium prices or differential costs. That this need not be a permanent situation is suggested by the fact that during the recent expansion the managerial, technical, and leadership resources available to the Negro have been enlarged and improved through the sheer doing of things that were never done before by Negroes.[14] Along with political strength, these become

[13] Another indication of the elaboration of real estate services and of enterprise is the recent formation of a Negro-controlled corporation with capitalization of $25,000 to deal in second mortgages. There are numerous stories—some of them no doubt apocryphal, and all difficult to check—of persons in the area who have become very wealthy as informal and unadvertised dealers in second mortgages.

[14] An important feature of this growth is the fact that within the Negro community itself there has developed almost a full complement of housing skills and services: there are in addition to the financial institutions already mentioned, approximately seventy-five real estate brokers and salesmen (the Empire Realty Board has a membership of sixty-three), approximately twenty-five

important resources as the Negro becomes more skillful in utilizing his potential—both within the system and probably to an increasing extent, outside it and despite it. One of the first by-products will probably be the reduction of cost differentials.

The Case of Mrs. Y.

This document is presented here not because it tells a typical story, but rather because it shows the roles played by the home-seeker, the real estate agent, lending agencies, white residents and protective groups, and very significantly, local law enforcement agencies in "a pocket of housing resistance" on the West Side.

The northwestward expansion, which resulted in the Negro settlement of Collier Heights—previously referred to—and other neighborhoods, leapfrogged a large area occupied by several hundred white families. In the summer and fall of 1955 the first tentative breaches of this all-white area were attempted by real estate dealers and Negro home-buyers. Among those involved in this attempt was Mrs. Y.

Mrs. Y., a widow with a grown daughter, has for several years been employed by one of the West Side educational institutions in a nonteaching capacity. The daughter is an employee in a Negro bank. The family was originally from Birmingham, Alabama, where they still own a home. Following the death, many years ago, of her husband, a dentist, Mrs. Y. had managed to rear and educate her daughter and a son—the son graduating with honors from Harvard, the daughter pursuing training in art and design in the East prior to coming to Atlanta. Because Mrs. Y. lived on the campus and did not own a home, her daughter had lived in rooming houses since coming to Atlanta.

Wishing to have a home so that she and her daughter might be together and so that her daughter might have a suitable place for entertaining her friends, Mrs. Y. decided in the fall of 1955 to buy a home. She got in touch with one of the better-

---

active construction firms or individual operators, a building supply firm, a fire and casualty insurance firm, a mortgage company, a registered architect, and a designer. A commentary on the function and contribution of the university center is the fact that the leaders, the idea men, and the men with inventiveness and managerial skill have, for the most part, been men who came to Atlanta to teach at or to attend one of the schools and who remained or returned after further experience and training.

known Negro real estate agencies and was told that there were some homes available in the Collier Heights neighborhood. When they drove through this neighborhood, Mrs. Y. saw "For Sale" signs up in front of several properties. The home she was shown and which she eventually purchased was located on a street which had no Negroes at that time, although at least two other Negroes had just purchased homes in the area. The agent said that sales of several other homes on the street were in the process of negotiation and that he and other agents were attempting to sell enough homes in the neighborhood to Negroes so that all the buyers might move in at approximately the same time. Since the whites she saw during the period when she was examining the house and completing the sale were either courteous or noncommittal, she anticipated no real difficulty.

The home which Mrs. Y. decided to buy was a four-room-and-bath house, built originally through a VA loan. In order to purchase the home, Mrs. Y. had to take over the loan amounting to $7,500. She had on hand $1,500 for a down payment, but when she began seeking further financing she ran into some difficulty. She was a middle-aged woman whose salary was not impressive and whose daughter had been working in Atlanta for only a short time. Finally, a conventional loan was arranged through the Jefferson Loan Society, a white downtown financing agency. The terms of the loan required payments of $42 per month. Plans were made to move furniture from the house in Birmingham to Atlanta. By December, 1955, there were at least seven Negro families who had purchased homes in the area. But already there were rumors of opposition, mostly from the West Side Protective Association. The other seven Negro purchasers decided not to move into their homes, but Mrs. Y., her daughter, and a cousin moved into their house in March, 1956. By this time one of the Negro-owned homes in the area had been bombed. Shortly after Mrs. Y. and her family had taken occupancy another of the unoccupied homes was bombed.

Mrs. Y. and her family had been living in their new home for about a month when they were visited by a delegation of four members of the West Side Protective Association. Mrs. Y.'s new neighbors suggested that she move out of her home; the discussion, as Mrs. Y. remembers it, was calm and orderly and there were no threats of violence—though all those present were aware of the bombings that had already taken place. Mrs. Y. said she had spent all of her resources in buying the house and moving her belongings from Birmingham. Although some suggestion was made that the association might repurchase the new home, the meeting concluded with no definite decision.

Police had been detailed to patrol the area after the bombings, and a special detail was supplied to keep an eye on Mrs. Y.'s house. After about two weeks the patrol cars were withdrawn. A few days later one of the police officers who had been a member of the detail told Mrs. Y. that he was worried and felt that she should move before something happened. During this period Mrs. Y. was especially concerned because her work kept her at the dormitory during the evening hours and her daughter was alone except for a teen-age cousin. She put in a call to the chief of police asking for continued protection and reports his attitude as being "rather ugly." According to Mrs. Y., he informed her that he had given her all the protection he could afford, and that it was too expensive to keep two squad cars assigned to patrol duty in the area.

One evening about two weeks after the detail was withdrawn—and within a day or two of the conversation with the police chief—the daughter came home from choir rehearsal at about midnight and went to bed; the mother was working at the dormitory that night. At about 1:00 A.M. the daughter and the cousin were awakened by the long-dreaded explosion. A bomb, evidently thrown at the front bedroom, had rebounded into the street where it tore a hole in the pavement, the impact of the explosion shattering windows in the house and driving nails through the wall. The daughter called the police immediately. No member of the police force arrived until more than twenty-five minutes later. But within two minutes of the explosion a crowd of whites had gathered in the street in front of the house. The daughter estimates this crowd as having exceeded two hundred persons. Although certain of the neighbors had appeared sympathetic earlier, there was now no offer of either sympathy or assistance from this group. Evidently brought to the scene by the noise of the explosion, a Negro motorist drove into the street. Certain persons in the crowd attempted to attack this man. Following her call to the police, the daughter phoned her mother at the dormitory and next phoned the real estate agent, both of whom shortly arrived.

After having made certain that neither the daughter nor the cousin had been injured, the mother went out to the street where the police car which had finally arrived was parked. Mrs. Y. reports that she said to one of the officers: "I'd like to know if you intend to give any protection to my daughter and her cousin?"

"I ain't worried about your daughter or your cousin either," the policeman replied. "I ain't got time to stay around watching them."

The daughter and cousin left the house on that night and never spent a night there again. Evidence that the policeman's retort to Mrs. Y. possibly had higher sanction was given on the following day when a relative of Mrs. Y.'s, a clergyman, called the mayor and asked if further protection would be provided in the event she and her family remained in their home. The mayor is reported to have said that while no neighborhood was zoned exclusively for either Negro or white occupancy, he could not promise to provide further protection.

Three days after the bombing, Mrs. Y. received a call from representatives of the West Side Protective Association offering to repurchase her home on the same terms as the group had set for the repurchase of the other homes bought by Negroes in the area: the association would buy the house for the same amount she had paid for it. Although the other Negro buyers had evidently accepted these terms, Mrs. Y. refused to agree to a settlement which did not take into account other expenses involved in buying the home and moving her furniture from Birmingham. She was also concerned about the problem of buying a new home and of finding suitable temporary quarters in the meantime. Eventually, a meeting was held in the offices of the Jefferson Loan Society at which it was agreed that Mrs. Y. would resell the house at a higher figure than she had paid for it, that she would be allowed to remain in the house for an additional month rent-free, and that she would be compensated for any furniture-storage charges incurred while she was trying to find another house.

Mrs. Y. finally found, through another Negro real estate

agency, a house listed some six or eight blocks south of the house she had bought previously. The street had formerly been all-white, but here the transition to Negro occupancy had been completed. The home which Mrs. Y. decided to buy was approximately the same size as the previous home, but the lot was only half as large, and the problem of financing proved to be more difficult. An attempt to secure an FHA loan fell through when Mrs. Y.'s age and salary were considered as constituting insufficient security. The daughter's job was ruled out of consideration. Finally, a loan was arranged through Atlanta Federal Savings and Loan Association. The terms for this loan were somewhat stiffer than for the previous loan, with higher monthly payments.

Mrs. Y. tends to look back on the events connected with the first house with a fair degree of objectivity, but she is understandably bitter about certain aspects of her experience. She agrees with her daughter that the real estate agent who represented them in the venture stuck with them through all the troubles that followed, but she feels that the head of the firm for which the agent works encouraged a false estimate of the amount of tension in the area, and she resents the fact that the original agreement to resell all the homes at the flat purchase price was entered into by the firm without any consultation with the owners themselves. This feeling is strengthened by the fact that certain stipulations of the agreement finally negotiated in her case were not lived up to. In spite of the agreement, she was charged a portion of the rent on the house before she moved out, and was never reimbursed for the charges connected with the storage of her furniture. She further feels that the mayor, the chief of police, and the policemen with whom she came in contact did not accord her the treatment she would have received had she been a white citizen. The daughter, looking back on the night when she and her cousin were awakened by the explosion, is wryly bitter about the rapidity with which the white "mob" formed and the contrasting tardiness of the police—called to a home which they had been "guarding" a few days before. She feels too that the entire situation might have turned out differently if the other seven or eight Negro buyers had actually occupied their homes at a mutually agreed upon time, rather than leaving the Y. family to move into the area alone.

The victim's bitterness is shared in some sections of the Negro community. Others, however, view the episode more dispassionately as a tactical error on the part of Negro housing leadership. Some of the Negro real estate brokers who listed homes in the neighborhood predicted that, with the semiencirclement of the area by the Collier Heights, Crestwood, and Simpson Road Negro settlements, it is only a matter of time until racial transition will take place. According to this line of thinking, Mrs. Y. was just unfortunate in being caught in a move that was premature in its timing and poorly planned and coördinated.

BIRMINGHAM

The Setting

Founded in 1871, Birmingham has been called "The City of Perpetual Promise"—a southern city without a past.[15] Its promise was tied to the combination of iron, coal, and limestone found in it and its environs. Employment is heavily concentrated in mining, manufacturing, and construction. Compared with other metropolitan areas of the South, wage levels are relatively high.

The Birmingham Standard Metropolitan Area (Jefferson County) had a 1950 population of 559,000, of which 209,000, or about two-fifths, were Negroes. These populations may be compared with the Atlanta Standard Metropolitan Area's 672,000, including 166,000 Negroes (one-fourth). In Birmingham, as in Atlanta, the white population has been growing more rapidly than the nonwhite, especially since 1940. Even so, the proportion of Negroes in the population of the Birmingham area is equaled in only one other metropolitan area of comparable size (Memphis, Tennessee).[16] In total population, the Birmingham area ranks eighth among metropolitan areas of the entire South, and third among those of the lower South, being exceeded by New Orleans and Atlanta.

---

[15] George R. Leighton, "Birmingham, Alabama: The City of Perpetual Promise," *Harper's Magazine*, August, 1937.

[16] The Negro proportion in the Memphis metropolitan area was 37.4 percent in 1950, compared with 37.3 percent in the Birmingham area. Five other metropolitan areas in the Deep South had Negro proportions higher than Birmingham's, but all were below 200,000 in total population (Charleston, South Carolina; Jackson, Mississippi; Montgomery, Alabama; Savannah, Georgia; and Shreveport, Louisiana).

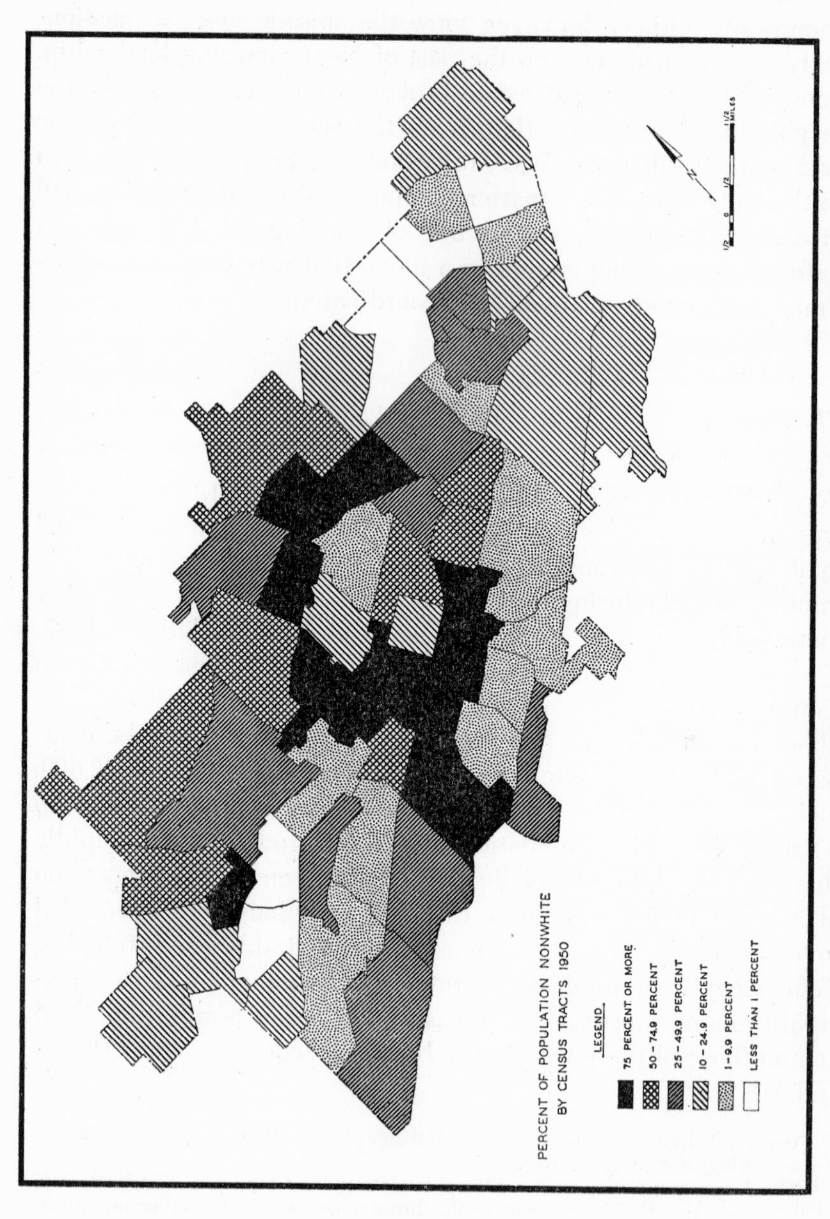

Map 2. City of Birmingham, percent of population nonwhite by census tracts, 1950.

The lack of diversification, the vulnerability of Birmingham's economy to economic fluctuations, and the manner in which human and natural resources were exploited during much of its history give substance to the local maxim, "Hard times come first to Birmingham and stay the longest." And these adverse factors appear to have delayed realization of the "promise." Although Birmingham is a city without a romanticized past tied to the Civil War and antebellum days, the way in which it was settled, its industries developed, and its people used and misused do constitute a heritage that colors much in its economic, social, and political relationships today.

The company town and cheap and captive labor set the social and economic tone and did much to mar and scar the social and physical landscape. The mines and furnaces, voracious in their demand for labor, made use of convicts who were leased to industrial concerns. Most of these convicts were Negroes. The notorious convict-lease system was not abolished until 1928. People in Birmingham today refer to certain settlements as having been started by escaped or released convicts. Many older persons remember the system and it is possible to talk with some who suffered directly from it. According to Leighton: "When a convict miner was worn out . . . his sentence would sometimes be cancelled, and he would make his way into town. There are families . . . today descended from such workers which can boast 'murderers in the third generation.'"[17]

Company towns, company housing, and the general frontier-like climate helped to fix the housing pattern also: "scattered about were tracts bought by land speculators and crammed with 'nigger houses,' then and now described as among the most profitable investments in the city."[18]

Birmingham's short history has been notable for both industrial and racial tension and violence. It was not until the 1930's, with the protection of federal legislation, that labor was successful in sustaining organization. The United Mine Workers and the steel workers' unions organized both Negroes and whites while soft-pedaling or evading the social equality issue.[19] By the

---

[17] Leighton, *Harper's Magazine*, August, 1937, p. 235.

[18] *Ibid.*, p. 236.

[19] Many union members and leaders in the Birmingham area have been in the forefront of the contemporary White Citizens' Council movement.

late 1930's, Birmingham had become a strong union town, and the income of its industrial workers had risen significantly. In 1936, the steel industry undertook a major expansion and modernization of its facilities and began to treat the local industry as something better than a stepchild of Pittsburgh. War and defense production fostered the further expansion of industry and increased payrolls.

The Birmingham Negro's Share

Birmingham Negro workers and families enjoy higher incomes than those of any other city in the Southeast, but their housing is among the poorest. The 1950 Census reported a median family income for Negroes in Birmingham of $1,849, compared with $1,695 in New Orleans, $1,681 in Atlanta, and $1,617 in Memphis. In 1955, a market survey conducted by Birmingham newspapers reported a median Negro family income of $2,348, a money increase of 27 percent over 1950.[20] The distribution of Birmingham Negro and white families by income class reported in successive annual surveys by the same agencies merits recording, as in table 9.[21]

TABLE 9

WHITE AND NEGRO FAMILIES IN BIRMINGHAM, BY INCOME GROUP

Color and income class	Percent distributions			
	1955	1954	1953	1952
White families				
$7,000 and over	20.3	16.7	14.5	14.1
$4,000 to $6,999	48.1	44.8	44.9	41.1
$2,000 to $3,999	23.2	27.3	31.3	36.0
Under $2,000	8.4	11.2	9.3	8.8
Negro families				
$7,000 and over	0.7	0.3	0.5	0.4
$4,000 to $6,999	10.4	9.3	8.3	5.6
$2,000 to $3,999	46.8	45.0	51.0	49.1
Under $2,000	42.1	45.4	40.2	44.9

SOURCE: Data compiled from *Birmingham News* and *The Post-Herald, Birmingham, Number One Test Market of the Deep South* (1955).

[20] *Birmingham News* and *The Post-Herald, Birmingham, Number One Test Market of the Deep South* (1955).
[21] *Ibid.*

These surveys show a continued heavy concentration of Birmingham Negroes in the lower-income groups as compared with whites, with evidence, however, of economic progress. The middle-income group of Negro families ($4,000 and over), while comparatively very small in both 1952 and 1955, nevertheless doubled in relative magnitude.

In table 10 are presented some summary characteristics of the housing occupied by nonwhites in Birmingham and three other metropolitan areas of the South in 1950. As will be noted, Negro dwellings in the Birmingham area are cheaper, of poorer quality, and more often crowded than those of the Atlanta, New Orleans, or Houston metropolitan areas. Owner-occupied dwellings in the Birmingham area were valued on the average a thousand dollars below the median value of owned homes in the Atlanta area. Fewer than 12 percent of Birmingham Negro households lived in "standard" dwellings—that is, units not dilapidated and equipped with private bath, toilet, and hot water.

TABLE 10

SELECTED CHARACTERISTICS OF NONFARM DWELLING UNITS OCCUPIED BY NONWHITES IN THE BIRMINGHAM, ATLANTA, NEW ORLEANS, AND HOUSTON STANDARD METROPOLITAN AREAS, AND IN THE UNITED STATES, 1950

Standard Metropolitan Area	Percent of dwelling units substandard [a]	Percent of dwelling units crowded [b]	Single-unit owner-occupied properties: median value	Tenant-occupied dwellings: median gross monthly rent
Birmingham	88.2	40.2	$2,800	$19
Atlanta	77.2[c]	39.4[c]	3,800	24
New Orleans	82.9	38.6	3,700	21
Houston	69.3	34.2	3,850	39
United States	61.2[d]	32.1	3,000	27

SOURCES: *U. S. Census of Housing: 1950*, vol. I, *General Characteristics*, chap. 1, "U. S. Summary," and chapters for respective states; vol. II, *Nonfarm Housing Characteristics*, chapters for respective states. Unpublished tables and special tabulations supplied to the Commission on Race and Housing by the Bureau of the Census.

[a] Dilapidated, or lacking private bath, toilet, or hot water.

[b] With 1.01 or more persons per room.

[c] Based on total nonwhite-occupied dwellings in the metropolitan area, farm and nonfarm.

[d] Based on total nonwhite-occupied dwellings in urban places.

The inferior housing of Birmingham Negroes as compared with Atlanta Negroes, although the former have higher money incomes on the whole, serves to focus attention on the differing characteristics of the two populations and on the different social climates in which they live. Birmingham Negro workers are heavily concentrated in unskilled industrial jobs. Many fewer, relatively, than in Atlanta are engaged in professional or business occupations. Resources of intellectual leadership, prominent in Atlanta, are much less highly developed in Birmingham. It is a reasonable theory that Birmingham Negroes, historically habituated to a low standard of housing, have not developed the same drive to improve their living conditions that is characteristic of large sections of the Atlanta Negro community. But too much weight should not be placed on this aspect of the matter, for, as we shall see, Negro housing aspirations have been more firmly suppressed in Birmingham than in Atlanta. Moreover, the possible demand of Negroes for better housing has never been tested, as it has elsewhere, by making a supply of such housing available to them.

The images which Birmingham Negroes have of themselves and their concepts of what is good and what is possible are most certainly changing. Informants in the Negro community, when asked about housing tastes, would say that there has been, in the past, little incentive among Negroes to buy or to build houses because the small professional and white-collar class provided no leadership in the field: "The big boys never had big homes, therefore, the little Negro didn't want much either." "Negro doctors and others had small two and three bedroom houses until recently." "Birmingham, unlike Atlanta, does not tend to hold college-educated Negroes. . . . It is not an educational center itself, as Atlanta is." One informant said that until after the war a $12,000 home was about the maximum for Negro professionals. Matters are now quite different, but Negro real estate operators and builders report that most white developers do not yet realize that the Negro client wants more and is willing to pay for it.

The following excerpts from the authors' field notes afford a vivid example of the underestimation of Negro housing wants and tastes and the necessity of "education" in this area:

Mr. M. (Negro real estate broker) told of some advice that

he had given the white developer of a series of houses on an eighty-acre plot. The developer had asked Mr. M. about the wisdom of building some "nice" houses for Negroes, and Mr. M. had said that the market would consume all of the "nice" homes that could be offered. Without further consultation, the developer had one house erected and called Mr. M. to look at it. Mr. M. got Mr. R. and went to see the house. Immediately, after they had seen the structure of concrete block with red brick trim, Mr. M. said, "So that's what that man called a 'nice' house. Let's go." Mr. R. said, "Let's take a look at the inside." Mr. M. said, "You go on, I don't care what the floor plan is, that thing isn't worth a damn." When Mr. M. reached his office, he called the developer and told him that he had looked at the house and asked him, "What happened? I thought you said you were going to build some 'nice' houses. I don't know anybody that I'd try to sell that thing to." The developer asked what was wrong. Mr. M. replied, "The house is wrong. I've seen some nice houses that you've built, but what do you think you'll get for that thing?" The developer thought the house should sell for $6,300. Mr. M. said the house was not worth more than $4,000. "You think you are going to get rich off of Negroes? Well, I'll have nothing to do with it."

The developer then got a house plan book and asked Mr. M. to show him a nice house. Mr. M. randomly opened the book to a page and said, "Now, I'd be interested in something like this." The developer said, "Why, that house would cost at least $9,000." Mr. M. then told the developer, "Apparently, you are trying to put all Negroes into the class that your chauffeur and maid are in. Now, I don't know either one of them, but if you use them as your guide to Negroes, you are always going to be wrong." The developer told Mr. M. that he would try to build another type house and proceeded to do so. A number of houses have been built and all have been sold. The developer later told Mr. M., "They probably won't appreciate you, but you are a man and I like that about you."

The Negro Residential Pattern

The proportion of the Negro population in the Birmingham metropolitan area living outside the central city is somewhat higher than in the Atlanta area (34 percent and 27 percent, respectively, in 1950). The difference is not due to any movement of suburbanization or expansion on the part of Birmingham Negroes but to the persistence of long established communities and industrial suburbs. Within the city of Birmingham, Negro residences are concentrated around the edge of the business district and in numerous small clusters throughout most of the city. The pattern is described in a report of the Birmingham Planning Board in commenting on school location problems:

> The map shows rather clearly some major differences between white and Negro residential areas which must be taken into account. . . . It will be noted that in white residential areas, except for housing projects, pupils are rather evenly scattered over the entire area. Negro residential areas tend to be much more concentrated and restricted . . . or there are small islands scattered over the city. . . . The heaviest concentration of Negro population also surrounds the transition zone of the business fringe areas of the city, which makes for very expensive and often very restricted school sites which may be of an impermanent nature.[22]

To the foregoing description, it should be added that the "islands" of Negro residence are in most cases surrounded by built-up white residence areas ("bottled up" is the Negro term) and do not have the possibility of expansion under prevailing racial mores. Where Negro communities are adjacent to unoccupied land, as in the western part of the city, such land has been regarded either as reserved for future white development or as "buffer" zones. Attempts of Negroes to expand into these vacant areas have been met with legal and illegal repression.

On the whole, the Negro residence pattern in Birmingham and environs has changed little in twenty years or more. A leading mortgage banker (white) remarked that "Birmingham has no transitional areas." This is substantially true, and this fact, in the face of a steadily growing Negro population, makes Birmingham virtually unique among the larger cities of the United States.

Between 1940 and 1950, the proportion of home-owning Negro families in the Birmingham area rose from 19 percent to 35 percent.[23] The drive of Negroes for homeownership was thus as much

[22] Birmingham Planning Board, "Preliminary Report," February 8, 1952, p. 50.

[23] Among whites, the rate of owner-occupancy increased from 43 percent to 59 percent.

in evidence in Birmingham as elsewhere. Unlike what happened in Atlanta, however, the increase in homeownership among Negroes reflects a change in status within established areas, both inside and outside the city, rather than the opening up of new areas to any significant extent.

The Control of Negro Residence

From the close of World War I until after the Second World War, the most decisive factors affecting the areas of residence of Negroes in Birmingham, and to a great extent the supply of housing available to them, were the legal, extralegal, and illegal acts and policies of local government and its representatives. These, combined with the violence and terror which in some measure they fostered and always permitted to go unpunished, have given a grim cast to the story of efforts by Negroes to expand their residential enclaves or to open up new ones. Birmingham, in common with many other southern and border cities, enacted ordinances for racial zoning during and after the First World War. Other cities abandoned such legal efforts after United States Supreme Court decisions had declared them unconstitutional, but Birmingham is unique in the persistence with which it has continued to apply such rules. It is also a curious fact that the city in which Negroes are as dispersed as probably any in the country should have insisted more strongly than any other on containment of the Negro population within prescribed boundaries.

Racial residential zoning enforced by city officials, although long invalidated by the highest court, was a fact in Birmingham until the 1950's. Legal penalties for violation of the zoning "laws" were never applied; they were not needed because of the rarity of challenge, the readiness of officials and others to use violence and threat of violence, and the important administrative device of "the certificate of occupancy" which could be withheld by the inspector's office for reasons within his discretion, including the race of occupants.

The early racial zoning ordinances,[24] dating from 1915, were

[24] This historical discussion is based on a study by Leavy W. Oliver, "Zoning Ordinances in Relation to Segregated Negro Housing in Birmingham, Alabama" (unpublshed Master's thesis, Department of Government, Indiana University, February, 1951).

rather vague and general as to specification of areas, although explicit in laying prohibitions upon Negroes. A city ordinance adopted in August, 1919, declared it to be ". . . a misdemeanor for a member of the colored race to move into . . . or having moved into, to continue to reside in, an area in the city of Birmingham generally and historically recognized at the time as an area for occupancy by members of the white race."[25]

In 1926, under enabling authority granted by the Alabama State Legislature in 1923, Birmingham adopted a comprehensive zoning ordinance specifying the areas in which whites and Negroes, respectively, were to be permitted to live. The city was divided into five districts: white residential, Negro residential, commercial, light industrial, and heavy industrial. The white and Negro residential districts were further subdivided. Negroes were allowed to continue living in thirty-seven small areas where they were already residing, although only two were actually zoned for Negro residential purposes. In recognition of the fact that the large majority of the Negro population lived in areas zoned commercial or industrial, Negroes were permitted to continue living in such areas with the provision that any Negro-occupied building in such areas must be three hundred feet or more from any white residential zones.[26] Similar restrictions are placed on members of the white race, but none of the informants of the present study were able to recall an instance of a white person's being charged with a violation of the ordinance, although numerous Birmingham whites do actually reside in or near Negro residence areas.

The administration of these zoning laws is entrusted to three agencies of the local government. The chief building inspector, whose duty it is to approve or disapprove all plans and specifications for building, to issue building permits, and to inspect all buildings for compliance with regulations, also issues occupancy permits upon approval of such buildings. The Planning and Zoning Board of Adjustments has the duty of formulating plans for future building, zoning, hearing and deciding appeals in connection with the enforcement or application of zoning ordinances,

---

[25] *Ibid.*, p. 9–10.
[26] *Ibid.*, pp. 13, 14. (Sections 1606 and 1607 of the 1926 zoning ordinance.)

and making recommendations to the City Commission. The latter body may amend or repeal the regulations or district boundaries on recommendation of the Planning and Zoning Board.

The general effect of the racial zoning ordinances (and doubtless their intent) has been to "freeze" Negro residence within the pattern of thirty years ago. Negro informants are of the opinion that the zoning ordinances have been administered harshly and oppressively. The editor of the *Birmingham World* (Negro) states that practically every plan submitted by the Zoning Board of Adjustments for the purpose of expanding Negro residential sections has been rejected by the City Commission. Frequently, however, the City Commission has approved zoning changes to enlarge the areas reserved for white occupancy, with the result, among others, that Negroes have been deprived of the use of property owned by them in such areas. In Atlanta, Negro ownership of land in undeveloped areas was a major instrument in the Negro housing advance in the postwar period. In Birmingham, similar use of Negro-owned property was barred by the zoning laws and the method of their enforcement.

It is reported that the Chief Building Inspector has, on several occasions, refused to issue building permits to Negroes on the sole ground of their race. He has also refused to issue occupancy permits to Negroes after having previously issued them building permits, and after they had completed the building of their homes in accordance with approved plans. Negroes claim that it is often very difficult to determine what areas are actually open to them and that any controversy involving the interests of white persons is automatically resolved to the latter's advantage. In Atlanta, the voting power of Negroes has brought them some consideration at the hands of local officials; Birmingham officials need consider only the interests of their white constituency, since the vast majority of Negroes are disfranchised. According to local informants, although Negroes make up 40 percent of Birmingham's population, they represent only 3 percent of the electorate.

Prior to 1947, so far as can be ascertained, Negroes brought no legal challenge of the Birmingham racial zoning laws. In that year, and subsequently, several legal actions were undertaken with the expectation that the legislation would be declared contrary to the Constitution. But this has not solved the problem.

Postwar Expansion and Resistance

As previously noted, the phenomenon of "transitional areas" is all but unknown in Birmingham. Nevertheless, in the early postwar period, several areas came into dispute between Negroes and whites. Most notable as the source of litigation and the scene of violence was the district known as North Smithfield.

Located in the northwest portion of Birmingham, North Smithfield was not, as might have been expected in a different city, a white residential area being invaded by Negroes. It was originally a 500-acre farm owned by a Dr. Joseph R. Smith, a former slave owner. Before Dr. Smith died, he donated the land to the city of Birmingham as an area for Negro dwellings. The tract was subdivided and most of the lots were purchased by Negroes for future building sites. But when attempts were made to secure building permits on these lots, it was discovered that many of them had been zoned for white residence only; if Negroes built homes there, they could not occupy them without violating the zoning ordinance. About one-third of the area was zoned for white residence only; the rest was zoned for commercial use. Negroes lived in the commercial part of the area and owned 90 percent of the lots in the "white" zone, which they were not allowed to use. Only three white families lived in this zone; the rest of the area was undeveloped.

In 1946, Mrs. Alice P. Allen, secretary to the president of Miles College, bought a home in the North Smithfield area, on the street where the three white families lived. Negro residents were on the other side of the street and in the surrounding area. The house had been advertised as for sale to whites, but the real estate agency handling the property was unable to find a white buyer. Believing that no whites would consider buying the house, the agency offered it for sale to Negroes. Upon finding it had been sold to a Negro, the whites who lived in the block exerted pressure to prevent Mrs. Allen from moving into the house. They told her that Negroes could not live on that side of the street in that block. Before she moved in, several windows were shattered by rocks thrown by unknown persons. Mrs. Allen reported the violence to the police, and inquired at the city hall concerning her rights. A few days before she was to move in, the city officials advised her that she could not live there, but that she could lease or sell the house to some white person to get a return on her investment. Determined to live in her new house, she leased it to a white tenant, while investigating further the possibility of living there herself. In December, 1946, Mrs. Allen filed a suit against the city of Birmingham, challenging the validity of the zoning laws. Before the case came to trial, the City Commission rezoned the block for residential purposes with no race stipulation, thereby making it possible for Mrs. Allen to move into her home.[27]

The city was not, however, to avoid a court test of its racial zoning. In January, 1947, Mr. and Mrs. Samuel Matthews, after having ascertained from city officials that the property which they desired to purchase for a new home was subject to Negro occupancy, purchased a lot and built a home in what is known as the East Thomas area.[28] It was located about three blocks from the nearest white resident, and a block and a half from a thoroughly built-up Negro neighborhood. After the home was completed, a city official refused to grant them a permit to occupy it, on the ground that the area had been zoned for white residents. With the aid of the National Association for the Advancement of Colored People, they filed suit against the city, alleging that racial provisions of the city's general zoning code were in violation of the Fourteenth Amendment.[29]

The U. S. District Court, Judge Clarence Mullins, ruled the ordinance unconstitutional and issued an injunction against its further enforcement. The Court noted that the U. S. Supreme Court and the Supreme Courts of North Carolina, Georgia, and South Carolina had declared similar ordinances in violation of the Fourteenth Amendment.[30]

Less than three weeks after the court decision, the house owned by the Matthews was dynamited and destroyed by unknown persons. The bombing occurred about eleven o'clock at night, but, according to newspaper reports, police did not come to investigate until the following day, after a visit was made to

[27] *Birmingham World*, January 14, 1947.

[28] This is not located in North Smithfield, but is in the same general area.

[29] *Matthews* v. *City of Birmingham*, 87 Fed. Supp. 538.

[30] *Birmingham World*, August 1, 1947.

the city hall by the Matthews' attorney. No one was apprehended for the bombing.[31]

The decision of the District Court in the Matthews case did not settle the issue. City officials continued to withhold building and occupancy permits from Negroes in the disputed area; the City Commission enacted further and more specific prohibitions of Negro residence in certain areas; "unknown persons" continued to bomb Negro homes.

Between March, 1949, and April, 1950, seven houses, purchased or built by Negroes in the North Smithfield area, were bombed.[32] In several other reported instances, Negroes were warned by city officials against moving into houses which they had purchased.[33] No one was ever apprehended in connection with the bombings.

A focal point in the controversy between Negro property owners and the city was a proposal to create a "buffer strip" 150 feet wide separating the white and Negro zoned areas. Negroes opposed the scheme on the grounds that it would deprive them of the use of building lots which they owned, both within the proposed strip and in the white-zoned area. The buffer was, nevertheless, established by city ordinance, and all persons, Negro or white, were prohibited from moving into the strip under penalty of a fine.[34]

In September, 1949, fifteen Negro owners of lots in the North Smithfield area brought suit in the District Court to restrain the City of Birmingham from enforcing the racial zoning ordinances preventing them from building or living on their properties. The case was heard in December, 1949, by the same Judge Mullins who had tried the Matthews case more than two years before. Again, the Court declared the racial zoning ordinances unconstitutional and enjoined the city from their further enforcement. On appeal, the decision was affirmed by the Circuit Court of Appeals, and the Supreme Court refused to review the case.[35]

Local inquiries turned up four other small areas where Negroes were succeeding whites. Characteristically, the process begins

[31] *Birmingham News-Age Herald,* August 19, 1947; *Birmingham Post,* August 19, 1947.

[32] *Birmingham World,* March 29 and August 16, 1949; April 18 and 25, 1950.

[33] *Birmingham Post,* May 31, 1949; *Birmingham News,* June 1, 1949.

[34] *Birmingham World,* August 16, and September 9, 1949.

[35] 185 F 2nd 859 (5th Cir. 1950). 341 U. S. 940 (1951).

with Negroes buying and building on vacant lots. Transfer of existing houses comes later, after the Negroes have gained a foothold in the area. Of the four transitional areas which were located, one consists almost entirely of vacant land; two others are deteriorated old residential sections, changing to commercial use; and the fourth is a middle-class district, partly built up, with homes ranging in price from twelve to fifteen thousand dollars or more. In one of these areas, known as Fountain Heights, white property owners reacted to the arrival of Negroes by forming a "civic association," which issued an appeal to whites not to advertise or show property to "any whom you would not deem socially equal and morally qualified."

Public Housing

The contrasts between Birmingham and Atlanta apply as well to public housing. One indication is the fact that since World War II 1,990 units for Negroes have been constructed in the Atlanta area; this figure is 500 more than the total number of projects constructed for Negroes in Birmingham both before and after the war.[36] One-third of the 1,492 units now available to Negroes were built after World War II. All units in the Birmingham area are within the central city.

At present, there are seven public housing projects in Birmingham, of which three are occupied by Negroes. The seven projects contain a total of 4,862 units, including 1,492 for Negroes and 2,270 for whites. This more nearly approximates a division based on population proportions than one based on the racial equity formula (relative proportions in substandard housing), as in Atlanta. Two-thirds of the Atlanta units are for Negroes, although there are proportionately (and absolutely) fewer Negroes in Atlanta than in Birmingham, and fewer of them are in substandard housing.

Newly Acquired Housing, 1945–1956

The figures in this section are based upon official reports, field observations and counting, and interviews. They give the picture as of August, 1956.

[36] A contract was let during the summer of 1956 for 1,250 additional units for Negroes. The addition of these units will mean that Birmingham Negroes will have just about one-half the number of units that Atlanta Negroes have.

Between 1945 and 1956, an estimated 4,300 units were added to the housing supply available to Negroes in Birmingham. Approximately $26,000,000 in mortgage money was involved.[37] Three out of every four of these newly acquired units were new houses, and they involved almost four-fifths of the total mortgage investment. The estimates are presented in table 11.

TABLE 11

ESTIMATED DISTRIBUTION OF NEW AND USED OWNER- AND RENTER-OCCUPIED NONWHITE DWELLING UNITS, AND ESTIMATED MORTGAGE, BIRMINGHAM, ALABAMA, 1945–1956

Total and type of occupancy	Number of units		Estimated mortgage	
	Number	Percent	Amount	Percent
Total	4,300	100.0	$25,681,504	100.0
New housing	3,170	73.7	20,036,504	78.0
Used housing	1,130	26.3	5,645,000	22.0
New housing	3,170	100.0	20,036,504	100.0
Owner-occupied	1,905	60.0	12,286,000	61.3
Renter-occupied	1,265	40.0	7,750,504	38.7
Used housing	1,130	100.0	5,645,000	100.0
Owner-occupied	1,130	100.0	5,645,000	100.0
Renter-occupied	...	...	...	...

Three out of every five of the new units were occupied by owners, and practically all of the used housing acquired was owner-occupied. These percentages, which are higher than the comparable figures for Atlanta, reflect the relatively more meager supply of rental units, both used and new, in Birmingham rather than a greater tendency to purchase homes. The chances were high that if a Birmingham Negro acquired new housing—and relatively few did—that he would have to buy it. This, of course, left untouched the needs of a great part of the lower-income and middle-income group.

Further indications of the nature of the supply and selective factors operating in the Birmingham market are the facts that about 60 percent of the newly acquired owner-occupied homes were in subdivisions (table 12). Our investigations indicate that less than 100 new individually built homes have been built in

[37] In gross terms, two and one-half times as many units were added to the Atlanta area and nearly three times as much mortgage money was involved.

Birmingham during this period[38]—less than 4 percent of the new owner-occupied units built. Used homes acquired by owners accounted for nearly 30 percent of the total acquisitions in all categories. The majority of these were acquired from white owners within existing Negro areas.

TABLE 12

ESTIMATED DISTRIBUTION OF OWNER- AND RENTER-OCCUPIED NONWHITE DWELLING UNITS, BIRMINGHAM, ALABAMA, 1945–1956

Type of housing	Number of units			Estimated mortgage
	Total	Inside city	Outside city	
Total	4,300	3,650	650	$25,681,504
Owner-occupied	3,035	2,405	630	17,931,000
New homes in subdivisions	1,830	1,205	625	11,236,000[a]
New individually built homes	75	70	5	1,050,000
Used homes	1,130	1,130	...	5,645,000
Renter-occupied	1,265	1,245	20	7,750,504
New government-insured apartments (608)	659	659	...	2,627,400[b]
New nongovernment-insured apartments	106	86	20	416,000
New public housing	500	500	...	4,707,104
Used apartments[c]	...	...	...	...

[a] Average mortgage on houses in subdivisions was $5,930.
[b] FHA commitment.
[c] Data not available. On-the-spot inspection and questioning reveal negligible number. Some few apartments in one of the fringe areas are due to be turned over to Negroes in the very near future.

Of the rental units made available, more than half were Section 608, FHA-insured units and about 40 percent were new public housing.

Between 1945 and 1956 about 14 percent of the new government-insured Section 608 rental units became available to Negroes in Birmingham. For whites, there was one apartment for each 87 persons; and for Negroes, one apartment for each 317 persons.

Nearly 85 percent of all newly acquired housing was located

[38] In Atlanta, about one-fourth of all newly acquired owner-occupied units were individually built.

inside the city of Birmingham. Even of the new homes in subdivisions, two-thirds were inside the central city. The limited extent of suburban development reflects the lack of organization to supply better quality housing to the Negro population. Potential opportunities for development of good, new residence areas for Negroes are not lacking but the motivation, permission, and "know-how" to exploit them have not existed up to now. A report to the Birmingham Housing Authority observes that suburban expansion areas for Negro development are actually more abundant in the Birmingham district than in Atlanta.[39]

Financing Houses for Negroes

In the present study, the authors were concerned with exploring the differences and similarities between Atlanta and Birmingham —particularly the presumed differences between the Negro communities of the two cities. In one interview, a Birmingham business man said: "Birmingham is about a generation behind Atlanta. We've got a different kind of Negro here and we've got a different kind of white man." Another respondent believed that the white power groups in economic and political affairs operated on the principle: "Don't let the Negroes want too much. If they do, they will get to desiring other things." Much of the foregoing material has indicated reasons why the quality of life for the Negro in Birmingham is different from that of Atlanta. The "climate"—a product of historical and situational factors—has at once been fostered and reinforced by greater rigidity, restriction, and literalness in applying the "rules" of the regional racial system; hence, "a different kind of Negro and a different kind of white man." The talent, ambition, money, and experiences of the Negro community appear to have been blunted, diffused, or diverted to a greater degree than in Atlanta. Birmingham has not exhibited or provided opportunities for the same kind of expansion and elaboration of economic activities in the Negro community. In general, economic activity has been truncated and confined to a few areas—small service enterprises, insurance, and fraternal organizations.

In contrast to Atlanta, there are less than a half dozen nonwhite

---

[39] *Residential Re-use in Avondale "Site C,"* A Report Prepared for the Housing Authority of the Birmingham District by Hammer and Company, Atlanta, Georgia.

real estate brokers in Birmingham serving Negro homeseekers. The small number of articulate and experienced nonwhite brokers plus the dearth of organized financial resources means that the Negro homeseeker has been relatively more dependent on white agents and lending institutions than his counterpart in Atlanta. Birmingham does not have an Urban League or similar agency with a program designed to promote more and better housing for Negroes.

The headquarters for the nonwhite Booker T. Washington Life Insurance Company and the Most Worshipful Prince Hall Grand Lodge, F. and A. M. of Alabama, are in Birmingham. These two lending institutions with rather limited assets have relieved some of the housing shortage in the state by investing $1,839,092, or one-third of their combined asserts, in first mortgage loans. Even with limited financial resources, the nonwhite lending institutions in Birmingham have put proportionately more money—34 as compared to 24 percent—in first mortgage loans than have the institutions controlled by Negroes in Atlanta.

A significant recent Negro action in the financial field has been the organization of a federally chartered savings and loan association. An application for a charter was submitted to the Federal Home Loan Bank Board in 1955. The application was supported by the Governor of the State, a Senator, the First National Bank of Birmingham, and several real estate brokers, mortgage bankers, and builders. The nine existing savings and loan associations in Birmingham (all white) opposed it. Portions of the testimony, pro and con, at the hearing before the Home Loan Bank Board are worth quoting.[40] One of Birmingham's largest mortgage brokers submitted in writing that:

> It is undoubtedly true that it is practically impossible for the average member of your race to secure home financing on a conventional basis or even on a government-insured basis. This situation is one over which we in Birmingham have no control in that the bulk of first mortgage loans, whether FHA-insured or VA-guaranteed, that are originated by a brokerage company such as ours must of necessity be sold to investing institutions . . . in the East and Midwest. These institutions have not been at all active in purchasing mortgages based on an ownership by members of your race. In some

[40] "Hearings before the Home Loan Bank Board, Washington, D. C., Application of A. G. Gaston, *et al.*, January 12, 1956" (typewritten).

few cases they have done so; however, the discount required has been prohibitive.[41]

A lumber company official wrote:

. . . I am constantly faced with situations where worthy colored families seem to be deprived of the privilege of building or purchasing their own homes because of the difficulties inherent in the obtaining of mortgage loans for colored people. This would seem to work a hardship not only on the colored families, but also on the white businessmen who need and would like to do business with these colored people.[42]

A white builder who has constructed over four hundred homes for Negroes stated that "there have been only two failures to keep up payments, and only one foreclosure." He wrote further that:

We had the greatest difficulties in placing the mortgages even though they were guaranteed by the government, and carried strong recommendation from the then executive vice-president and now president of the First National Bank of Birmingham. We had to comb the country to find takers. . . . The above-mentioned bank official finally placed them at 10 percent reduction.[43]

In opposition, representatives of the existing white savings and loan associations made three points: (1) that an additional association was not needed in the Birmingham area, (2) that the proposed association would probably fail, and (3) that the Negro population could not or would not sufficiently support an association primarily dependent on their savings. Excerpts from testimony follow:

Q. Mr. Yeilding, based on your experience in the savings and loan business over a period of approximately thirty years, having seen the associations grow and develop, is there a need for an additional savings and loan association in the Birmingham area?
A. I wouldn't think so.
Q. On what do you base that opinion?
A. I base that opinion on the fact that I believe we are filling the needs of all the people. We are growing as fast as we should grow from a conservative standpoint. We are growing faster than associations over the nation are growing. We have progressive

[41] *Ibid.*, p. 8.
[42] *Ibid.*
[43] *Ibid.*, p. 7.

management. I can't see why another institution would be necessary because it would have a small beginning and would take many, many years to grow to where it would be a power in the community.

Q. In your opinion, can a new association within the first five years make loans, government-insured loans, VA and FHA, with safety?

A. I don't believe they can, because the government-insured loans call for a low rate of interest and it is necessary for you to pay 3 percent dividend on your accounts, and the spread is not sufficient for it to be a good business proposition.

Q. Would you say in your opinion any new association could not make government-insured loans for a number of years after its organization?

A. It would be many, many years before they could make any sizable number of government loans.

Q. Mr. Yeilding, you have said there is no need for a new association. In your opinion, what is the probability of success of a new association in the Birmingham area?

A. I think that the competition it would have from the other existing associations would be hard to overcome, and it would be difficult to attract any sizable sum of capital with which to operate.

. . . .

Q. In your opinion, Mr. Yeilding, would you say that the probability of success of a new association is doubtful in the Birmingham area?

A. I would say so, yes, sir.[44]

Further testimony along the same line:

Q. I notice that there seems to be quite a bit of difference between the amount of savings accounts that the Negroes have in the various associations that you named as contrasted even to the amount of loans. . . . In your opinion, what would explain why the associations have not been able to cultivate savings from the Negroes?

A. In my opinion, the Negro in our area is essentially not a saver, in the first place. In the second place, a large part of the Negro population in our area is industrially employed and there are two very large industrial credit unions that operate in the steel manufacturing industry particularly, and there are numerous smaller credit union operations in the smaller operations in the Birmingham district. It is my opinion that the existence and operation of these credit unions in necessary manufacturing operations get the bulk of the savings that the industrially employed Negro is able to accumulate.

---

[44] *Ibid.*, p. 29.

Q. In other words, you don't feel that a Negro savings and loan association would necessarily be able to cultivate savings in any great number.

A. I don't think they are available. In all honesty, and all sincerity, I am sure all of us in the business in Birmingham have made a diligent effort to get savings, just as diligent to get savings from the Negro as we have from the white. The figures as to what they are speak for themselves.[45]

Statistics submitted at the hearing by the opposing savings and loan associations indicated that the nine associations together had 985 savings accounts by Negroes, totaling $511,791, or approximately $520 in the average account. Mortgage loans to Negro borrowers were reported to number 2,243, with an outstanding balance of $5,350,678, an average of $2,386 per loan.[46] The unpaid balances of loans to Negroes represented 7.2 percent of the nine associations' total investment in first mortgage loans. One association—Avondale Federal—reported more than 30 percent of its total mortgage investment in loans to Negroes. This was, however, next to the smallest of the nine associations, and accounted for only 13 percent of the total investment in Negro mortgages. The largest of the nine associations, with more than nineteen million dollars invested in first mortgage loans, reported only 3 percent of its loans made to Negroes. Another association, with total mortgage loans in excess of $8.3 million, had less than 1 percent of its investment in loans to Negroes.

The type of loans made to Negroes was not reported in the hearing. However, a representative of one of the larger associations stated in an interview with the authors that "this institution makes most conventional loans to Negroes at 6 percent for periods of seven to twelve years and no VA loans. FHA loans are made at 4½ percent for from twenty to thirty years." The official further said that most of the financing for Negro homes in Birmingham was done by savings and loan associations and that no outside insurance companies had "put a dime into Negro mortgages." This statement appears to be not wholly accurate, however. The authors learned of one subdivision of ninety-four

[45] *Ibid.*, p. 37.

[46] The loans to Negroes totaled originally $7,614,000 which, according to the testimony of the protestants, had been reduced by $2,264,000 as of December 31, 1955. *Ibid.*, p. 33.

units in the "Belvedere Circle" area financed by the Metropolitan Life Insurance Company. Other mortgage brokers indicated that a few outside life insurance companies had put small amounts of money into Negro housing, but that it was generally difficult to get these companies to accept mortgages on Negro property.

Approval of the proposed savings and loan association was granted by the Federal Home Loan Bank Board in April, 1956, with the requirement that capital of $250,000 should be raised from 250 local investors. At the end of August, 1956, over $375,000 had been subscribed by more than 375 investors. The organization was named the "Citizens Federal Savings and Loan Association of Birmingham." With this step, the Negroes of Birmingham have embarked on the road of mobilizing their financial resources in order that they may help pull themselves up by their own "boot straps."

The Case of Mr. B.—Builder

Probably the most successful Negro builder in Birmingham is Mr. B., a native of the city, now in his thirties. He is one of only three Negroes licensed as general contractors in the state of Alabama—and the only one to secure his license by passing the state examination. B. is not only a competent practical operator in the field, but is also a student of the complex of customs and attitudes involving the Negro builder, artisan, and home-buyer in Birmingham. His experiences and observations may therefore be of some value in augmenting the more objective findings which define the housing picture for Negroes in Birmingham.

B. has been interested in the building trades for as long as he can remember. His father is a well-known plumbing contractor, and two of his uncles have plumbing and heating businesses in other cities. B. learned the plumbing trade while he was still a youngster and is a licensed plumber, but from childhood he wished to be a general contractor.

He attended Hampton Institute in Virginia, where he could get training and experience in the trades along with his college degree. After a term of service as an Army lieutenant, he went back to school, taking work in architecture and engineering at Howard University and later pursuing similar studies at the

University of Michigan, after which he went home to Birmingham.

There was only one Negro contracting firm which offered any opportunities, but B. was unable to obtain employment with it. B. decided there was nothing to do but strike out as an independent, even though it meant operating on a shoestring. For the first year or so he worked mainly on alterations and repairs—doing most of the work himself or using a skeleton crew. During this period he came to know a white civil engineer, with whom he talked over some of his problems—one of them being the difficulty of getting licensed as a general contractor. In the state of Alabama the applicant for such a license must be recommended by an engineer, an architect, and a licensed contractor. Through the efforts of the civil engineer, B. was introduced to a contractor and an architect, who, after talking with him and inspecting the remodeling and repair jobs he had done, agreed to recommend him for the general contractor's examination. In trying to weigh his chances, B. had one of his white sponsors inquire as to the treatment Negro applicants received when they came before the state licensing board. The conclusion arrived at was that there was no way of telling, since no one could remember hearing of any Negro who had applied to take the Alabama examination before. The one substantial Negro builder in Birmingham had obtained his license by having been actively in business at the time the licensing law was passed.

In due time, B. received a notice from the state licensing board telling him to report to the capital for the contractor's examination. He was careful to arrive earlier than the time set in the letter and to take his place in the room indicated. The other applicants, all whites, began to gather, and after a time the clerk began calling off names. Finally, B. was left alone in the waiting room. When he questioned the clerk, he was told that the examination had been set for only a certain number and that he evidently had not been included in the group. B. went to a telephone and called his sponsor, the engineer, in Birmingham. The engineer advised B. to return to Birmingham while he and others attempted to find out what had happened. Within sixty days, B. was called back to the capital for a special examination. He worked on written problems until noon, then went to lunch. When he returned, the members of the licensing board called him in and began quizzing him on problems and information in the field. After two or three hours of this, B. was asked to step outside. When he was called in again, the board members stood and shook hands with him one by one and informed him that he had been licensed as a general contractor in the state of Alabama. He was assured that the members of the board stood ready to help him whenever he called upon them, and his relations with them have been good in subsequent years.

Now that he was licensed, B. found that he still had several handicaps to contend with. One of these was the negative attitude of the people in Birmingham who had known him as a boy. They could not seem to take him seriously as a qualified builder. For this reason, most of B.'s early work was done in the outlying areas of the city, or outside Birmingham altogether. During his second year, he got his first job of any consequence. He was selected by a church official to do a remodeling job originally figured at $6,000 but which eventually climbed to $16,000 as the official asked for additional changes. Throughout most of 1949 and early 1950, B. worked mainly with churches, with some house repairs and alterations thrown in. In 1950, B. did his first house within the city limits—a job for a white real estate company which wanted a house for one of its clients. B. contracted to do this house for $6,000—a figure which proved so disastrously low that the real estate company voluntarily paid B. an additional $700. The real estate company, meanwhile, sold the house for $10,000. Next, a lumber company contacted B. and had him build three houses for Negroes. Again, according to B., he found himself exploited. He was using material provided by the lumber company, and as the time came to wind up the jobs, he discovered that he was being billed for $200 on items for which the price originally quoted had been $100.

At about this time, B. discovered that if he did not work for the lumber companies or real estate companies, he was limited to only the smallest jobs. Financing was a pressing need, and he decided to seek money in the Negro business community. He went to one Negro businessman after another, telling them that he was willing to pay the same interest a bank would charge. Each man told him the same thing: Go to the banks; we don't lend money for building purposes. When B. did go to the banks, he was told that loans of the kind he wanted could not be made unless he were bonded. The bonding companies, in turn, told him that he had no work in progress which required bonding. In order to get the kinds of jobs which required bonding, B. needed at least $10,000 in immediately convertible assets. Although he had transacted considerable business at some downtown banks since his return to Birmingham, he found it impossible to borrow any sizable amount of money. He finally decided he would use the funds he had on deposit as a lever—either he would get a satisfactory loan or he would withdraw his funds. This approach proved to be effective with those who had turned down his loan applications earlier. From that time on, B. has been able to get money more readily—although not in the amounts nor on the terms which he feels would be open to him if he were a white builder.

With some financing at his disposal, B. was able to move into the heart of the Negro community. Even so, his first jobs in this area were done for representatives of concerns with headquarters outside Birmingham. A cosmetics company with headquarters in Chicago and an insurance company with headquarters in Jacksonville provided the first showcase in midtown for B.'s work. Contracts for houses followed, and by 1952–1953 B. was able to take on additional help and to justify the office building and garage he had built for himself.

B. did not find it difficult to get workers, but did have a problem getting skilled men. He found relatively few Negroes who responded satisfactorily to the program of on-the-job training he attempted to provide. One source of the difficulty is that Negroes in Birmingham were and are excluded from most of the building-trades unions. They can belong to the carpenters, bricklayers, plasterers, and cement finishers unions but are barred from the electrical, plumbing, and painters unions and from all the machine-operating unions such as the crane operators, bulldozers, and truck drivers. He also could not find competent help on the management end. His original hope of making large profits through a large gross could not be realized in view of the unavoidable waste and slow-ups growing out of a one-man managerial setup. This became clear to him when he found that he had netted a smaller amount in the year during which he did a gross of a half million dollars than he had netted in the year when he cut back his operations to an $80,000-plus volume of business. At present, B. maintains a stable crew of twelve to fourteen people, including his secretary (he once employed forty). He and his foreman split the on-the-job supervision, switching from one job to another when they have more than one project going.

The cost of the houses B. was putting up during the early 1950's ranged between $9,000 and $10,000. He feels that the relatively low value of homes built for his Negro clients during his first years as a contractor not only reflects the financing difficulties met by his clients but may also in part be attributed to the modest "image" of suitable housing held by most middle-class Negroes in Birmingham up to that period. For years, the Tennessee Coal and Iron Company and other industrial firms had put up $2,000 shacks for their workers, both Negroes and whites; therefore, the Negro teacher or doctor could build a home in the $6,000 to $10,000 category which seemed more than adequate by comparison. In 1952, when a well-known Negro professional man summoned B. to discuss building a home, he was the first client B. had ever heard talking in terms of a $35,000 home or a 100-foot frontage. So unaccustomed were most Negroes to houses of the size B. was building for the professional man that he received numerous calls from people who thought he was building apartments and wished to rent. According to B., the new idea provided by this house, along with the influence of Negro-owned homes in Atlanta and other cities, which Birmingham professionals noted as they began to travel about more often, has resulted in the building of homes ranging from $15,000 to $30,000. B. says that he has not built a house costing less than $12,000 in the past several years. Part of the higher price, of course, is due to the rise in building costs.

B. is now enjoying what he calls a "band-wagon boom" with people bringing him more business than he can handle within the limits he has had to set for himself. In part he feels this can be accounted for by the satisfaction his clients have found in the homes he has built for them. All of his homes are built to the special requirements of his clients and he refuses to duplicate any design. But even more important, he feels, is the fact that he can now get financing for his clients. He has the reputation of being able to secure financing even after others have failed. In several cases he has sent applicants back to the same man who turned them down previously, and they are always impressed to find that a telephone call from B. has removed the obstacles which blocked the loan only a matter of days, or hours, earlier.

Nevertheless, as B. points out, his situation is far from ideal. Although a licensed contractor, he cannot belong to the white professional groups in the city and is therefore denied access to the inside information, the day-to-day exchanges which facilitate success in the field. In spite of some coöperation from city officials and occasional aid from friendly materials men and others, B. is largely limited to the kind of knowledge which the general public can find in the newspaper. An instance of this was the building of the public library branch in the Negro community, less than six blocks from B.'s home. When B. read one day that the library was to be built and that an architect had been chosen, he called another architect asking about the procedure for getting plans so that he might bid on the project. He was told that an announcement would appear in the papers advising contractors when they might get plans and prepare their bids. Since the job was not large enough to attract the big firms, and since it was in the Negro community and represented public funds, B. felt that his chances of getting the job were fairly good. For several weeks he watched the papers carefully, and then one day as he drove along the street he saw bulldozers at work excavating the site. When he called his friend, the white architect, he was told that the other architect had evidently winked at the law and accepted a secret bid. B. feels that the fact that a Negro contractor was planning to seek the job was probably a deciding factor in the architect's decision.

The matter of financing is still a problem, though not an acute one so long as B. stays within safe limits. Large-scale financing, however, is still unavailable. B. has observed a young white contractor who began work on the outskirts of Birmingham at about the same time B. was handling a $45,000 job in the same area. Since that time the young white contractor has begun taking $100,000 jobs. According to B., the banks and other lending agencies will let such a promising young white builder have money on little more than his signature and the recommendation of an established businessman in the community who has faith in the young man. B. points out that white lenders still refuse to treat Negro loans as normal business transactions. Too often they not only charge higher rates and ask stiffer terms, but insist on insulting Negro applicants and trying to make them feel that they are recipients of special favors in being allowed to borrow money at high rates of interest.

Although B. has won the confidence of most Negroes in the community, he finds that certain attitudes suggestive of envy or malice continue to persist. B. owns a station wagon which he uses for business purposes. At the time he bought the vehicle, he was in the process of discussing the building of new homes with two prospective clients. In talking with one of them one day, he stated his intention of next visiting the other prospective client. "I don't think there's any use of seeing her any more," the first person said. "She says she don't intend to buy that new station wagon for you." In two other cases Negroes who had employed white contractors to build their homes passed the word around that they had previously gone to B., only to have him quote an outrageously high figure. In neither case had B. even seen the plans, let alone submitted figures.

But as serious as are the problems of financing, of finding managerial assistance and skilled labor, of adverse attitudes on the parts of Negroes and whites, B. sees another problem as potentially more serious. As race relations worsen in Birmingham and as the power of the White Citizens' Councils and other anti-Negro groups increases, more and more Negroes begin thinking of leaving Alabama. This is particularly true of those Negroes who make up the professional class—the same group which, in the main, provides clients for B. and other builders. In recent months, at least three professional men who had planned to build homes ranging in cost from $15,000 to $35,000 have decided not to build. One of these had his FHA commitment in hand and had secured approval of a loan, but has now decided to leave Birmingham as soon as he can get his affairs in order. Another client for whom B. built a home some three years ago has sold his home, disposed of his medical practice, and moved to the Midwest. Those who are leaving or thinking of leaving include both young people and those who are in their middle years, both relative newcomers and families whose members have lived in Birmingham all their lives. Unless this situation changes, B. foresees a gradual shrinking of his opportunities as a builder. If this happens, the time may come when B.—a married man with four children—may also have to decide whether it might not be necessary for him to leave his native city, to which he returned with such high hopes following the war.

SUMMARY AND CONCLUSIONS

The present study has drawn a picture of sharply contrasting housing conditions and opportunities for Negroes in two big cities of the Deep South. In both, the Negro lives under the regional system of segregation and white dominance. Yet, in one the Negro has been able to achieve a significantly better life and larger opportunity (as measured by housing) than in the other.

The quantity and quality of housing services for Negroes depend on the intricate interplay of many factors. The three major factors that appear to make the difference are the economy, the social climate, and the structure and quality of life in the Negro community.

The diversified and expanding economy of Atlanta is based primarily on commerce, communications, and services. This affects the occupational structure of Negroes as well as whites, and despite lesser economic rewards, produces a more buoyant and self-confident community. There are large numbers of businessmen, white-collar workers, and professionals, and this means a different community from one based on workers almost exclusively.

Birmingham is an industrial city that has moved belatedly to achieve diversification and balance. Workers are more aware of their dependence on what happens in one industry and on economic policies that might be set outside the region by a few interests. Birmingham is profoundly affected by big company policies and the swings of the business cycle. The occupational structure, styles and levels of living, community morale, and day-by-day exigencies of life for both whites and Negroes reflect this. Birmingham shows to a greater extent the dilemmas and anxieties of a city not sure of its ability to cope with its many besetting problems.

Atlanta is more permissive and fluid. It does not have the industrial, company-town heritage. It has had an economic and political leadership that has given (or has been able to give) priority to civic advancement and national reputation rather than to maintaining rigid control of the racial minority. And that minority itself has been able to establish its claims through its own leadership and resources, partly because the expansion of the minority community *within the system* is viewed by the whites as a matter of pride and profit rather than a threat to the system itself.

Birmingham is more restrictive, rigid, and tension-prone. A kind of racial dominance, which in its beginnings was probably motivated primarily by an economic interest in cheap labor and control, has its own dynamism now. It is hard to combat because of lags in development of an outside orientation and also because of the truncated political, economic, and educational development of the Negro community.

In both cities, the direct impact and the backwash of postwar changes in national and international affairs, and the recent court decisions, have raised the sights of Negroes and provided specific examples and techniques of change. It is symptomatic of the differences in the social climate of the two cities that Atlanta has been less adamant and strident in racial relations than Birmingham. Thus it has accepted desegregated public golf facilities, for example.[47]

We do not mean to suggest that Atlanta is lacking in restrictions, adamant people, a die-hard opposition, public affection for tradition, and its quota of violence and threats. All of these are present. But our point is that these features are more contained, less condoned officially, and more effectively combated or ignored by both Negroes and whites. This is due to the social climate—a result of the interaction between the design for stable, big-city progress, responsible city government, and the increasing sophistication, know-how, and leadership in the Negro

[47] Atlanta politics are different from Georgia state politics. In some instances, such as this, Atlanta can and does resist strong state-level political pressure to conform.

community. The relationship among these is reciprocal. Given Atlanta, literally it could afford nothing else; given Birmingham, the powers that be appear to think that they could afford nothing else but what they have—hence it is a more troubled city in which both the white and Negro communities lag in many respects, of which housing is only one.

It is clear that the resources and organization of the two Negro communities have also made a difference in their housing stories; but it should also be clear that the quality of life in the Negro community in neither instance is an independent variable. Atlanta's pattern is one of dynamic segregation; Birmingham's is more static. The Negroes of Atlanta have struggled against segregation barriers which were neither as high nor as rigid as those set up before the Negroes in Birmingham. The lesson of Atlanta is not, we believe, "see what can be accomplished under segregation," but rather, "see what can be accomplished under a little freedom."

If there is one difference between the two Negro communities that appears to be telling or perhaps decisive, it is the fact that Atlanta has been since Reconstruction a center of higher education for Negroes. The impetus, the leadership, and the personnel for most of the significant achievements in business, professions, finance, politics, and welfare have come from or been closely associated with staff members, former students, and students of the six schools—Atlanta University, Morehouse, Spelman, Clark, Morris Brown, and Gammon. Aside from providing the leadership and much technical know-how, this group has also provided leadership in consumption and taste. They have provided images of performance as well as consumption within the community and have transmitted important images of the good and possible from outside the local community. This is important, even though the influence of the Negro intellectual community, particularly with regard to housing, was not much in evidence until very recently. When the opportunity arose to do something in housing during the years immediately after the war, a base of resources and skills was available. This was not true of Birmingham; what happened in Atlanta could not have happened in Birmingham, even if the opportunities had been the same, because Negro resources were smaller and less organized.

Another commentary on the differences between the two cities is the fact that much of the housing story among Negroes the past ten years in Atlanta has been tied up with the efforts of the Housing Division of the Atlanta Urban League; without the Urban League's efforts, there would have been gains, certainly, but of quite different dimensions and extent. Birmingham has no Urban League. Efforts to establish such an agency there were abandoned after the strong opposition of powerful groups and leaders. Like the Negro bank and other crucial institutions, Atlanta was lucky to have an Urban League and fortunate to have a situation in which it could operate effectively. It should be stressed that operating effectively for any agent or any institution active in housing in either community has meant acting to some degree with the coöperation, sponsorship, or collabortaion of whites and Negroes. The quality and range of coöperation and *laisser-faire* in Atlanta are different because they have been mutually rewarding. Significant changes in images—those that the Negro has of himself and of his community and those that important figures in the white community have of him and his community—are occurring, more rapidly perhaps in Atlanta than in Birmingham. Nowhere under the current restrictions of segregation is it reflected more graphically and poignantly than in the tough stuggle for and the premium price paid for more and better—and in these communities, still segregated—housing.

JACK E. DODSON

II

Minority Group Housing in Two Texas Cities

The purpose of this study is to describe and analyze the housing situation of Mexicans and Negroes in San Antonio and of Negroes in Houston, Texas. There are virtues to studying these two situations together. We see how the same variables take different values in two different social situations, producing different total effects. In each city, and for each ethnic community, we will examine the demand for housing as affected by the size and demographic character of the minority group, its income, and its attitudes on housing, and the availability of housing for the group, as determined by the attitudes and activities of builders, general community attitudes, the practices of the real estate brokers, the availability of finance, and the state of the general housing market. We will see that the common picture of a uniformly negative situation for Negroes in the South must be modified to take account of local circumstance and variation, and that there are wide differences between the situation of Mexicans and Negroes in San Antonio, and wide differences between the situation of Negroes in San Antonio and Houston.

The evidence for this study has been collected from official figures and reports and from interviews in both cities with all relevant parties—leaders of the various groups, builders, real estate brokers, offices of financial institutions, government officials, and others. At many points, we have not been able to go as far as wished. In particular, we were unable to evaluate systematically the role of public housing. In both San Antonio and Houston, public housing supplies a good deal of housing for

Mexicans and Negroes, but the complexity of the public housing issue in both cities and limitations of funds and time have led us to exclude it from this study. We concentrate thus on the role of the private housing industry in supplying housing for these minority groups.

Although the report is written in the present tense, the field work for the study took place in the first months of 1956. The reader is asked to remember that reference is always to 1956 unless some other date is specifically given.

MINORITY GROUP HOUSING IN SAN ANTONIO

San Antonio is marked by a number of features which sharply differentiate it from most American cities of its size and from other southern cities particularly. It has maintained features of a special subculture, derived from its unique role in the history of Texas, its strong links with Mexico and its large Mexican population, its role as a frontier military station, and its place as a trading center for the neighboring ranches. Its failure to develop a strong industrial base has, in a measure, shielded San Antonio from the modernizing and secularizing impact of industrialization.

Politically, the city gives a mixed picture. It is the city which produced Maury Maverick, the distinguished Texas Congressman, but it also has been plagued almost continually by corrupt local government. It led all other metropolitan centers of Texas in desegregating its schools, but it has also had a particularly vociferous group of superpatriots, who a few years ago led an assault on the public library in an effort to remove all the books they considered objectionable.

Military personnel coming from all over the United States give a certain cosmopolitan character to the city, as does the Mexican-Spanish influence. Its military role has been maintained and expanded, despite the decline of the significance of the Mexican border. San Antonio and its environs contain four Air Force bases, Fort Sam Houston, Brooke General Hospital, and an Army armory, as well as numerous lesser installations. A large part of the population is on the payroll of the armed forces.

San Antonio is a poor city. An unusually small proportion of the city's labor force is engaged in manufacturing, and it has a low median income per family compared with other Texas cities. Nevertheless, it is a rapidly growing city. Between 1940 and 1950 the San Antonio Standard Metropolitan Area registered a population increase of 48 percent, and in the latter year contained 500,460 people: this was not much less than the rate of growth of the metropolitan areas of Houston (52.5 percent, to 806,701 people) and Dallas (54.3 percent, to 614,799 people). The central city grew even faster than these two larger Texas cities, with an increase of 67 percent (to 408,442) as against increases of 55 percent (to 596,163) and 47 percent (to 434,462) for Houston and Dallas.

About 40 percent of the population of the city bears Spanish surnames;[1] no other metropolitan city in the United States has such a high proportion of Spanish-surname population. On the other hand, the Negro population of San Antonio is relatively small; in 1950 it was only 7 percent of the total population.[2]

There is no question that there exists an institutionalized pattern of "Anglo"[3] supremacy in San Antonio. There are large differentials between the average educational attainment, income, and occupational achievement of the Anglo population and the two minority groups. There is also a definite pattern of social segregation, and the Anglo group is dominant politically. However, there are important differences in the social positions of the two minorities.

From the point of view of formal segregation practices, the Negroes are much worse off. There is clear residential segregation, and the rule of "Jim Crow" prevails in restaurants, hotels, and

[1] The proportion of persons of Latin-American cultural background is undoubtedly larger than 40 percent. It is recognized that the Bureau of the Census' use of surname as a means of identifying Latin-Americans, or Mexican-Americans, is approximate. All data derived from census data for 1950 pertaining to the Latin population of San Antonio used in this report is recognized as being approximate. For a discussion of the limitations of the 1950 Census for the Latin population, see: *U. S. Census of Population: 1950*, vol. IV, *Special Reports*, part 3, chap. C, "Persons of Spanish Surname," pp. 3C-4–3C-6.

[2] Census data are ordinarily given for the ambiguous "nonwhite" category rather than for Negroes separately. Because in San Antonio and Houston all but tiny fractions of the nonwhite populations are Negro, the term "Negro" rather than "nonwhite" is used in presenting census data for the cities' nonwhite populations.

[3] The term "Anglo" is used in this report to refer to all non-Latin white persons. This term has obvious deficiencies but is used because of fairly general acceptance of the word with the meaning assigned here.

places of public entertainment. The public schools and the municipally operated junior college, however, have been recently desegregated. The city buses and some parks have also abandoned segregation. In these respects, San Antonio has generally led the major cities of Texas and has done so with little public excitement.

The segregation of the Latin-American population is neither as rigid nor as formal as that of the Negro. There is no traditional "Jim Crow," no pattern of "etiquette" to govern intergroup contacts. There has never been official segregation of the Mexican population in the public schools, the parks, or public transportation. Mexicans are not categorically barred from hotels and restaurants; those who bear the marks of high social status are admitted. However, there is *de facto* residential segregation, and as a result, a high degree of *de facto* segregation in the schools.

One of the most striking ways in which San Antonio differs from other southern cities is in the political role of the minority groups. Rather than being excluded from politics, they have been important as a means of maintaining the power of the local political machine. This machine has been in almost continuous control of the city government: only in recent years has a reform coalition wrested power from it. The Negro vote has generally been delivered to the machine by local Negro political leaders. At times, this vote has been paid for in the form of paved streets in the Negro districts, parks, schools, public housing, and other improvements. There can be no question that the Negro community has benefited to some degree under machine rule. At the same time, as the consciousness of the possibility of greater equality grows among the Negro population, this tradition of Negro voting in San Antonio is potentially capable of playing an important role in affecting municipal decisions relating to race relations. The experience of using the vote to get local improvements may easily develop into the idea that it may be used to get even more.

The Mexican-American vote, despite the much greater size of the population, has played a smaller role in local politics. There is little political participation by Mexican-Americans and no large important vote that might be delivered by local political leaders. Members of this group, if they vote, do so as individuals. A few Mexican-Americans have been elected to public office.

The belief is common in San Antonio that there has been, on occasion, considerable "buying" of Mexican-American votes by the local political bosses when needed in a close election. This participation in politics is on a lower level of political consciousness than that of the Negroes: among the latter, the vote may be delivered, but for concrete goods, by leaders; in the Latin-American group, the vote is not exercised or is often given by an individual in return for money, with no advantage accruing to the group.

Negro Housing in San Antonio

In 1950 there were only 29,500 Negroes in a population of 408,000 in San Antonio. But their proportion is rapidly growing. In the decade from 1940 to 1950, San Antonio's Negro population increased by 68 percent, as compared with an increase of 47 percent for the white population, and it has probably been growing at the same rate since 1950. It shows a slightly smaller proportion of married persons than does the white population, but considerably fewer children. If one measures fertility by the number of children less than five years old for each 1,000 women between the ages of 15 and 44, the Negro population has a fertility ratio of 393, as against 453 for the Anglo population and 696 for the Latin group.

In 1949 the median income of Negro families in San Antonio was $1,461, as compared with $2,196 for white families. Since the white group includes the large Latin-American population, the difference between Negro and Anglo income is much greater than this spread suggests.

These circumstances of rapid growth and low income would alone suggest that the housing situation of Negroes cannot be good, and indeed it is not. Negro housing is more crowded than Anglo housing: almost one-quarter of Negro dwellings have more people than rooms, as against one-fifth of Anglo-white dwellings (see table 13). Because the Latin population lives under considerably worse conditions than the Negroes, the Negro percent of overcrowding is somewhat lower than that for the city as a whole. Sixty-three percent of the Negro dwelling units are either dilapidated or lack private bath, toilet, or hot running water, while only 39 percent of all San Antonio dwelling units (Anglo, Mexican, and Negro) are in this condition.[4]

TABLE 13

PERCENT OF DWELLINGS SUBSTANDARD OR OVERCROWDED, BY ETHNIC GROUP OF OCCUPANTS, SAN ANTONIO STANDARD METROPOLITAN AREA, 1950

Classification of dwellings	Total dwelling units	Dwellings occupied by		
		Anglo	Negro	Latin
Substandard [a]	39.0	20.6	63.4	79.0
With 1.01 or more persons per room	26.3	19.9	23.8	55.4
With 1.51 or more persons per room	14.1	7.5	10.5	34.9

SOURCE: *U. S. Census of Housing: 1950*, vol. I, *General Characteristics*, chap. 43, "Texas."

[a] Dilapidated, or without private bath, toilet, or hot running water.

In general, the supply of housing for Negroes has not kept up with the increase of Negro population. From 1940 to 1950, against a nonwhite population increase of 68 percent, dwellings occupied by nonwhites increased by only 37 percent; whereas the white population, which increased by 47 percent, showed a 74 percent increase in number of dwelling units.

These summary statistics conceal what is actually a wide range of housing conditions for Negroes in San Antonio. There are small areas of the worst possible slums, in which streets are almost completely unimproved, many dwellings have pit privies for toilets, running water is not available, and water vendors are the only sources of usable water. On the other hand, since 1950 there have been a few developments of high quality housing for Negroes, built to FHA or VA standards at prices of seven to ten thousand dollars. There are areas of almost complete Negro segregation, areas of mixed Negro and Latin occupancy, and even areas of mixed Negro and white occupancy.

The additional housing needed by San Antonio's growing Negro population comes from three sources: public housing, houses vacated by the white population, and new houses built for sale

[4] *U. S. Census of Housing: 1950*, vol I, *General Characteristics*, chap. 43, "Texas."

directly to Negroes. The transfer process of white to Negro ownership of old houses tends to provide deteriorated housing, for the most part, on which it is difficult or impossible for Negroes to get reasonable financial terms. New housing did not begin to be built for Negroes until after 1950.

New housing for Negroes was dependent on the entry of builders into this market, and, unfortunately, builders in San Antonio were generally pessimistic concerning the possibility of building and selling to Negroes. Most believe the Negro population does not constitute a desirable market because of moral inferiority and financial irresponsibility. There is also the feeling that commercial relations with Negroes affect one's status in the community. As one builder said, "I do not want to become known as a 'nigger' builder." One finds that builders for the Negro market have indeed suffered a loss of repute among fellow builders. Builders went to pains in interviews to indicate their lack of familiarity with the operations of those builders who have entered the Negro market; while the latter appeared to be highly defensive about the fact that they did build for Negroes.

Builders also tend to be uninformed about the Negro market. Their prejudice tends to keep them from acquiring information, while their ignorance tends to heighten their prejudice, or at least their discriminatory behavior. In recent years, however, builders have shown somewhat greater interest in the Negro market. The key event was the entry into San Antonio of an out-of-town company in 1952 which built a development of some 200 houses for Negroes. These houses qualified for FHA or VA financing; they were a marked success, and were sold quickly and without much difficulty. Very shortly thereafter, a number of San Antonio builders became interested in building for Negroes, and several other developments were begun. Today, Negroes who are financially qualified can buy houses in the seven to ten thousand dollar range which are roughly comparable to houses in the same price class in the Anglo market.

Even though builders' prejudice and ignorance have to some extent broken down, other effects of prejudice and discrimination tend to hamper the development of good housing for Negroes. Desirable sites for Negro housing are very difficult to find. Many factors affect the availability of good sites for Negroes: inlying sites are reserved for expensive Anglo housing; most areas are white and builders would hesitate to introduce a Negro housing development in them; the outlying areas suffer from lack of city facilities, and it is not easy to get the city to extend sewers, streets, and utilities to service new Negro developments.

Nevertheless, community attitudes in general are not quite so rigid as in many other parts of the South. Thus, one small development, which had been planned for whites—although adjacent to a Negro area—was opened to Negroes when it turned out that all the houses could not be sold to whites. The development thus became mixed and remains so, without arousing any great excitement. There is only one such case, but its acceptance is significant. Equally significant is the fact that there has been no effort to maintain the boundaries of Negro areas by terror, bombing, or strongly organized pressures. Negroes have been moving into a number of transitional areas without excitement.

Real estate agents reflect the dominant community attitudes. When interviewed, they asserted they would not handle any transaction which resulted in the entry of a Negro into an exclusively white neighborhood. However, there are a number of agents who concentrate on transactions involving Negroes, and on properties in or near Negro neighborhoods, and there is reason to believe that these, on occasion, do handle transactions which bring Negroes into white neighborhoods. But where this occurs, the neighborhoods involved are deteriorated; in some cases, Mexicans have moved in previously. The agents who played a role in this expansion of the Negro market were wary in discussing their operations: they were aware that these would not be looked upon with favor by the community.

Also affecting chances for better housing for Negroes are the possibilities of financing. Local commercial banks, savings and loan institutions, and mortgage companies make some loans to Negroes under FHA and VA programs, but Negro applications do not appear to be treated as casually as other applications. The Negro applicant, it would seem, is acceptable to local institutions only if he is a prime risk on the basis of income and character. All other things being equal, a Negro applicant for a loan is less likely to be successful than a white applicant. In a number of interviews it was pointed out that there were sound reasons for such selectivity which had nothing to do with personal prejudice and the acceptance of stereotypes: segregated Negro neighborhoods, it was asserted, do lack the stability of white neighborhoods, and deterioration is much more likely; and in addition, Negro occupational security and income is much lower than in the case of whites.

Negroes who cannot get loans from regular banks and lending institutions may resort to the private market for mortgages in San Antonio. This is particularly important where the property purchased by Negroes is old or substandard. Interest on such loans is exorbitant.

In each of the recent large developments for Negroes, mortgage financing was arranged by the builder with an out-of-town institution. Contacts with eastern financial institutions for financing are apparently necessary for large-scale building for Negroes in San Antonio.

To sum up, housing for Negroes in San Antonio is affected by a variety of factors: the rapid growth of the Negro population, its poverty, the pattern of segregation in certain neighborhoods (though this is less severe than elsewhere), the prejudice and lack of knowledge of builders, the dominant community attitudes in favor of limiting areas into which Negroes may move or in which housing for them may be built, the stricter scrutiny they must undergo for financing home purchase.

Despite all these negative factors, under certain circumstances it seems some large-scale building will take place for Negroes. But, as we have seen, the builders will enter the Negro market last; and, one may assume, will leave it first. In terms of human need, the quantity of this housing is quite insufficient. Even when one takes into account the limited economic capacity of the Negro market, it seems that the Negro market will be served last, and only when builders have idle resources.

Latin-American Housing in San Antonio

Paradoxically, the Latin-American population of San Antonio meets less discrimination than the Negro population, but it is worse off. The West Side of San Antonio, the Mexican section, has long been notorious for its slums. One may still see many examples of what are called "corrals," in which up to twenty or thirty families share one pit privy and a single cold-water tap. There are great numbers of shacks on rutted, wholly unimproved streets, without inside plumbing or running water. Some areas of newer housing have been ramshackle slums from the day they were constructed, and their undersized septic tanks in clay soil have rendered the inside plumbing almost unusable.

Statistically, the Latin-American group shows far more overcrowding and a much higher proportion living in dilapidated dwellings, or dwellings without bath, toilet, or hot running water, than the Negro population (see table 13).

Probably more than three-fourths of the city's Latin-American population lives on the West Side. By one measure, this is a very high degree of segregation. The West Side, to a degree, is an isolated and autonomous Latin-American community, with Spanish the most common language; signs on stores and business establishments frequently appear in Spanish alone, moving pictures show only Spanish movies, and the like. However, at the same time, one may find Latin residences in all but the most exclusive Anglo neighborhoods of San Antonio. We find that there is no rigid line of segregation, even though the vast majority of the Latin-American population is concentrated in one large area.

There are no census data for 1940 to compare with housing data for 1950 to indicate the trend in the housing of the Latin-American population in recent years. However, there is some evidence of moderate improvement. There have been three trends which have increased the quantity and quality of housing available to Latin-Americans: developments of new houses designed specifically for Latin-American occupancy, the movement of Latin-Americans into predominantly Anglo areas, and a widespread tendency toward home improvement in recent years in older Latin areas, under the FHA home-improvement loan program. (Once again, we must note the omission from our account of public housing: the West Side has five such developments with about 2,500 rental units.)

For the Latin-Americans, as for the Negroes, 1952 was the year in which for the first time private developments of low-cost homes were built specifically for the minority group, breaking the previously universal refusal of San Antonio builders to consider this market. In that year, a pioneering builder began a development of about 750 houses for Latins on the West Side, and had great success in selling them. The houses sold for between eight and nine thousand dollars, and were financed under the FHA or VA programs. With this demonstration of the profitability of home developments for Latins on the West Side, other developments were begun. The builder of the first project completed a second development in 1955, with a multimillion-dollar shopping center adjoining. In all, between 3,000 and 3,500 houses in developments for Latin Americans have been put up since 1952. The prices were in the $7,500 to $9,500 range, and financing has been under either the FHA or VA programs.

There were some new houses built for Latin-Americans before 1952, but they were not in large-scale developments. In those years, a number of lumberyards and a few smaller builders originated a program of building houses on lots owned by Latin-Americans. The lot gave the purchaser an equity in the property and served as a down payment of sorts in mortgage financing. The builder who first launched a large-scale development for Latin-Americans began building individual housing on lots owned by members of the minority group in 1947. The number of houses built in this manner has varied greatly from year to year. The houses have had to be built at minimum costs, and the market for mortgages on this kind of house has varied greatly in the post-war years. Even a rough estimate of the numbers of houses built in this way is impossible. One builder estimates that he alone has put up 1,500 houses under this system since 1947.

Some new housing for Latin-Americans has come through another channel. A San Antonio businessman has established an integrated building and real estate organization—combining a lumberyard, collection office, title company, and mortgage finance facilities—for the purpose of building houses, generally for Latin-Americans, for purchasers who cannot qualify for mortgages through regular channels. The mortgages are privately held by the builder. Interest rates are reported to be extemely high, and so too are repossessions. Because there is no recourse to regular financing channels, the houses do not usually meet FHA or VA standards of construction. Many in building and financing circles unhesitatingly condemn this builder-financier as an exploiter of an ignorant and impoverished group; others point out that he supplies new housing to those who could not otherwise get it.

As we have said, Latin-Americans live almost everywhere in San Antonio, and everyone agrees that the sentiment among Anglos in favor of segregation of Latin-Americans has weakened considerably in recent years. Thus, before the war there were no Latins in North San Antonio, the principal Anglo area of the city, but now Latins are scattered through the area. Of course, the absolute numbers are small. Low incomes, as well as prejudice, still hamper any general movement.

Finally, considerable improvement in the quality of Latin-American housing has been effected in recent years by general repairs, additions, and the like under the FHA program. A large number of salesmen from lumberyards and contracting firms are reported to specialize in providing this kind of service to Latins.

But it is very unlikely that all this has made any radical change in the statistical picture we presented at the beginning of this section. The need for housing for Latin-Americans is great; we have already pointed to the very large number of children in this group. But poverty sharply restricts funds available for housing expenditures for the majority of families. Census data on family income are not available for the Latin-American group. Their family incomes, however, probably average lower than those of Negro families in San Antonio. Latin households in 1950 paid somewhat lower gross rents than did Negro families (medians, $23.06 and $25.39), and occupied owned homes worth far less on the average than those of Negroes ($3,211 versus $4,062).[5] Latins are held back economically by many things. Many are poorly educated and do not speak English well. Family income is depressed by the strong patriarchal family tradition, which tends to limit the employment of women outside the home. The position of the group has improved greatly since the war, and the gap between Latin-American and Anglo has been somewhat reduced. But the Latin-American group is still the most impoverished in the city.

But is there, in addition to these economic factors, some factor in the cultural attitudes of this group which leads Mexicans to be content with very poor housing, and to have little desire for

[5] *Ibid.*, p. 55.

something closer to the American ideal home? This point of view is widely held by Anglo informants. But it seems doubtful there is much truth in it. The experiences of the builders who pioneered in the Latin-American market attest to the contrary. They report universal enthusiasm for new housing among former slum-dwelling Latins, and they say there is no problem in interesting Latins of all degrees of acculturation in new housing: there is only a problem of finding Latin customers who can qualify as home purchasers.

Certain special problems do arise in selling new houses to Latin-Americans. In dealing with other groups, particularly "gringos," Latin-Americans are frequently nonaggressive and somewhat suspicious and untrusting. Real estate agents report that, as a group, Latin-Americans are reticent and undemanding. This means that if something arises in the selling situation to disturb them, to suggest they are being unfairly treated, to offend them, they will silently withdraw from the negotiations, despite their interest in buying a house. Thus, one builder found great difficulty in selling to Latin-Americans at a time when others were selling easily. His salesmen used high-pressure techniques and were condescending, and they consequently found it difficult to make sales. The builder who pioneered in this market, it is interesting to note, took special pains to instruct his sales force on the mores and customs of the Latin-American group. Thus, he did not allow female sales agents to serve prospective customers and required that his salesmen not wear ties when selling to Latin-Americans. The standard house he began to build (on lots owned by Latin-Americans) in 1947 was given the trademarked name of "Joe Doak's Dream House," and this name became a symbol to Latin-Americans for nondiscriminatory treatment and fair business practices. When he began to build on a large scale in 1952, he had established an excellent reputation in the group.

The attitudes of builders have affected the supply of housing for Latin-Americans in the same way that they have affected the supply available for Negroes. There is some evidence of a prevailing pattern of prejudice and discrimination, and a related ignorance of the Latin-American demand for housing. However, this was never as clearly defined as in the case of the Negro group, and following the example of the first builder, there was a general willingness to build for this market. Indeed, a good deal of competition developed among builders in trying to reach this market. Just as in the case of the Negroes, the pattern of segregation, even though it is less severe, limits the availability of sites for housing developments for Latin-Americans. The slum areas of the West Side are too expensive for private redevelopment. Other sites are too expensive for the cheap houses that Latin-Americans can afford. Others are much too far from the city. And all this is combined with an unwillingness to break the general pattern of Latin-American segregation by building on sites in Anglo areas.

In the same way as in the case of the Negroes, the behavior of real estate agents and lending institutions tends to limit the housing chances of Latin-Americans—even if less severely than for Negroes. Real estate agents will be very careful about introducing Latin-Americans into Anglo areas—and they will admit this ("Too many Mexicans can ruin a neighborhood," or "People never can tell about Mexican neighbors") at the same time that they deny there is any discrimination. There are many Latin-American real estate agents in San Antonio, but they are as unwilling to introduce Mexicans into any areas in which they might be unwelcome as the Anglo real estate men. We see in the behavior of Latin-American real estate agents, and elsewhere, a tendency to withdraw from a situation in which discrimination is sensed, rather than to oppose it. In this respect, the Negro minority, in San Antonio and elsewhere, appears to be much more militant than the Latin-American.

Mortgage-lending institutions give Latins special scrutiny as a high-risk group—just as they do Negro applicants. Several representatives of mortgage-lending concerns indicated that Latin-Americans had some advantages over Negroes in obtaining mortgage financing, because the Latin-American family was more cohesive than the Negro family and it could be expected that all members of the family would take responsibility for repayment. But despite this advantage, the problem of finance is a serious one. The small builders who have tried to build inexpensive houses for Latin-Americans have found great difficulty in obtaining financing from local institutions, even when FHA or VA commitments were obtained for prospective Latin-American buyers.

Mortgage loans are easier to obtain for houses in the large developments that have gone up since 1952. In every instance mortgage financing for these developments was obtained by the developer from an out-of-town institution. In these developments, Latin-Americans have been able to obtain mortgage loans on about the same terms as Anglos.

Again as in the case of the Negro, the difficulty of obtaining credit leads to resort to the private mortgage market, where interest rates are high and sharp practices common.

It is not easy to disentangle the complex factors of prejudice and discrimination and of economic incapacity in considering the housing of minority groups in San Antonio. The factors of prejudice and discrimination play a role in the segregating of these populations, and in the behavior of builders, real estate agents, the community at large, and financial interests. And yet, the poverty of these groups alone is sufficient to explain the bad housing conditions they endure. If we were to assume that these populations could bid for housing under conditions of strict equality with the Anglo group, and at the same time their economic position were to remain the same, no great improvement in their housing would result. Insofar as there exists an economic demand for housing by members of the minority group who can afford it, this demand, it appears, is now being met, even if somewhat sluggishly and with some degree of prejudice and discrimination.

HOUSING CONDITIONS OF NEGROES IN HOUSTON

Houston is the largest city in the South, by far; in 1955, the population of its Standard Metropolitan Area was estimated at more than one million—the first city in the South to achieve this size. It is also one of the most "urban" of southern cities. Tradition has little weight; the population is heterogeneous and diverse; the behavior of its inhabitants suggests the metropolis rather than the Old South, of which it historically may be considered a part.

It is metropolitan too in the diversity of its economic life. Houston's first economic significance was as a port, and it grew because of the volume of cotton and petroleum shipped through

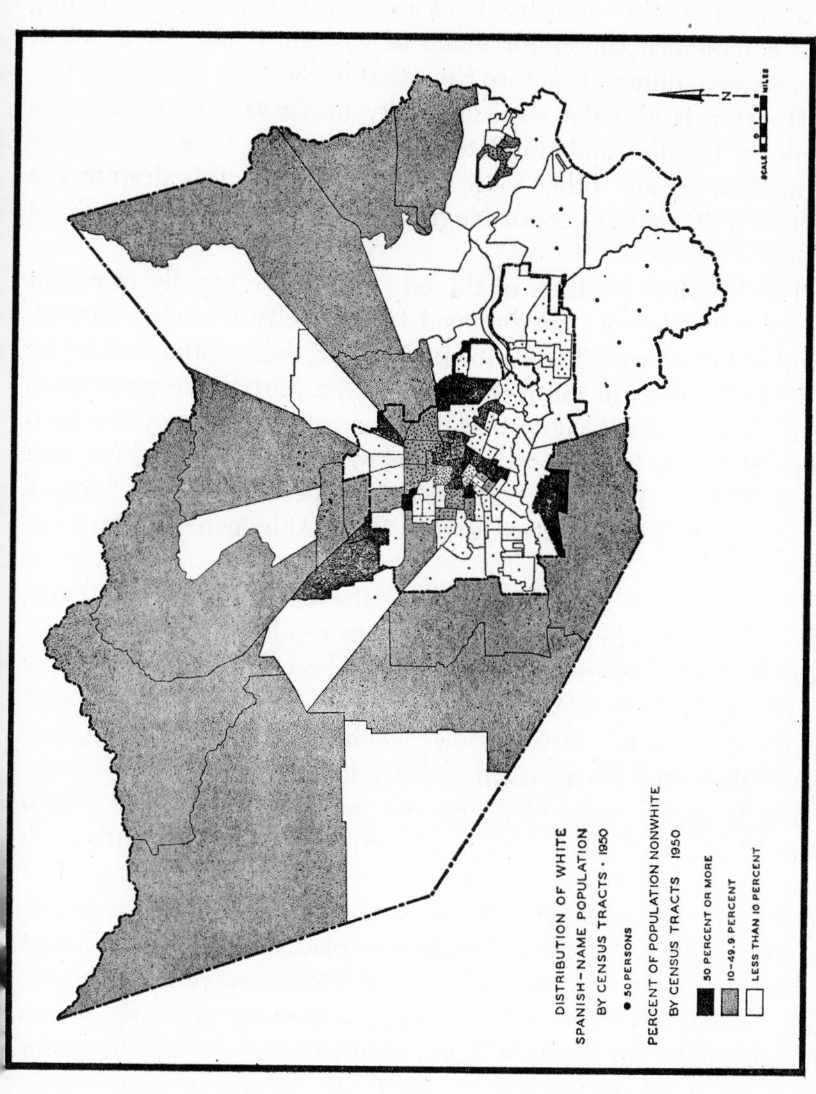

Map 3. Houston and adjacent area, distribution of white Spanish-name population by census tracts, 1950.

it. Its recent growth, however, which has moved it from twentieth place among American cities in 1940 to fifteenth in 1950, has been based largely on the growth of the petroleum and chemical industries, and other industry, light and heavy. It is also the trading and commercial center for much of eastern Texas. All in all, it gives a very different picture from that of San Antonio.

Houston is also the wealthiest city in Texas. The median income of families and unrelated individuals in 1949 was higher than that for any other large Texas city. And this despite the fact that it contains more Negroes than the other large Texas cities.

The Negro population of the city has grown rapidly in recent decades, as Negroes have moved into the city from the agricultural areas of east Texas. In 1955, there were estimated to be 176,211 Negroes in the metropolitan area. But Negro population growth has recently not been quite as rapid as that of the total population, for the proportion of Negroes in the metropolitan area dropped from 19 percent in 1950 to 17 percent in 1955.[6] There is also in Houston a considerable Latin-American population—39,000 in 1950.

Race relations in Houston follow the pattern usual for Texas cities. Negroes are restricted to certain residential areas, are not admitted to white restaurants, and until recently were restricted to the rear of buses. As of 1956, no plans had been made to end segregation in the city schools. Negroes vote in Houston, but have not been a strong political force in the past.

But there are signs of a growing militancy among the Negro population. The traditional "racial etiquette" of the South is in scant evidence. Whites cannot expect to receive, as a matter of course, the honorific "sir." Negroes do not automatically and universally make way for whites in public places, but generally adopt a "first come, first go" attitude. In 1956 Negroes were sufficiently bold to boycott Alan Shivers, the race-baiting governor, when he was invited to speak at Texas Southern University, the major Negro state-supported college in Texas, by the predominantly white board of the institution.

In 1950, Negro housing in Houston was worse than that of the

---

[6] These estimates were obtained from a special census conducted by the Houston school district, financed by the Houston Chamber of Commerce.

white population, although better than that of the Latin-American population. But there was great variation, from area to area, in the quality of Negro housing. In certain census tracts, less than 20 percent of the residences of the Negro population were dilapidated or without private baths—a proportion lower than that for the Anglo population of the city, as we may see from table 14. At the other extreme, there were tracts in which more than 85 percent of the Negro dwellings were either dilapidated or without private baths. And of course, even within each tract Negro housing was not uniform. Yet there were Negro areas in which the housing was comparable to that of most white residential areas.

TABLE 14

PERCENT OF DWELLINGS SUBSTANDARD OR OVERCROWDED, BY ETHNIC GROUP OF OCCUPANTS, HOUSTON STANDARD METROPOLITAN AREA, 1950

Classification of dwellings	Total dwelling units	Dwellings occupied by		
		Anglo	Negro	Latin
Substandard [a]	26.1	23.1	52.3	66.1
With 1.01 or more persons per room	19.0	16.5	25.0	52.7
With 1.51 or more persons per room	6.2	4.0	11.7	33.1

SOURCE: *U. S. Census of Housing: 1950,* vol. I, *General Characteristics,* chap. 43, "Texas."
[a] Dilapidated or without private bath, toilet, or hot running water.

The Negro population in 1950 was fairly widely scattered throughout the city. There were two large districts which contained about 50 percent of all Negroes in the metropolitan area. Some other quite large Negro concentrations were in the downtown area, had long been centers of Negro population, and generally had poor housing. The smaller districts, some of which were located on the periphery of the city, were not markedly better. Although living in many separated districts widely distributed through the city, the Negroes were almost completely segregated within these districts. Some of them were expanding into old and deteriorating white neighborhoods.

That was the situation in 1950. Since then, there have been

spectacular changes in the distribution of Negro population and the quality of its housing. New areas of residence have become available for Negroes on a large scale, first, through private housing developments, and second, through "invasion" of a middle- and higher-income white residential area, which has created, for the time being, an "integrated" area of high-quality housing.

Since 1950, there have been many private housing developments built for Negroes in various areas of the city: some on the northern and western fringe, more in the largely industrial eastern part of the city, and most extensively, on the southern periphery, known as the Chocolate Bayou area. At least five thousand new houses have been built for Negroes since 1950 in these private housing developments.

Around 1950, too, Negroes began buying houses in previously white areas east and south of Texas Southern University, which was established in 1948 on the "line" between one of the old downtown Negro concentrations and a white area. The white area, comprised of the Riverside and Washington Terrace districts, was middle-income, and the houses ranged from ten to fifteen thousand dollars in price. More recently, the movement has penetrated farther to the south, into an area where houses are considerably more expensive. In mid-1955, a conservative estimate by a reliable and knowledgeable organization placed the number of houses occupied by Negroes in this movement at approximately two thousand. But the total number of dwellings potentially made available to Negroes is much greater, for the invasion has been by leapfrog jumps, and sizable white or partly white areas are now mixed in with the Negro-occupied areas and dwellings. In these interstitial areas, many of the houses are for sale or vacant. Unquestionably, much good housing has thus been made available to Negroes, and, owing to the very large numbers of houses on the market, property prices have declined precipitously, and consequently homes are available very reasonably.

The poorer Negroes have also benefited by this great increase in the number of houses available to the more prosperous element. For the older Negro areas have lost population to the newer areas, and rents and property prices have declined there also.

Negroes have thus been able to "move up the housing ladder" all along the line.

As a result of these developments, the supply of housing for Negroes has more than kept pace with the growth of the Negro population since 1950, although before that date it lagged behind. Among various factors that have made possible this striking improvement in the housing situation of Negroes, three may be singled out as most important: the somewhat better family and economic situation of Negroes in Houston, the favorable attitudes among builders toward building for the Negro market, and community attitudes which, while they have not been friendly toward or tolerant of Negro invasion, have not resisted it forcefully.

Consider first the special aspects of the Negro demand for housing in Houston. While the Negro population growth has not kept pace with that of the whites, in absolute terms it has been substantial—from less than 100,000 in 1940 to 176,000 in 1955. The Houston Negro population also has a high birth rate. If we use the measure of total fertility, which is adjusted for differences in the age distribution of various populations, we find a rate for the Negro population of 291, compared with a total fertility for the Anglo population of 269. This suggests that the Negroes of Houston may have a more stable family pattern than those of San Antonio, which would have some effect on the strength of their motivations to acquire new housing and their ability to bear the economic demands and pressures of homeownership.

More significant in this respect, however, is the fact that they are economically in a stronger position than the Negroes of other Texas cities. The median income of Negro families and unrelated individuals in 1949, as reported by the Bureau of the Census, was $1,681 in Houston, compared with $1,461 in San Antonio and $1,439 in Dallas.[7]

It is also the feeling of this writer that there is a distinctively strong desire for better housing among the Negroes of Houston. Occupancy of better quality housing has come to serve as an effective symbol of rank for Negroes. Similarly, for a good part

[7] *U. S. Census of Population: 1950*, vol. II, *Characteristics of the Population*, part 43, "Texas."

of the Negro population, the possession of a certain make of car gives status. It is understandable that a group which is deprived of status in so many different spheres should seize upon the few areas where it can express itself freely—such as car purchase—and place great weight upon them as status markers. Perhaps the mere fact that relatively so much good housing was available to Negroes in Houston served to make home-owning, and the owning of a good and expensive home, an important source of status.

There is strong awareness of the relative status of different kinds of housing. The term "Sugar Hill" is in current use in Houston, as elsewhere, to designate the areas of high-quality housing available for Negroes, and this term, or some variant, has been used by builders to name developments for Negroes. The same words will often preface advertisements for single houses.

This concern for the status of housing was remarked upon by informants who had studied the fanning-out of Negro homeowners in the areas south and west of Texas Southern University. Prospective homeowners often attempted to purchase homes that were beyond their means even when good, less expensive houses were available, and the reason usually was the desire to keep up with someone else. This strong desire for housing of higher status thus had negative as well as positive effects, from the point of view of bettering the Negro's housing situation: many families which had bought houses beyond their means sold or were attempting to sell after only brief occupancy. Of course, one should not overstress these factors of special values emphasized by a certain subculture as against the simple utilitarian need, even though the writer believes they did play a role.

Perhaps the most crucial factor in the improvement of Negro housing has been the attitude of Houston builders. Since 1950, at least, they have shown great interest in the Negro market and a minimum of prejudice, and have made serious efforts to acquire reliable knowledge of the Negro housing market. Shortly after 1950, the builders of Houston formed a committee to explore needs of Negroes for housing and the possibilities offered to builders by the Negro market. The work of this committee appears to have induced a number of builders to begin developments for Negroes. This committee also coöperated with Negro leaders in planning developments and in attempts to study the market. A grant was made to Texas Southern to support research on the market for Negro housing.

This interest, as we have said, has resulted in at least five thousand new houses for Negroes. Indeed, it has been so successful that by mid-1956 the market for houses in private developments for Negroes in the eight to fifteen thousand dollar price category in Houston had been almost glutted. Intense sales competition has been necessary to move houses in new developments, and there has been at least one bankruptcy as a result of the failure of a development for the Negro market. Other developments that had been planned or were already under way have been stopped or postponed.

Most of the builders who went into the Negro market have been satisfied by the results; but, as we might expect after such serious competition developed, others have been disappointed and have even become bitter at the selectiveness of Negro buyers. Some builders reported that Negro buyers tended to be unreasonably demanding and arrogant in home-buying negotiations. Other builders pointed out that the success of future all-Negro developments was threatened by the successful Negro movement into previously all-white areas. Centrally located and priced so as to compete with new houses in all-Negro developments, these older houses are often more attractive to the Negro homebuyer than the new house inconveniently located at some distance from the city center.

What explains this great home-building activity by builders in Houston? It is probably not without significance that the builders taking the lead in this relatively organized effort to develop the Negro market were mostly Jewish. They were, perhaps, sensitive to discrimination and therefore sympathetic to the plight of Negroes. The atmosphere of Houston, as a rapidly growing, commercial-industrial metropolis, must also have had some effect on builders: community attitudes are determined more by rational economic considerations and are less bound by tradition and prejudice.

These general community attitudes have been significant in making possible the second large expansion of the Negro housing market in Houston: that created by the movement into all-white areas. We do not mean to suggest that there has been any popular feeling in favor of breaking down Negro residential segregation. But the opposition that this movement has met has been relatively weak, weaker than in most other cities, both North and South. The newspapers, for example, have larely ignored this development, whereas in other cities they have played an inflammatory role.

There was one bombing of a home bought by a Negro in the area of invasion in 1953, but there was no popular support for this action. The police acted promptly and arrested a neighbor, who was later indicted—although, as of mid-1956, he had not been brought to trial. In 1952, an organization, the Greater Riverside Home Owners Association, was formed in an effort to stem the Negro movement by getting the residents to refuse to sell to Negroes and by raising money to buy property that came on the market and "buy out" Negroes who had already moved in. The organization went out of existence after only a few months.

In one small section of this area another organization exists for the same purpose, and at the entrance to the chief street leading into the neighborhood a sign proclaims that it is a white area and will continue so. However, the writer noted that more than 50 percent of the houses in the neighborhood bore "For Sale" signs.

The white population is bitter at the drop in property values (caused by its own flight), but there has been little organized effort to prevent the Negro movement.

Just as builders and the general population seem less affected by prejudice, so do the real estate agents. They do not appear to be as cautious in transactions involving Negroes as those in San Antonio. They were less evasive in discussing the "conversion" of areas from white to Negro occupancy and less defensive about their role in such conversions. They admitted they were frequently under pressure from whites in the affected areas not to sell to Negroes, but this pressure seemed to carry little weight with them. The informal rule of the local real estate board in recent years has been that the realtor may freely sell white property to Negroes if there is already one Negro resident on the block. The limitation contained in this rule is no great restraint because of the effective techniques for "block-busting" which have been developed by Negroes (use of white dummies and other devices). The real estate men still assert they would not handle a transaction which inaugurated a new Negro invasion. Their official views are still as restrictive as those of the real estate men in San Antonio. But they seem freer in their actual behavior.

As in San Antonio, the Negro applicant for a loan is screened carefully; there is no indication that Negroes at an equivalent economic level find it easier to get credit in Houston than in San Antonio. Nor have the local financial institutions financed the extensive housing developments for Negroes in recent years—the support for these has come from out-of-state institutions. However, as in San Antonio, a Negro who wishes to buy a house in a new development and can qualify for either an FHA- or VA-supported loan appears to have no difficulty in getting a mortgage loan, and the FHA and Veterans Administration, here, as in San Antonio, appear to be nondiscriminatory in evaluating loan applications from Negroes. In mid-1956, Negroes who could qualify for either FHA or VA support for mortgage loans could buy houses in the eight to fifteen thousand dollar price category in private developments on very easy terms.

There also seems to be no great difficulty in getting mortgage loans on houses in the Washington Terrace-Riverside area. Almost all of the houses in this area can qualify for either FHA or VA loan support. Since property prices have declined drastically, the loans required are small in relation to what the houses would be worth in a more normal market situation. As a result, there is a good demand for these mortgages in out-of-town mortgage markets.

Negroes who cannot afford houses as expensive as those in the existing housing developments—above eight thousand dollars—have great difficulty in obtaining mortgage loans of any type. This includes, of course, a great majority of the Negroes of Houston.

The over-all picture for Houston, then, is that one problem of Negroes in seeking housing has been met: that of obtaining relatively expensive housing by the part of the Negro population which can afford it. A good deal of such housing has been supplied—indeed, in mid-1956, there was a surplus. However, this does not mean that discrimination and prejudice do not play a role in restricting the chances of Negroes for good housing in Houston. Residential segregation still limits the Negro's choice of an area of residence. The pattern of segregation creates special problems in finding sites for Negro developments. The greater difficulty in obtaining mortgage finance is still a special problem for Negro home-purchasers. But the major restriction on Negroes in acquiring better housing in Houston today is their poverty rather than the direct expression of prejudice and discrimination.

SUMMARY AND CONCLUSIONS

The chief conclusions to be drawn from this investigation are that members of minority groups in both San Antonio and Houston face special problems in obtaining housing; that the quality of their housing is markedly inferior to that of the nonminority population; that up until recent years prejudice and lack of interest in minority-group housing on the part of builders and mortgage lenders played an important role in restricting the supply of housing for minority groups; that since 1950 this situation has changed, and there have been considerable additions to the housing supply available to the more prosperous parts of the Negro population; but that relatively few members of minority groups are economically able to take advantage of these positive changes.

This study provides strong evidence that the chief cause of the inferior housing of minority groups in the two cities today is their poverty. It follows that any large-scale improvement in their housing conditions involves either a rise in the level of income of the minority groups or more extensive subsidized housing.

Thus, the poor housing of minority groups is part of the total fabric of economic and social disadvantage. For an increase in income involves such significant and extensive changes as greater equality in educational opportunities, greater equality in occupational opportunities, greater equality in remuneration for work —in short, nothing less than the extensive revolution which would produce equality for the minority groups in all spheres.

Greater subsidy for cheap minority housing, in one form or another, is perhaps a more reasonable immediate prospect. Thus, one specific change that would benefit minority groups would be measures to make mortgages on cheaper houses more attractive to lenders. As we have pointed out, for houses costing more than eight thousand dollars there is no great problem in placing mortgages. But builders report they cannot obtain financing for less expensive homes under present conditions in the credit markets. Of course, it is questionable whether minimum adequate houses can be built for less than eight thousand dollars.

Aside from this and other measures, such as more extensive public housing, which might increase the numbers of cheap houses available for Negroes and Latin-Americans, the improvement in the housing conditions of minority groups must involve a general improvement in their economic and social status, with all that this implies for the social fabric of the South.

FORREST E. LAVIOLETTE
with the assistance of Joseph T. Taylor and Giles Hubert

III

The Negro in New Orleans

New Orleans is distinguished from the other great cities of the South by a rich and even romantic past which has left a heritage of varied social elements, to add to the omnipresent juxtaposition of white and black, and by the enormously complex physical problems created by its location in the Lower Delta. Both aspects of its distinctiveness affect the housing problems of Negroes.

New Orleans, even before it became an American city, was divided between Creoles of French origin and Anglo-Americans. Today, this basis of division is no longer important: Creole and Anglo-American fused long ago into a homogeneous upper class, which has maintained a certain degree of continuity and stability since the middle of the nineteenth century and today sustains a strong interest in the management of the affairs of the community—business, educational, religious, philanthropic, and recreational. During the latter part of the nineteenth century, New Orleans was the only city in the South that attracted large numbers of white immigrants. Thus, there developed important groups of Irish, German, and Italian extraction, the last of these being particularly numerous: 12 percent of the population is of Italian descent. There are lesser groups of Syrian and Greek origin, groups from Herzegovina and Croatia, and some 20,000 from Spanish-speaking areas. Descendants of the Acadian French, who are moving from the swamps and prairies of western Louisiana, form an important part of the middle- and lower-class parts of the white population. Most of these ethnic elements have long

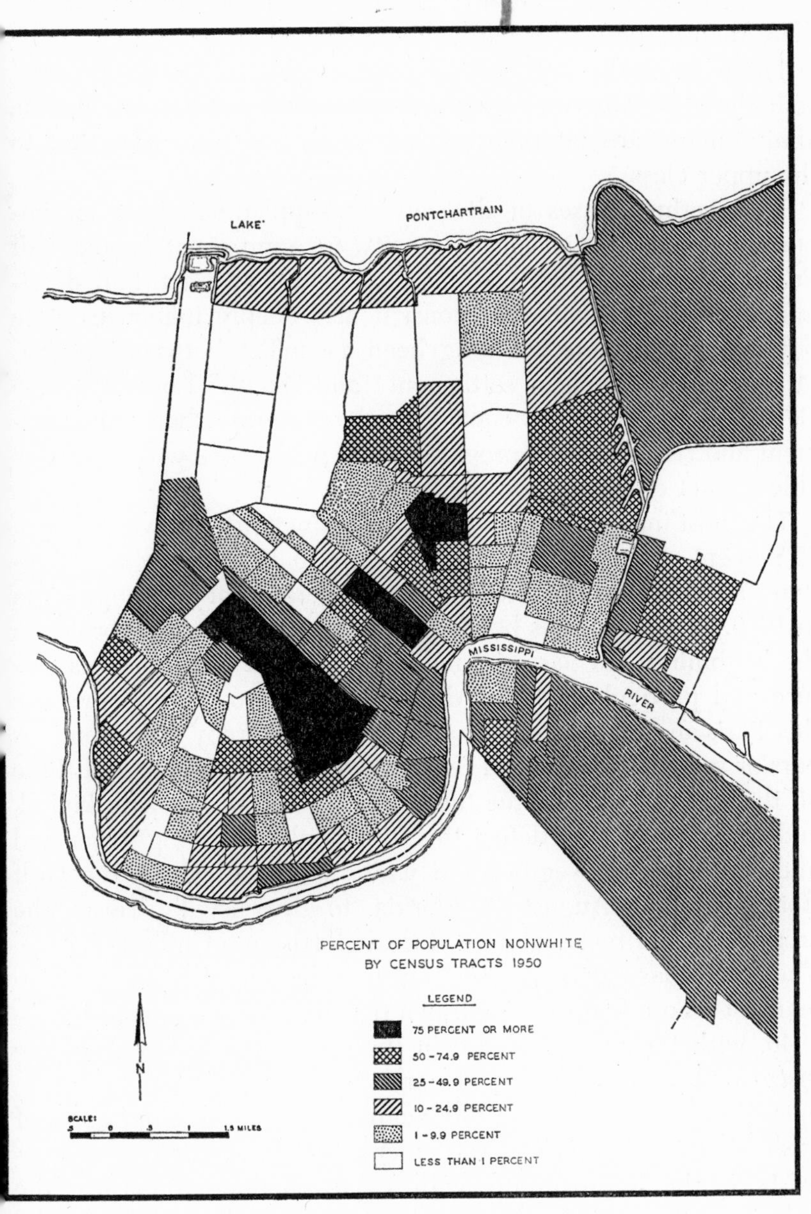

Map 4. City of New Orleans, percent of population nonwhite by census tracts, 1950.

been resident in the country and city; of the total population more than 90 percent is native-born.

There is also a long-settled Jewish group, one of the most assimilated in America. Prominent Jews take active roles in civic affairs, many are intermarried, but none are fully admitted to the upper class.

These ethnic bases of division are supplemented by an important religious division. The city is approximately one-half Protestant and one-half Catholic. Religion is an important determinant of Negro-white relations; it also deeply influences state politics, where there has long been a conflict between "North" (the Protestant area of settlement) and "South" Louisiana (the Catholic area), and this conflict has bearing on urban redevelopment and rehabilitation programs in New Orleans, with considerable impact on Negro housing.

The most important basis of social distinction, however, is race: 32 percent of the population was Negro in 1950, and the proportion had risen steadily from about 26 percent of the population in 1910. The Negro has been part of the New Orleans story from the beginning. He has contributed heavily to New Orleans culture and particularly to its distinctively *bistro* culture—we use this Parisian term to refer to the pattern whereby unpretentious bars or small neighborhood restaurants, tucked in here and there off the main street, become the center for socializing with kinfolk and friends. We may detect this *bistro* culture among lower and middle classes of Negroes and whites alike, all along the Gulf Coast, from St. Augustine, Florida, to Brownsville, Texas, the area which has received a good deal of Hispano-Gallic influence. The Negro has participated in and to a degree adopted a culture many of whose features are drawn from the Mediterranean. Since 1946, with the great increase in the use of the automobile, the *bistro* culture has been in decline, but one may still see it in operation, not only among the Negroes, but in the older areas of Irish, German, and Italian settlement, too. The *bistro* culture coexists, in the Negro group, with a pattern that emphasizes the culture of the gang for boys and men and of the matriarchy for girls and women.

The *bistro* culture has had considerable influence on patterns of settlement and living in New Orleans; the break-up of this culture contributes to the current situation in relation to housing in the city.

The Physical and Economic Setting

The fact that New Orleans is built on low, swampy land and squeezed in between the Mississippi and Lake Pontchartrain means that land is extremely scarce and expensive. An officer of the Federal Housing Administration said that residential property which would cost $2,000 in most cities would cost $3,500 in Baton Rouge and $6,000 in New Orleans. An officer of the Chamber of Commerce who lives in a middle-class neighborhood owns a lot 90 by 110 feet whose market value is $10,000. A banker who provided the credit for a large subdivision of modest homes reported that the land was worth $6,000 an acre before it was even cleared, and after preparation for building was worth between $3,500 and $4,500 a building lot. This subdivision is some distance from the city center.

Land is expensive because all of it must make some contribution to costs of the ever-present problem of keeping back the waters of the river and lake and pumping out rain water and sewage. Since all the land is below the level of the levees and much of it below river and gulf level, drainage has been one of the foremost problems of the city. In the early days, canals sufficed; these were replaced by windmill pumps, then steam pumps, and then, in 1903, by electric centrifugal pumps. In 1910 the problem of moving sufficient water was finally solved by the invention of an electrically driven propeller-type pump. The present drainage system can pump out sixteen and a half billion gallons per day.

The second great charge on land is created by the need for expensive preparation. The water table is so close to the surface and the type of soil such that the land can be made stable only with careful preparation. Streets and highways are notoriously difficult to build and to keep in repair; roadbeds and building foundations settle unevenly. Piles must be driven, and a special type of foundation used.

There has been a continuous search for land which could be used for building and for an improved technology for better drainage. In the past, swamps between the river and the lake were drained; more recently this has been done in swamps east and west of the older city, the so-called "Crescent," cradled in a great bend in the Mississippi. South, beyond the river and toward the gulf, the sand and spongy soil make building costs prohibitive; to go north across Lake Pontchartrain involves the addition of twenty-four miles of travel each way—the length of the causeway across the lake.

For this scarce land not only do Negroes and whites compete but also industrial and commercial uses, for New Orleans is economically a rapidly growing city. The city is a center of wholesale and retail trade for southern Mississippi and Louisiana, a manufacturing center, and a great port ranking second in tonnage in the United States. In December, 1957, a tidewater channel was begun to Mississippi Sound and the gulf, to eliminate the vagaries of the Mississippi River passage and make more land available for industrial development by dredging and filling.

New Orleanians are optimistic about the economic future of the city. The building industry has been stimulated by a continuing demand for new homes, by office and factory building, and an extensive city improvement program. The first bridge across the river was completed in 1937, a second was opened in April, 1958, and already there is talk of a third. There is heavy migration into the area (it is estimated that 40 percent of population increase comes from migration), and income is rising. The Chamber of Commerce reported:

> . . . Effective income in 1956 rose 4.1 percent to an estimated $1,797. By contrast, the estimate for 1940 was a mere $592, less than one-third the current figure. Considering that the cost of living has risen 97.8 percent in New Orleans since 1940, the per capita income necessary to maintain a comparable standard of living in 1956 would be $1,171. Instead, last year's figure of $1,797 means that the average family today (3.5 persons) has an additional $2,191 per year, which may be spent on better housing, better food, education, recreation. . . .

Population has increased by nearly 70 percent since 1910 (see table 15), and New Orleans has begun to expand out of Orleans parish—the central city—into neighboring Jefferson and St. Bernard parishes. It is in this social setting and physical and economic situation that Negroes must compete for decent housing.

TABLE 15

GROWTH OF POPULATION IN ORLEANS PARISH, BY COLOR, 1910–1950

Year	White		Nonwhite		Total	
	Population	Percent increase	Population	Percent increase	Population	Percent increase
1910	249,403	19.2	89,672	14.7	339,075	18.1
1920	285,916	14.5	101,303	13.0	385,219	14.2
1930	327,729	14.5	131,033	29.3	458,762	18.5
1940	340,503	3.9	149,034	13.7	494,537	7.8
1950	387,814	13.9	182,631	22.5	570,445	14.7

The Negro in New Orleans—1950

Almost immediately after the Louisiana Purchase of 1803, the population of New Orleans began to increase markedly. Two low ridges, slightly higher than the surrounding low land, offered building room to the Creole and American sections of the population, respectively. Close around these two settlement areas was a Negro residential fringe. Expansion and invasion have transformed this early pattern, of course, but the effects of the old distribution may still be seen. One of them is the mingling of Negroes and whites. The two groups lived in close propinquity in old New Orleans, and even today New Orleans is not a highly segregated city. The shortage of land, the expansion of the city so as to incorporate farms on which Negroes lived and worked, the need for the Negro to be close to his domestic work—all these have imposed a closer geographic connection between whites and Negroes than in many other cities.

This residential pattern forms an important part of the image of Negro housing for white and Negro alike. It means, for example, that there is no "block-busting"—no furtive effort by Negroes to move into all-white areas, because there are so few all-white areas. Nor are there any legal or quasi-legal restrictions on where Negroes can live, as in Birmingham, nor any history of restrictive covenants.

The available statistics bear out this picture of a relatively nonsegregated city. In 1950, of 142 census tracts in the city, only 21 were all-white (less than 1 percent Negro); and only 33 were predominantly Negro-occupied. Considerably more than half of the census tracts were mixed (1 to 50 percent Negro). The census tract is a rather large unit, but an analysis of blocks bears out the claim of New Orleanians that their city is not highly segregated. The racial composition of 5,381 blocks, according to the 1950 Census, is shown in table 16.

TABLE 16

RACIAL COMPOSITION OF NEW ORLEANS CITY BLOCKS, 1950

Percent of dwelling units occupied by nonwhites	Percent of total (5,381 blocks)
Less than 1 percent	57
1 to 24 percent	13
25 to 74 percent	10
75 to 99 percent	12
All nonwhite	8
Total	100

SOURCE: Census data tabulated in Leonard Reissmann, K. H. Silvert, and Cliff W. Wing, Jr., "The New Orleans Voter: A Handbook of Political Description," *Tulane Studies in Political Science,* vol. II, 1955.

A second group of compelling facts with broad significance for Negro housing is the economic condition of the Negro community. New Orleans is not a wealthy city, despite its recent economic expansion, and the Negro population is its poorest element. Median income in 1949 for Negro males was $1,469; for white males, $2,603. Considering all income recipients, $3,000 was virtually the ceiling for Negroes. Less than 4 percent of them earned more than that amount, as compared with roughly one-third of the whites.

The Negro was worse off in New Orleans than in other big cities of the South as shown by the following figures of Negro median personal income in selected cities in 1949:

Houston	$1,336
Birmingham	1,076
Dallas	1,076
Atlanta	1,045
New Orleans	986
Memphis	986

And yet, the Negro position has been unquestionably improving. The 1940–1950 period witnessed a significant occupational upgrading of Negro workers, as shown in table 17.

TABLE 17

DISTRIBUTION OF NEW ORLEANS NEGRO WORKERS BY MAJOR OCCUPATION GROUP, 1940 AND 1950

Occupation group	1940	1950	Percent change, 1940–1950
Total Negro workers[a]	50,408	68,751	26.7
Professional, technical, etc.	1,922	3,513	46.4
Clerical, sales, etc.	1,762	3,333	44.1
Craftsmen, foremen, etc.	3,025	4,861	39.8
Operatives and kindred workers	8,976	13,716	41.8
Private household workers	15,677	11,443	−27.0
Service workers	5,577	7,415	25.6
Laborers	10,081	16,370	38.5

SOURCE: *U. S. Census of Population: 1950*, vol. II, *Characteristics of the Population*, part 18, "Louisiana."

[a] Unclassified workers are not shown but are included in totals.

Nonsegregation, the pressure of population increase on a crowded city with high land costs, and low income produced the following housing picture for Negroes in 1950.

They were tenants, rather than owners: fewer than one Negro family in four owned its home, compared with 44 percent of white households. Negroes paid a median rent of $21 a month, white renters, $34. Negro owner-occupied homes (single unit) had a median value of $3,800, much less than half the white median of $10,100. More than four-fifths of all Negro dwellings were either dilapidated or lacked essential sanitary facilities. More than 40 percent of Negro-rented dwellings and nearly a third of those owner-occupied were crowded (fewer rooms than persons).

During the 1940's, Negroes gained only 18 percent of the dwelling units built although they made up 44 percent of the total population increase during that decade. Nonsegregation for Negroes in New Orleans seemed to mean the right to crowd into old and poor dwellings as whites left them for new housing.

But the trends were not all negative. There had been an increase in the status of Negro employment during the decade (see table 17) and, although we have no figures for Negro income since 1949, there are indications it has been going up. Inspection of the annual reports of the New Orleans Housing Authority reveals that each year more than a hundred Negro families are required to move because they exceed the maximum income limit for public housing. This means that some of these families are now earning well over five thousand dollars.

In addition to improved income, there is reason to believe that the Negro community now includes more stable families. The proportion living under common-law arrangements is probably in decline, and this would mean more families able to get credit and to maintain loan repayments.

The Negro community is developing greater unity of action and self-consciousness. The NAACP, until outlawed in 1956, was a strong organization; in October, 1957, having met the requirements of the state law, it again emerged to take leadership in the Negro community. The Urban League, although it also has been affected by the recent heightening of tensions (in May, 1957, its support from the Community Chest was terminated as a result of pressure by the White Citizens' Council), is still very much alive and active, particularly in the field of housing and community organization.

We now turn to action undertaken in recent years to meet the problem of Negro housing.

Housing for Negroes

Public Housing.—As early as 1929, civic-minded citizens of New Orleans were investigating the possibility of a housing project which would supply modern and satisfactory homes to low-income Negro families. Edwin Embree and Alfred Stern of the Julius Rosenwald Fund were interested in the possibility of supporting the development of two squares near the Flint-Goodridge Hospital as a housing project. A special committee was organized in the Council of Social Agencies, and a New Orleans architect, Moise Goldstein, was asked to make plans and estimates. Then the Depression struck and the Rosenwald Fund was unable to follow up its initial interest.

In the early days of the New Deal, when the Public Works

dministration was active in supporting public housing in a number of cities, this interest was revived. A staff was made available) Mr. Goldstein to prepare plans for two projects, one white nd one Negro; and thus, for the first time, it was assumed that ublic housing in New Orleans would be segregated. These plans 'ere ready in 1935, but were delayed to await state enabling egislation required before federal funds could be granted. This ame in July, 1936, with an act authorizing housing authorities in ouisiana cities. The New Orleans Housing Authority was created n March, 1937, and became the first in the United States to benefit from the funds made available by the Wagner Act for the learing of slums and the building of publicly subsidized housng.

By the end of 1941, the New Orleans Housing Authority had uilt two projects devoted exclusively to white families, conaining 1,826 dwelling units, and three projects for Negroes, with ,309 units. An additional Negro development was under contruction, making a total of 3,053 units of public housing proided for Negroes at the time of American entry into World Var II.

During and after the war, demands on New Orleans housing ncreased steadily. In 1948, the director of the New Orleans Housing Authority reported he had on hand 46,000 applications, 0 percent of which were eligible for public housing. Under the Housing Act of 1949, New Orleans hoped for an allocation of 12,000 units. It actually received 6,000 units, and funds for only 5,000. By 1956, when the Desire Project was completed, there were available 3,102 units for whites and 7,173 units for Negroes. This was not expected to be the end, but the City Council withheld approval of any additional projects until mid-1958, probably as a result of political pressures which had developed against expansion of public housing.

Low-rent public housing is now involved in a number of problems. It is proving hard to keep the white projects fully occupied. In 1957, Negro informants claimed there were 400 vacancies in the Florida and St. Thomas projects for whites. This was a potentially explosive situation. On what basis could the maintenance of entire projects as white be justified when they could not be filled? But this situation did not continue long. Through appeals in the press and by signs on the premises, the vacancies were filled with low-income, elderly white families.

However, the problem is a chronic one. There is a much heavier rate of move-out from white than from Negro projects. The whites have 34 percent of the units assigned to them; yet in 1950, 1951, and 1952, the Housing Authority reported that about two-thirds of all move-outs were white. Under these circumstances, the new project would have to be Negro. And then the great problem arises, where shall it be located? There is great competition for land in New Orleans; the city is growing and various rebuilding schemes are in the air. The City Planning Commission reports that "we have given the Authority a general area, but not a site." The general area which the City Planning Commission thinks would be appropriate for a low-income Negro housing project is becoming more attractive to private interests, for the business center of the city is shifting in that direction.

Public housing is one instance of the general problem that Negroes in New Orleans (and elsewhere) make disproportionate use of services for low-income groups; consequently the expansion of such services is affected by the general atmosphere surrounding Negro-white relations and the political situation affecting Negroes. Thus, in the Charity Hospital of New Orleans, maintained by the State of Louisiana, and servicing low-income groups, three-quarters of those treated are Negroes, even though they form only one-third of the population.

The effect of urban renewal on the Negro housing situation remains for the future, since no project has been actually undertaken in New Orleans. Two projects have been proposed, but local interests affected were successful in obtaining legislation which has so far prevented any urban renewal project.

The city's efforts under urban renewal have consequently been limited to the establishment of a Division of Housing Improvement and Slum Clearance, designed to take advantage of the rehabilitation provisions of the 1954 Housing Act. How successful rehabilitation will be in improving Negro housing remains to be seen, but it seems unlikely that a program of such limited scope will have much impact on Negro housing.

Private Housing—It is difficult to form any reliable estimate of the total amount of new housing made available to Negroes in recent years. There have been eleven multiple-unit private developments, most of them small, providing about 1,200 units in all. They are as follows:

	Number of units
1. N. Tonti, Tricou, N. Miro and Delery Streets	17
2. Square 2684, Foy Subdivision	10
3. Harvey Canal	130
4. Garden Plaza	94
5. Bunche Village	256
6. Tricou, Delery, and N. Prieur Streets	18
7. N. Tonti and Tricou Streets	5
8. Harold Homes, Inc.	16
9. Pontchartrain Park Homes (to date)	463
10. Truman Park	114
11. Gentilly Gardens (rental units)	86
Total	1,209

So far as could be learned, no further private subdivisions for Negroes are now planned, but Pontchartrain Park Homes is expanding and will eventually house 900 families.

In 1957, the writers interviewed private builders, developers, and financiers to try to learn why there had been so little building in developments for Negroes. Informants agreed that there was still a good market for housing for whites, and the building of houses for Negroes must await the saturation of this better market, which may not occur for years. The white market is preferred by builders because of its stronger and more varied housing demand, fewer difficulties of selling and financing, and greater abundance of good building sites. This market is far from saturated, because New Orleans—for long one of the most urban cities in the country, with a very high proportion of renters—is just now getting used to the idea of homeownership in distant subdivisions. The housing pattern that has become typical throughout the rest of America has only recently become popular there.

The concept of the Negro market which dominates the housing industry in New Orleans is that based upon the traditional notions of the Negroes as income-earners, debt-payers, and property-owners. With very few exceptions, the Negro population has been lower-class in income, in stability of family life, and in attitudes toward the acquisition of homes and their maintenance. White real estate dealers, financiers, and developers are aware of the consequences of Negro status, and the housing industry in all its branches agrees that housing for Negroes is a "tough problem." Those who have attempted subdivisions for Negroes have had mixed experiences. Some say, "Never again." Others feel that under the "right conditions" they might attempt another.

But slowly these images are being somewhat modified, and the housing industry is becoming more aware of the growing Negro middle class. "Panic selling" when Negroes move in, for example, is becoming more discriminating. On Paris Avenue, when whites discovered that incoming Negroes were middle-class people who took as much pride in home maintenance as they did, "For Sale" signs were taken down, and this experience seems to have made an impact in the real estate world. But it is still the case that the Negro cannot expect much from the building industry on economic grounds alone; altruistic motives, as we will show, have played a major role in getting the Negro the limited housing he has been able to acquire.

There have been alternatives, even if limited ones, to dependence on the subdivision builder, and the financial institutions that generally support him, and some new housing has been acquired through other channels: building by individuals on land they own, usually in an undeveloped or fringe area, and building by small builders, who have put up single houses here and there. The houses that individual homeseekers have put up demonstrate considerable persistence and initiative, but unfortunately the city has been negligent in requiring these houses to conform to city codes. Many such houses have been built since 1950, and one area below the Industrial Canal abounds in them, but they have been below standard, and the area in which they have been concentrated has already taken on the appearance of a slum. Financing for such houses has been that typical for poor risks, and lenders generally expect the properties to be "lost" and "resold" several times.

A few builders are reported to specialize in single houses for Negroes. One of these, a Mr. R——, after forty years in real estate and building, has built exclusively for Negroes during the past nine years. During this time he has constructed almost two hundred homes. According to the City Planning Commission, the homes constructed by him conform to the codes and are superior. His houses range in price from $10,000 to $12,250. The earnings of his purchasers, he reported, range between $60 and $150 a week; the wives usually work too, and bring in $20 to $40 a week in addition. Most of his buyers are longshoremen and postal clerks. Terms of sale usually require a down payment of $369, with $425 closing costs, and carry a thirty-year, FHA-insured mortgage. At present, Mr. R—— reports that not a single purchaser is behind in his payments. Unquestionably, this successful operation depends on the builder's own deep personal interest in building for Negroes, and probably involves for him a much greater investment in time to find appropriate purchasers than would be necessary if he were building for whites. Yet, when these motives are added to normal commercial interests, it is apparently possible to build for a middle-class Negro market in New Orleans.

In New Orleans, it has not been possible for the Negro community to undertake directly any major economic role in providing housing. As previously pointed out, the Negroes of New Orleans form one of the less prosperous Negro communities of the urban South. There are no banks, savings and loan associations, or mortgage companies headed by Negroes. However, a savings and loan association is now being formed. The only existing financial institutions are seventeen small life insurance companies with combined assets in 1955 of eight and a half million dollars and unassigned (surplus) funds of less than one million dollars. One of these, the Good Citizens Life Insurance Company, undertook a small housing development, and did so successfully. However, it was not planning any further ventures in housing because of preferred alternative investments for its limited funds.

A more significant effort undertaken by members of the Negro community was a rental housing development, Gentilly Gardens. This development, near Dillard University, was built with FHA assistance and completed before 1950. The response suggested untapped possibilities in the Negro market. After a slow start, Gentilly Gardens has a very low vacancy rate, and was recently expanded. The rents, ranging from $55 to $86, the long waiting lists, and the low rate of turnover suggest the presence of an upper-income group in the Negro community whose housing demand is not being met.

Pontchartrain Park and Bunche Village—A Comparison

The two largest private housing developments for Negroes in New Orleans are Pontchartrain Park homes and Bunche Village. The story of these two developments illustrates many of the circumstances that must be considered in providing housing for Negroes.

The Industrial Canal runs north and south through the city, connecting Lake Pontchartrain with the Mississippi River. During the war, the area immediately west of the canal, toward Lake Pontchartrain, was partly filled with temporary wartime housing for workers in nearby industries. The rest was still forested swamp. This area, close to the center of the city, was one of the few choice sites available for either residential or industrial developments. It was zoned for residential use, and the City Council resisted efforts of industrialists in 1950 and 1951 to rezone it.

Soon after the war, W. Hamilton Crawford, of Crawford Homes, Inc., Baton Rouge, secured City Planning Commission approval for a subdivision on this site. It was understood that there would be one development for whites, another for Negroes. The white project came first. Gentilly Woods was begun, and within a year of opening, Mr. Crawford had sold 1,500 homes. But nothing seemed to be happening about a Negro subdivision. Meanwhile, the city invested $186,000 for a 186-acre park, between the white development and the proposed Negro housing, and this, it was expected, would be for Negro use. The city administration was seriously interested in showing it was doing something for Negro housing; federal lending agencies were also interested in a good housing development for Negroes. The original builder, however, decided not to go ahead with the project and a new group was formed to undertake it. The people who came forth to underwrite Pontchartrain Park homes were well-to-do and public-spirited citizens whose prime concern was not in making a profit, but in demonstrating to builders and private investors that good housing for Negroes was economically feasible. They considered, nevertheless, that the worth of the project as a demonstration depended on its being at least reasonably successful financially. It is worth noting that some of the leading figures involved in Pontchartrain Park are related to the philanthropists who, almost thirty years before, first tried to build modern housing for Negroes in New Orleans. In both cases, members of the Jewish community figured prominently.

The new developers provided much of the necessary funds from their own resources and secured additional financing from the New York Life and Prudential Life insurance companies. Between 1955 and 1957 the city invested over $400,000 for improvements in the subdivision—rather more than it would have expended for an ordinary subdivision. The first units of what was planned to be a 1,000-home development were opened in mid-1955, and houses are still being built. A church is under construction and others are planned; a 515-pupil school will be located nearby; the park has been developed and now includes a golf course for Negroes, and there is talk of locating a branch of the state university for Negroes on the lake front nearby.

The developers of Pontchartrain Park provided fifteen different house styles, of two or three bedrooms, on lots of varying sizes, the smallest being 45 by 100 feet, the largest 90 by 135 feet. The houses range in price from $9,800 to $27,000, but most sell for $10,000 to $13,000. The project was provided with streets with concrete foundations and black-top surfaces, concrete sidewalks, and driveways. There is adequate plumbing, good water and sewerage facilities, and good drainage.

Pontchartrain Park has the appearance of a good residential neighborhood, and one that will probably get better, as churches and schools are completed, the trees grow, and the rest of the area is filled with new homes.

In striking contrast to Pontchartrain Park is Bunche Village. Built by the Delta Mortgage Company as an ordinary business venture without philanthropic backing, it opened in March, 1955, a few months earlier than Ponchartrain Park, and was completely occupied by September, 1956.

Bunche Village is located about twenty miles from midcity (as compared with six miles for Pontchartrain Park), directly west of the city in Jefferson Parish. It is directly off an arterial expressway and between two railway lines which are here only a few hundred yards apart. South of the Kansas City Southern Railway line is the Mississippi River levee. To the north are other residential areas, stretching to Lake Pontchartrain. The area between the tracks is largely vacant with clusters of semirural slum dwellings. Drainage was provided by the developers, but until 1958 it was poor.

The homes in Bunche Village are all of frame construction. None have any brick or stone work. Lots are uniformly small. There are concrete sidewalks and black-topped streets, standard plumbing and water supply. Since there is no public sewerage, each house is provided with a septic tank, despite the high water table in this low-lying area. The homes range from $9,500 to $10,500 in cost, substantially lower than the average in Pontchartrain Park.

Two years after occupancy, the general aspect of the community is fair to good. Some of the houses have been improved by addition of rooms, carports, fencing, and brickwork. But many show an absence of any improvement, and several are rather neglected and run-down.

The comparison of Pontchartrain Park and Bunche Village is of particular importance because of the contrasting evidence they provide on the question of the Negro as a homeowner. There has been little problem of payment delinquency in Pontchartrain Park and few resales of houses. In Bunche Village, on the other hand, only 100 of the 264 home-purchasers had good payment records, according to the person in charge of financial management. There is a scattering of "For Sale" signs, and from the appearance of some of these properties, it does not look as if new purchasers will be easy to find, or that the original owners will get back their equity. The financial manager stated that the delinquency rates for 1,200 white accounts which he handled was roughly one-third that among Negro accounts. He added, however, that delinquencies in Bunche Village were not much above the delinquency rate in a white project occupied by persons of the same income class (Greenlawn Terrace).

What explains the striking differences in the delinquency experience of these two ventures into private housing for Negroes? Part of the explanation, probably, is in the differing social origins and characteristics of the home purchasers in the two projects.

In both developments, the great majority of families have come from the heavily populated areas surrounding the principal business district of the city. Canal Street separates the city into an "uptown" and a "downtown" area, both with slums, but the uptown slums are considerably worse. Negroes of higher status tend to live in the downtown area. More than three-quarters of the Pontchartrain Park residents formerly lived in this downtown area; in contrast, more than two-thirds of the Bunche Village residents had lived in the uptown area.

The heads of families in Pontchartrain are considerably younger than those of Bunche Village, and both are much younger than Negro family heads in the city as a whole. Four-fifths of the Pontchartrain group were under 40 years of age in 1957, as compared with two-thirds of the Bunche Village family heads. Possibly differences in financing account for this age difference. Four-fifths of the Bunche Village loans were VA-guaranteed, while in Pontchartrain Park the FHA-guaranteed played a more important role. FHA insures no loan beyond the sixty-fifth year; therefore, the terms of older applicants must be shortened with heavier monthly payments or larger down payments.

Available data on income distribution reveal no significant differences between the two groups. With respect to occupations, however, a marked difference does appear. Nearly a third of the Pontchartrain family heads are professional and white-collar workers (mostly the latter) while 95 percent of the Bunche Village heads fall in the blue-collar group of occupations. Even though the incomes of the two groups may be similar, it is well-known that a difference in occupation will be related to a difference in style and use of income. A professional or white-collar person making five thousand dollars a year is likely to have a rather different social outlook than a blue-collar worker with the same income. The blue-collar category, large in both projects, probably conceals other important differences between the two groups. Pontchartrain Park has larger numbers of "upper blue-collar" workers such as postmen and mail clerks, skilled craftsmen and policemen; the blue-collar workers of Bunche Village include many more longshoremen, stevedores, truck drivers, porters, and laborers.

Discussions with the management of Bunche Village and officials of the VA pointed to a number of specific causes for payment delinquency in Bunche Village. The overobligation of small incomes seems to be most important. Easy credit on what appears to be favorable terms, and the pressures of salesmanship and advertising, lead many to acquire more debts than their incomes can support. Associated with this is the fact that the person buying a home for the first time—and in neither Bunche Village nor Pontchartrain Park have many of the residents had previous experiences with home purchase—is not likely to appreciate all the costs involved. There is fencing to be purchased, lawns to be seeded, a mower to be bought, flowers and shrubs to be planted. The old furniture may not look right in the new home, and so on. Soon the home-buyer cannot keep up the payments.

A special factor in the blue-collar group is that the buyer's income comes in weekly payments, and he has long been accustomed to weekly rental payments. He is not accustomed to holding back expenditures to make up a monthly payment.

A third problem is that the applicants for loans were screened in a cursory fashion. The sales agents were under pressure to make sales rapidly so the developers could get their money out, and investigation was consequently not sufficiently thorough. Related to this is the fact that little weight was put on the kind of family that was buying the house. Some of the sales in Bunche Village were to families based on common-law marriages; the instability of the family, regardless of the reasons for it, makes unlikely the ability to maintain payments over many years.

Finally, there was unfortunately no counseling of prospective home-purchasers on what was financially involved in the contracting of large debts. Low-income people have had little experience in managing financial affairs, and it is the better part of both wisdom and charity to set up some arrangement whereby they can be told just what the undertaking of financial obligations entails.

Because of these various factors, it is not surprising that community morale should be high in Pontchartrain Park and low in Bunche Village. There are gripes in Pontchartrain Park, too. There are complaints about the noises coming from adjacent industrial areas, about industrial waste from one plant which stains woodwork and clothes, about seepage from the Industrial

Canal. But these are the complaints that might be found in many residential neighborhoods, and they have here resulted in co-operative efforts to resolve them. No one in Pontchartrain Park has expressed regret at having moved there.

But many in Bunche Village have expressed regret at their move. Having bought there because no other homes were available on the same easy terms, they have discovered its many drawbacks—its distance from the city, its dreary surroundings, the small size of house and lot. There are no community organizations in Bunche Village: a minister moved in to start a church, but the attempt was not carried through. In Pontchartrain Park, on the other hand, an active community organization exists which speaks for the community and has secured improvements from public utilities and the city. It has promoted a clean-up campaign, a lawn and garden beautification contest, a Christmas lighting campaign, playground activities, and other like undertakings. A church and community center is under construction and more are expected to follow. A community spirit and a sense of belonging are clearly emerging in Pontchartrain Park.

In the light of New Orleans' previous history of racial mixing, what, one wonders, is the reaction of the Negro community to the emergence, as in Pontchartrain Park, of the pattern of complete Negro residential segregation? Feelings are mixed. Some residents wish the promoters would invite in whites; others are afraid whites would then take over the area. Some are afraid that if Negroes do not move fast to buy the undeveloped part of the project area, it may become a white development. The desire for nonsegregated living conflicts with the fear that even the little that Negroes have in the way of good housing will be taken away if they do not accept segregation.

Despite the success of Pontchartrain Park as a community, and despite the good housing it has provided, it is not likely that this experience will be repeated and that other such developments will be made available to Negroes. Pontchartrain Park proved that Negroes wanted good housing, that they could pay for it, and that they would be stable homeowners. But Pontchartrain Park was not a uniformly positive demonstration to private developers. First, the Negro market responded much more slowly than the white market has to developments of this quality. It has taken longer to sell Pontchartrain Park homes to Negroes than it would have, had they been sold to whites. Second, the job of selection of qualified buyers has been more difficult than in the case of whites. Third, the money market has been tighter for Negro home-buyers. The builders of Pontchartrain Park have not lost money; they have recovered their investment and made a profit, but more slowly and with greater effort than is usual in the housing business. Without philanthropic and civic motives—as well as the strong support from city government and federal agencies—they would not have undertaken this development; and the supply of builders operating from these motives and with these aids is not large.

The Negro Political Potential

The impact of politics on housing does not have to be argued; it will determine what is done in low-cost housing, in urban renewal, in decisions as to sites and development of city services. And the impact of voting on politics is equally undeniable. Perhaps in New Orleans potential Negro political strength may come to compensate for economic weakness. For there has been a striking increase in the numbers of Negroes voting in New Orleans and in their ability to make use of this vote. Louisiana is one of the southern states which has not made an all-out effort to keep Negroes from voting, and since the Smith-Allwright decision of the Supreme Court in 1944, there has been a steady increase in Negro voters in the state. Between 1948 and 1956, the number of Negro registered voters in Louisiana increased from 22,600 to 161,400. In the latter year more than 30 percent of the potential Negro voters were registered, compared with less than 5 percent in 1948 and a negligible fraction before the war.[1]

In New Orleans the mayoralty election of 1958 marked a high point in Negro participation in politics. It is still not possible for white candidates to campaign openly for Negro votes, but the candidates did campaign "behind the scenes." In that election, 31,000 Negroes were registered; their number will certainly go higher in the next few years. Eventually, it may not be possible for candidates *not* to campaign for Negro votes. In the 1958

---

[1] John Fenton, "Negro Voting in Louisiana," *Research in Action,* vol. I, no. 6 (October, 1956), p. 1.

election, only one candidate was violently prosegregation; he received fewer than 3,000 out of 156,000 votes cast. Mayor Morrison was reëlected, after twelve years in office, with 90,494 votes, including, one may assume, most of the Negro vote. He has been, in southern terms, a moderate. He has sponsored no programs unfair or unjust to Negroes, and he played an important role in making Pontchartrain Park possible. He has placed no obstacles to Negroes' registering and voting; under his administration the number of Negro voters in New Orleans has grown from 1,000 to more than 30,000.

Another significant outcome of the 1958 election was in the race for councilman. A Negro candidate, Earl Amedee, received 19,409 votes out of a total of 265,181 votes cast for the election of two councilmen; he placed fifth in a field of eight. He did not secure every Negro vote, and one may speculate whether this was because Negroes voted for the "best candidate" independently of color, or because a good part of the Negro vote is controlled by local bosses working with local white politicians. But Mr. Amedee —and the Negroes of New Orleans—did gain something tangible from this showing, for the winning candidate for district attorney announced that Mr. Amedee would join his staff. This is the first time in the history of New Orleans that a Negro attorney has had such an appointment.

Reviewing the election, the Negro *Louisiana Weekly* was concerned with the lack of unity displayed by the Negro voters. But in other respects the Negro community has recently shown remarkable capacities for unified action, which suggests that its political force may be wielded with increasing effectiveness in the future. Here are a few examples of recent action by the Negro community:

Each Spring, the school children of New Orleans visit the memorial to John McDonough, a benefactor of New Orleans public schools, and place flowers upon it. Traditionally, white children have completed their ceremonies first, and then Negro children have followed. The Negro participants attempted unsuccessfully to get this practice changed, and failed; at this point, a complete boycott of the ceremonies by Negroes was instituted. Everyone coöperated; Negroes no longer take part in the ceremonies, and the reasons for their protest are clear.

Each year, during the traditional Mardi Gras season, balls, parties, and celebrations take place. Negroes have their carnival clubs which conduct elaborate balls at this time, just as white clubs do, and they are as old and important, relatively speaking, as the white ones. During 1956–1957, when the NAACP was banned in the state, the job of conducting Negro protest fell for a time upon a group of representatives from Negro organizations, called the United Clubs. This group felt that the economic potential of the Negro in New Orleans had not been sufficiently brought to the attention of the people of New Orleans. To accomplish both aims, the United Clubs proposed that the Negro carnival clubs forego their elaborate carnival dances and contribute the money thus saved to support the Negro fight for freedom. The Negro community was mobilized and not a single elaborate ball was staged by a Negro group, saving, it was estimated, $300,000. To be sure, all this did not go to support the causes which Negro organizations were then fighting for—yet the unified protest of the Negro community was impressive.

The Urban League in New Orleans has not played the role in housing that the Urban League in Atlanta has. It has been a much weaker organization. Organized in 1938, it did not get its first full-time staff member—an industrial relations secretary—until 1952. It was a member of the Community Chest in New Orleans, securing its funds from the United Fund. As the White Citizens' Council pressure rose, it was feared in the United Fund that a $3,000,000 campaign drive would be jeopardized if the Urban League were retained in the Community Chest, and consequently it was removed. At this point, the Negro community rallied to its support, raising more funds for it than it would have obtained had it remained in the Community Chest. The trade unionists raised their contribution from about $1,000 to $7,000. The Urban League was able to increase its budget to $30,000, move to a more central location, and undertake a more extensive program of community organization work, some of which involves housing and neighborhood improvement.

The Urban League has accomplished a good deal in exploring the Negro market for private housing and has placed the results of its research before the relevant parties. Together with Dillard University and Xavier University, the Urban League has initiated surveys in two areas for the purpose of educating Negro residents in the procedures necessary to get neighborhood improvements from the city. These organizations also expect, as a result of these surveys, to secure data which will help the rehabilitation work which the city's Housing Improvement Division is trying to encourage.

All of these signs indicate an ever-stronger, more self-conscious, more capable, and better-organized Negro community. One element in the Negro community, not previously mentioned, that has played a role in these developments and may play a larger one is the Negro trade unionists. They number between 12,000 and 15,000, have been central in the political awakening of the Negro community, and, as a relatively stable economic group with earnings quite high for the Negro community, may play a role in expanding Negro housing opportunities. The combination of well-paid Negro workers with solidly established unions suggests the possibility that the unions may help their members to build and buy houses. Nothing has occurred along these lines, but something may.

The Negro in New Orleans has not yet put forth his full political strength. In the past, he has been hampered by, among other things, the dispersed pattern of settlement we have referred to. Negro segregation when accompanied by certain other conditions, as in Atlanta, may be an aid to the development of political organization, political leaders, and group self-consciousness. In New Orleans, Negro political leaders have been essentially the minor mercenaries of white political organizations. But even this is changing. The new public housing and private housing areas are segregated, and solidly Negro. The areas within the cities where Negroes have been acquiring homes as whites move out to the new suburbs are becoming more completely Negro. Thus, segregation, which the Negro community dislikes, is paradoxically increasing their potential political power—making it easier for them to organize and ultimately to elect officials. But the second paradox that is likely to arise is that as Negro segregation increases Negro political power, that power may be turned against segregation itself, in the schools, in the public parks and facilities, and in housing. When Negro power is great enough, it will not be possible for an enlightened mayor to build new, segregated parks after Negroes have won the right in the courts to use all parks; to engage in elaborate legal maneuvers to prevent Negroes from exercising their legal rights to unsegregated public transportation; or to prevent Negroes from entering empty apartments in white public housing projects.

What, then, is the outlook for New Orleans? The statistics of population increase and minimal need indicate a widening gap between the demand for Negro housing and the supply. And despite increasing Negro political power, income, and rising standards of expectation affecting housing, the market forces at work in New Orleans still seem to be incapable of supplying sufficient good housing to this part of the community. The community managers responsible for the growth of New Orleans, despite their commitment to a policy of moderation, have, up until now, been unable to stimulate and guide local forces to the extent necessary to fill this need.

Under these circumstances, the best qualified observers see the need for action "off the top": new high-level policies, both at federal and local levels, seem necessary if the problem of sufficient housing for Negroes in New Orleans is to be solved.

ELIZABETH L. VIRRICK

IV

New Housing for Negroes in Dade County, Florida

The population of Dade County, which includes Miami, its suburbs and related towns, and a good part of southeastern Florida, has been growing phenomenally in recent decades.[1] In 1940, there were about 268,000 people in Dade County; in 1950, 495,000; in 1955, 704,000. The Negro population has also been growing rapidly, but, as elsewhere in the South, not as fast as the white population. Negroes in Dade County, in round numbers, increased from 50,000 in 1940 to 65,000 in 1950 to 98,000 in 1955. While the white population was increasing by almost three times in those fifteen years, the Negro population doubled. Its proportion of the county population has declined from one-fifth to one-seventh.

[1] In this report, the writer draws on her observations and experiences as a student and participant in movements for better housing in the Miami area over a period of years. Many of the specific data are from a personal survey of Negro housing developments made at the request of the Commission on Race and Housing in 1956. In addition, the following published materials have been utilized: United States Census data, 1940 and 1950, and Special Census of Miami, 1955; Planning Board of the City of Miami, Slum Clearance Committee of Miami, and Dade County Health Department, *Dwelling Conditions in the Two Principal Blighted Areas* (Miami Central Negro District and Coconut Grove), 1949; Planning and Zoning Department, Dade County, *Survey of Negro Areas*, 1950; National Urban League and Council of Social Agencies, Dade County, *A Review of the Economic and Cultural Problems in Dade County, Florida, as They Relate to Conditions in the Negro Population*, 1943, and *An Appraisal of Progress*, 1953; Reinhold P. Wolff and David P. Gillogly, *Negro Housing in the Miami Area* (Bureau of Business and Economic Research, University of Miami, 1951); *The Miami Herald*, series on slums in the Miami area, with major attention to Negro housing conditions, by Lawrence Thompson, December 11–18, 1955.

But Negro population growth, even if not as fast as the white growth, has required a great increase of housing. Contrary to experience in many other cities, the expansion of housing for Negroes in Miami and vicinity has been achieved mainly by new construction and not by transfer of dwellings from white to Negro use. Beginning in 1949, builders have gone heavily into the market for housing for Negroes, putting up both large projects of homes for purchase, generally with VA financing, and apartment houses, with FHA financing. Many of the apartment houses built in the early 1950's were financed under Section 608 of the National Housing Act. Apartment building has continued steadily since then and was still going on in 1959. Although, as we shall see, there are many drawbacks to most of the new housing made available to Negroes, a great quantity of housing has been supplied by private industry for Negroes in Dade County.

The purpose of this chapter is to describe the kind and quality of housing that has been provided, and to give a general picture of the changes in Negro housing conditions in recent years.

There are now twenty-six segregated Negro neighborhoods in Dade County. Many of these areas have come into existence only since the war. In 1940, more than three-fifths of the Negro dwelling units in Dade County were in the Central Negro District, near downtown Miami. There were only two other large Negro areas: Liberty City, north of the Central Negro District, consisting mostly of a large low-rent housing project for Negroes (Liberty Square); and Coconut Grove, about five miles southwest of the Central District. These three areas together accounted for four-fifths of Negro dwelling units in Dade County.[2]

The Central Negro District differs from Negro areas of other cities in that it was built as a slum, for the purpose of cheap Negro housing; it is not an area of once good housing that has deteriorated. Miami is only fifty-five years old. In the early days, a shack could be built for probably a hundred dollars. One, two, or three rooms, one behind another, with a small front porch, no electricity, no running water, and no bathroom, was the typical dwelling then put up for Negroes in the Central District. The houses were

---

[2] Reinhold P. Wolff and David P. Gillogly, *Negro Housing in the Miami Area* (Bureau of Business and Economic Research, University of Miami, 1951).

built as close together as possible, so as to place the maximum number on one lot.

Conditions in the Central District and Coconut Grove were described in a survey of these two areas by the Planning Board of the City of Miami, the Slum Clearance Committee, and the Dade County Health Department in 1949. At that time the Central District contained 8,505 dwellings and 36,906 people. It covered 284.2 acres or 144 city blocks. Less than 9 percent of the units were owner-occupied. Nearly 40 percent of the households were overcrowded. A large proportion of the houses lacked electricity, screens, bathing facilities, or hot water.

The situation in Coconut Grove was somewhat better. It extended over 37 residential blocks or 85.5 acres, and had approximately 3,600 inhabitants, which indicates less severe crowding than in the Central District (42 persons per acre, as against 130). Twenty-seven percent of the dwellings were owner-occupied. None was served by city sewers.

Since 1949, there have been three principle channels for increasing the supply of housing for Negroes. One is public housing, another is the building of houses for sale, and third is the building of apartments for rent. The two latter activities are by far the most important. Recently, a large number of individual homes have been sold to Negroes by white owners in an area undergoing transition from white to Negro occupancy.

The public housing project called Liberty Square, which formed the center of the Negro district in Liberty City, was started in 1937, and now contains 973 units, accommodating 4,580 people. Since World War II, there has been considerable public discussion about more public housing, but only one project for Negroes has been built in Dade County. A great deal of difficulty was involved in finding a site for this project. Again and again the county commissioners refused to approve sites proposed by the Housing Authority. Finally, a site was selected in Para Villa Heights, not far from Liberty Square. This had been a Negro settlement before the public housing project was built, and thus Negro homes had to be demolished to build it. The project was completed in 1954, contains 762 units, and houses 3,940 people. The difficulties with the site suggest one of the reasons why there have been no other projects. The private building industry's opposition was another important reason: it claimed it could do the job, and indeed, since 1949, when the white market seems to have been satisfied, at least temporarily, there has been considerable building for the Negro market. Two main centers have been developed at some distance from Miami in which individual homes in large developments have been built and sold to Negroes. These are Richmond Heights, about eighteen miles south of Miami, and Bunche Park, a similar distance to the north.

Richmond Heights was begun by a private developer, Captain Frank C. Martin, whose main concern was to improve housing conditions for Negroes. He brought together a committee of Negro leaders and sought their advice at every step. He built houses that gave his purchasers more than their money's worth, and screened purchasers carefully with the aim of insuring permanent residents and a stable community. Many who moved into Richmond Heights were professional people—teachers, ministers, and the like.

The first houses were available in 1950. By 1956, 647 homes had been built and sold. They contained two or three bedrooms and sold for $7,000 and $8,030. The houses were VA financed, with monthly payments of $37.50 or $47.50 a month, and included stove, refrigerator, washing machine, and Venetian blinds. They were better built than any other houses in projects for Negroes, then or later. The bathrooms were fully tiled, and the lots were large—75 by 100 feet.

Captain Martin also planned for community facilities. Ten acres were donated for a business section and five and a half acres were given to the school board. A wide area of land around the project was left for a park.

Richmond Heights is not without its drawbacks: the area was bulldozed and is completely bare and without trees. Its distance from the city is a serious handicap and adds a good deal to the living expenses of its residents. An elementary school for Negroes is nearby but high school children have to travel to Coconut Grove, fifteen miles away. There also have been changes in management since Captain Martin died, and some of the green belt that he reserved for a park has since been sold to speculative builders.

But Richmond Heights has been a marked success as a community. By 1956, only twenty-nine of the original occupants had sold their homes, and there had been only seventeen foreclosures. The foreclosed houses were offered for sale at increases of $400 to $900 over the original prices, and houses inferior to those in Richmond Heights are now being sold in nearby tracts at prices $2,000 more than those of the original Richmond Heights houses. There is a waiting list for Richmond Heights. People manifest considerable pride in their homes and neighborhood and feel the long trip to the city is worthwhile. They take a strong interest in the neighborhood and have succeeded in defeating a variety of proposed zoning changes, including one that would have brought a bar and cocktail lounge to the border of their community.

Contrasting markedly with Richmond Heights is the other large concentration of individual homes for Negroes to the north of Miami, the Opa Locka-Bunche Park area. Six developments have been built in this area, totaling nearly 2,200 units. Bunche Park is the largest development with more than 1,400 homes. These projects, too, were financed with VA mortgage guarantees for the most part. The houses in these developments are not as well built as those in Richmond Heights. One minor hurricane did so much damage that a VA investigation was conducted. It revealed that the houses were improperly constructed.

Intensive selling campaigns featured low monthly payments, but as a concomitant to this, purchasers were not properly screened. Many of the buyers lacked the financial ability or foresight to take on serious financial obligations. Many foreclosures resulted, and there were numerous cases in which occupants simply walked out. The creditors are now collecting payments weekly instead of monthly. Many families appear to take little pride in their homes or neighborhoods, and the whole area is rapidly taking on the aspect of a slum.

Substantial additions to the Negro housing supply have occurred also between Opa Locka-Bunche Park and the Central District, in the area around the first public housing project for Negroes, Liberty Square. When the project was put up, before the war, population in the area was sparse and little of it was Negro. Since the war, an estimated four to five hundred homes have been built in this region by Negroes. In addition, Negroes have begun to expand into areas of modest homes occupied by whites. Several hundred homes in Edison Center, directly east of Liberty Square, have been purchased by Negroes, leaving only a few in the hands of whites. This area has also seen extensive building of apartment houses for Negroes. At least 1,000 rental apartment units have gone up, both in large developments (Carver Village—500 units, Lincoln Fields—300, Sugar Hill Apartments—100, Caledonia Heights—75) and in the form of four-unit buildings.

But the most extensive apartment-house building for Negroes has taken place in Coconut Grove and the Central Negro District. Many of the shacks that filled these old Negro neighborhoods have been replaced by modern apartment buildings, constructed under Section 608 of the National Housing Act or other FHA financing. But this new supply has not been without its problems.

In 1949, while Coconut Grove was being surveyed by the County Health department and other agencies, the Coconut Grove Citizens' Committee for Slum Clearance came into existence. This organization sponsored an ordinance requiring running water in every household, and a toilet, sink, and septic tank. The local water company coöperated by installing water in every street. Within two years, the citizens' committee, working with the Health Department, eliminated every outdoor toilet in the area. The committee loaned money to those homeowners who could not get credit to help them install bathrooms.

This was only the beginning of the committee's activity. Up to 1949, only one Negro in Dade County had ever been able to obtain an FHA commitment to build a home.[3] One of the problems in getting FHA commitments was that the Negro residential areas were zoned commercial and industrial—as was Coconut Grove—and FHA asserted the lack of proper zoning made it impossible for it to insure mortgages. The citizen's committee consequently decided to get Coconut Grove rezoned in line with its actual land use—it was almost entirely single family homes, owned or rented. Four architects coöperated in developing a re-

[3] FHA records are not kept by race. However, it is well-known locally that Negroes in Dade County were refused FHA commitments until recently. The Negro who obtained the commitment prior to 1949 was a dentist, light-skinned, and planning to build a home in a non-Negro neighborhood. It is commonly believed locally that FHA was not aware that he was a Negro when the commitment was made.

zoning plan which would not only make it possible for Negroes to approach FHA for single-home financing but would prevent the area from being overcrowded by the rising tide of apartment building. The rezoning plan was submitted to the planning board and the city commissioners, but after numerous hearings was rejected. The citizens' committee then carried through the first successful initiative petition and referendum in the State of Florida in order to obtain the rezoning, but this was a two-year battle and in the meantime considerable apartment building took place.

Coconut Grove today presents a mixed picture. As the citizens' committee feared, the apartment houses have hurt the neighborhood, for they were put up hastily for profit, their construction is poor, there is almost no maintenance, and there is little space around them for children's play or other outdoor activity. Many of these apartment houses have already deteriorated badly.

The civic-mindedness which produced the citizens' committee and its achievements is also weaker than it was a few years ago. Many of the leading residents have moved to Richmond Heights; the new apartment-dwellers are not as civic-minded as the old residents and take less interest in the community. It is their carelessness, as well as the poor municipal housekeeping and the overcrowding of sites, that causes the new apartment houses to be surrounded by trash and garbage. Coconut Grove has never had sidewalks. Its two business streets are a hodgepodge of miscellaneous establishments. Its only recreation space is an open, treeless area owned by the city and by necessity used as a school playground. In the center of the town is an old incinerator, which is not only unsightly but malodorous and a fire hazard to the frame houses nearby.

And yet, there are many positive features, too, in Coconut Grove. The citizens' committee has carried through innumerable clean-up campaigns, and these have had some effect, at least temporarily. The area has recently been graced by a fine new building for St. Alban's Day Nursery, originally begun by the citizens' committee, but now run by its own biracial board. And there are the advantages, enjoyed even by $10-a-week shacks, of natural beauty in the form of magnificent old trees—citrus, mango, avocado, and palm—and other plants and shrubs.

The Central Negro District has none of these advantages. Its shacks are far more crowded (how they have survived hurricanes is a mystery), it contains little grass or shrubbery and few trees, and it too has inadequate garbage and trash collections. It does not have the active civic consciousness which has done so much for Coconut Grove. The Central District has been heavily invaded by poorly built apartment houses, with few amenities, crowded onto small plots. Our survey in 1956 found 248 apartment-house buildings, containing 3,808 units, and there have been more since. The space for these apartment houses came from "slum clearance" which, according to official figures, resulted in the demolition of 1,673 dwelling units. But they have been replaced by more than twice as many new apartment units. These latter, moreover, owing in part to their high rents, too often contain more people than they should. Thus, population density in the Central District has increased from 130 persons per acre in 1949 to approximately 170 persons per acre in 1956.

In summary, the housing needs of a growing Negro population in Dade County have been supplied very largely in recent years by new housing construction. The amount of new housing built for sale or rent to Negroes is large. Our 1956 survey, covering only the major areas of Negro residence, found 9,600 new dwelling units built between 1949 and 1956.[4] More have been added since then. Probably few communities in the United States can point to a comparable record of new housing production available to Negroes. The distribution of the new units by type and location is summarized in the following tabulation.

Nevertheless, one may question whether the housing needs of Negroes in Dade County have been met in the best way. The largest and poorest area of Negro residence, the Central District, contains more people than ever before, in the same space. Many are living in new apartment houses, but under conditions of severe crowding and on skimpy sites which preserve no space for play, for grass and trees, or for parking or laundry hanging. This crowding makes it easy—in fact, almost inevitable—for

[4] Adding the estimated number of existing houses transferred from white to Negro occupancy (300) and subtracting the 1,673 dwelling units demolished by slum clearance in the Central Negro District indicates a net addition of approximately 8,200 units to the Negro housing supply in the areas surveyed.

Housing type	*Number of units*
Public housing	762
Single-family houses for purchase	
Richmond Heights	647
Opa Locka-Bunche Park	2,183
Liberty City	426
Coconut Grove	60
Owner-built single-family houses in Coconut Grove	30
Rooming house in Coconut Grove	26
Apartment units	
Liberty City	1,015
Coconut Grove	644
Central Negro District	3,808
Total	9,601

trash and garbage to accumulate, demoralizing the residents and destroying whatever pride they might take in their new quarters. Similar conditions, although less severe, have developed in Coconut Grove with the building of apartment houses in the wrong locations with insufficient space and facilities. That these conditions could have been prevented by proper zoning and building controls makes their occurrence the more regrettable. Insofar as crowding and lack of space are basic features of slum life, it can be said that much of the new housing built for Negroes in Miami and Coconut Grove has intensified rather than relieved slum conditions.

MORRIS EAGLE

V

The Puerto Ricans in New York City

INTRODUCTION

The Puerto Ricans form the latest and very likely the last of the great waves of migrants that have again and again transformed New York City. Irish and Germans in the nineteenth century, Italians and Jews in the late nineteenth and early twentieth centuries, Negroes after World War I, and now Puerto Ricans have been accommodated in this city in such enormous numbers as to make New York, at various times in its history, the city having the largest Irish, Jewish, and Italian population in the world; it is now the largest Negro city in the United States and the city with the largest Puerto Rican population in the world.

New York is thus not ill-prepared to handle great migrations; the theme of this study is how has it managed with the vast Puerto Rican migration.

THE PUERTO RICAN MIGRANTS

At the end of 1956, there were an estimated 577,000 persons of Puerto Rican birth or parentage in New York City.[1] This is more than the population of Seattle, Kansas City, or New Orleans. The greater part of this population migrated to New York in the years after 1945, when regular air service was opened between New York and San Juan (see table 18). More than 400,000 Puerto Ricans migrated to the mainland in the ten-year interval, 1946–

---

[1] Migration Division, Department of Labor, Commonwealth of Puerto Rico, *A Summary in Facts and Figures,* April, 1957, ed., p. 17.

1955. At the beginning of this period, 95 percent were settling in New York; toward the end, about two-thirds.[2]

TABLE 18

ESTIMATED NET MIGRATION TO CONTINENTAL UNITED STATES FROM PUERTO RICO, 1939 TO 1957[a]

Year	Number of Persons	Year	Number of Persons
1939	3,035	1949	25,698
1940	−425	1950	34,703
1941	643	1951	52,899
1942	1,679	1952	59,103
1943	3,204	1953	69,124
1944	11,201	1954	21,531
1945	13,573	1955	45,464
1946	39,911	1956	52,315
1947	24,551	1957	37,704
1948	32,775	Total	528,688

SOURCE: Puerto Rico Planning Board, Bureau of Economics and Statistics, "Puerto Rico Passenger Traffic, by Route and Method of Transport," Monthly reports and cumulative balance.

[a] The figures represent the number of persons departing from Puerto Rico for the continental United States, or elsewhere, minus the number of arrivals in Puerto Rico. Transient passengers and tourists are excluded. Departures for and arrivals from places other than the Mainland are a relatively small proportion of these totals. The minus sign is used here to indicate a net outflow from the Mainland.

Under any circumstances, the housing of such large numbers would have been an enormous problem. But in the immediate postwar years, there was a combination of such factors as full employment, placing pressure on housing resources; the creation of large numbers of new families by marriage; their rapid increase in size by new births; and the fact that depression and war had for many years operated to reduce normal replacement building in New York. All this produced inordinate pressure on housing supply, and it was under these circumstances that Puerto Ricans had to compete for housing.

We will describe briefly the demographic characteristics of the Puerto Rican migrants to New York, making use of the 1950 Census.[3] Since in that year approximately 83 percent of all per-

[2] *Ibid.*, p. 16.

[3] *U. S. Census of Population: 1950*, vol. IV, *Special Reports*, part 3, chap. D, "Puerto Ricans in Continental United States." All census data relating to numbers and characteristics of the Puerto Rican population are taken from this volume.

sons of Puerto Rican birth or parentage in this country were living in New York City, we may with confidence ascribe the characteristics of the United States Puerto Ricans to New York Puerto Ricans. We will supplement the census figures with estimates from a demographic study of New York Puerto Ricans in 1953.[4]

Puerto Ricans are, to begin with, a youthful population. In 1950, Puerto Ricans in the continental United States had a median age of 24.3 years, compared with a median of 30.2 years for the entire population of the United States and 35 years for New York City. Only about 13 percent were 45 years and over, compared with 28.5 percent of the total United States population and about one-third of the New York City population. In 1953 the Puerto Rican population in New York City was apparently even younger, with a median age of about 20 or 21 years, owing to the large number of births to Puerto Ricans settled here and a decline in the age of migrants.

The 1950 Census reported a slight excess of females, but the 1953 estimate of Puerto Ricans in New York City suggested a small preponderance of males, especially in the ages between 15 and 34. However, as compared with other immigrant groups, it is a remarkably balanced population, reflecting both the ease and cheapness of migration (since Puerto Ricans are citizens, there is no problem about coming and going), and the fact that they come as settlers rather than to make money and return.

The Puerto Rican population tends to marry early, compared with the New York City population: 42 percent of the women in the age-range 14–24 are married, compared with 29 percent of the New York City population; 24.5 percent of the males in this age-range are married, compared with 14 percent of the New York City population. About four-fifths of those of ages from 25 to 44 are married, in both sexes, which is roughly the situation for New Yorkers, too. Beyond the age of 45, another contrast may be seen in the smaller proportion of Puerto Rican than New York women married; this is owing to an unusually high percentage of older Puerto Rican women who are widowed or divorced.

---

[4] A. Jaffe, ed., *Puerto Rican Population in New York City* (Columbia University, Bureau of Applied Social Research, January, 1954).

As would be expected from their youthful age and the high proportion married, the birth rate among New York Puerto Ricans is very much higher than among the population in general. But even holding the factor of age constant, Puerto Ricans have a much higher birth rate than the general population. Thus, births per 1,000 persons aged 15 to 44 in New York City in 1950 were as follows:[5]

Puerto Rican	135
White	82
Nonwhite	100

Puerto Ricans, as one might expect of migrants from a poor island, are not as well educated as New Yorkers in general. About one-fifth of the adults over 25, according to the 1950 Census, had graduated from eighth grade, and 10 percent had graduated from high school or attended college. This compares with nearly three-fourths of New Yorkers who had completed eighth grade and about one-third who had graduated from high school or had gone to college.

About the same proportion of Puerto Rican as New York males were in the labor force in 1950, if we take into account differences in age distribution; however, we find that 39 percent of Puerto Rican women were in the labor force, as compared with 35 percent of New York women. Unemployment is high among Puerto Ricans: 16 percent of the Puerto Rican males in the labor force in New York City were unemployed in 1950, compared with 12 percent of New York nonwhite and 8 percent of New York white males. Ten percent of Puerto Rican women were unemployed, compared with 9 percent of nonwhite and 6 percent of white women.

The dominant occupations of Puerto Rican workers, male and female, are those of "operatives" (semiskilled) and of occupations grouped by the Census under "service trades," except that we find few Puerto Ricans in domestic service. In New York City in 1950, these two categories (operatives and service trades) accounted for nearly two-thirds of all employed Puerto Rican men, as compared with 30 percent of all employed men. Women were even more concentrated: nearly four-fifths were in the "opera-

[5] *Ibid.*

tives" category, compared with one-third of nonwhite and one-fourth of white women.

The median income of Puerto Ricans in New York City with incomes in 1950 was $1,654, which was approximately the same as the figure for nonwhites, but about one-third less than the median income for all New Yorkers.

THE HOUSING OF PUERTO RICANS

We have pointed out that Puerto Rican migration to New York City occurred during a period of severe housing shortage. The 1950 Census showed a vacancy rate of 1.1 percent.[6] Surveys of about 50,000 FHA rental units during the years 1952–1955 showed an average annual vacancy rate of 1.8 percent.[7] Sample surveys of the 21,540 old-law tenement buildings in Manhattan showed average annual vacancy rates of 0.4 from 1946 to 1954.[8]

That a large number of impoverished newcomers should have been able to find shelter at all in such a crowded city is remarkable. Yet find it they did and not in small amounts but in many thousands of units. How was this feat accomplished?

A small percentage has been taken into the city's public housing projects for low-income families. At mid-1955, Puerto Rican families occupied 8,571 of New York City's 80,761 public housing units.[9] The proportion of units occupied by Puerto Ricans (11 percent) was somewhat higher than their proportion in the population (about 7 percent), but as a part of the low-income population they certainly had no more than a proportionate share of the subsidized, low-rent dwellings. Those in public housing were about 7 percent of the total estimated Puerto Rican population in New York. Undoubtedly, the number of Puerto Ricans in public housing and their percent share of total units have increased substantially since 1955.

The vast majority (over 90 percent) of Puerto Ricans in New York have sought and found housing in the private market. They

---

[6] *U. S. Census of Housing: 1950,* vol. I, *General Characteristics,* chap. 32, "New York," table 17.

[7] Communication from Office of the Director, Federal Housing Administration, New York City.

[8] Real Estate Board of New York, Inc., Research Department, *Tenement Areas in Manhattan, Occupancy Survey,* Tenement Series no. 17, March, 1955.

[9] New York City Housing Authority, "Racial Distribution in Operating Projects at Initial Occupancy and on June 30, 1955, All Programs." (Dittoed table.)

have been able to do so partly owing to the movement of older residents out of the city, partly by crowding and related adjustments. The Puerto Ricans, as we shall show, despite their low incomes, have proved able to compete effectively for housing with higher income groups by accepting less space per person and less building maintenance per unit of space. Many building owners have found their most profitable alternative to lie in subdividing their apartments into smaller units for rental to Puerto Ricans or in "turning" their buildings to Puerto Rican occupancy while maintaining or raising rents and often reducing costly maintenance or services.

In the historic pattern of immigrant groups, Puerto Ricans have settled mainly in the slums and blighted areas but they have also gained access to more than a few districts of comparatively good housing.

Unlike other immigrant populations at the same period of their history, and unlike the Negro population, the Puerto Ricans are not highly concentrated geographically. Thus, while 70 percent of New York Negroes in 1950 lived in census tracts that were 50 percent Negro or more, only 15 percent of Puerto Ricans lived in tracts in which they formed a majority of the population. They have not solidly occupied any large area of the city; rather they have settled in many different sections. Of course, they are not spread evenly throughout the city. In Manhattan in 1950, 57 percent lived in 14 of the borough's 286 census tracts (that is, 57 percent of the Puerto Rican population lived in 5 percent of the census tracts). These tracts of Puerto Rican concentration are located in three areas: "Spanish Harlem," the West Park area, and the Upper West Side. But this is a rather mild degree of concentration. The pattern is similar in the other boroughs; in the Bronx, slightly more than half live in ten of the borough's 447 census tracts, and in Brooklyn almost a third live in 17 out of 912 census tracts.

The Puerto Rican population has increased greatly since the 1950 Census and become even more dispersed through the city. A census of Puerto Rican and foreign students conducted by the New York City Board of Education in the fall of 1955[10] shows

[10] New York City Board of Education, Bureau of Administrative and Budgetary Research, *Census of Puerto Rican and Foreign-Born Pupils, Provisional Report,*

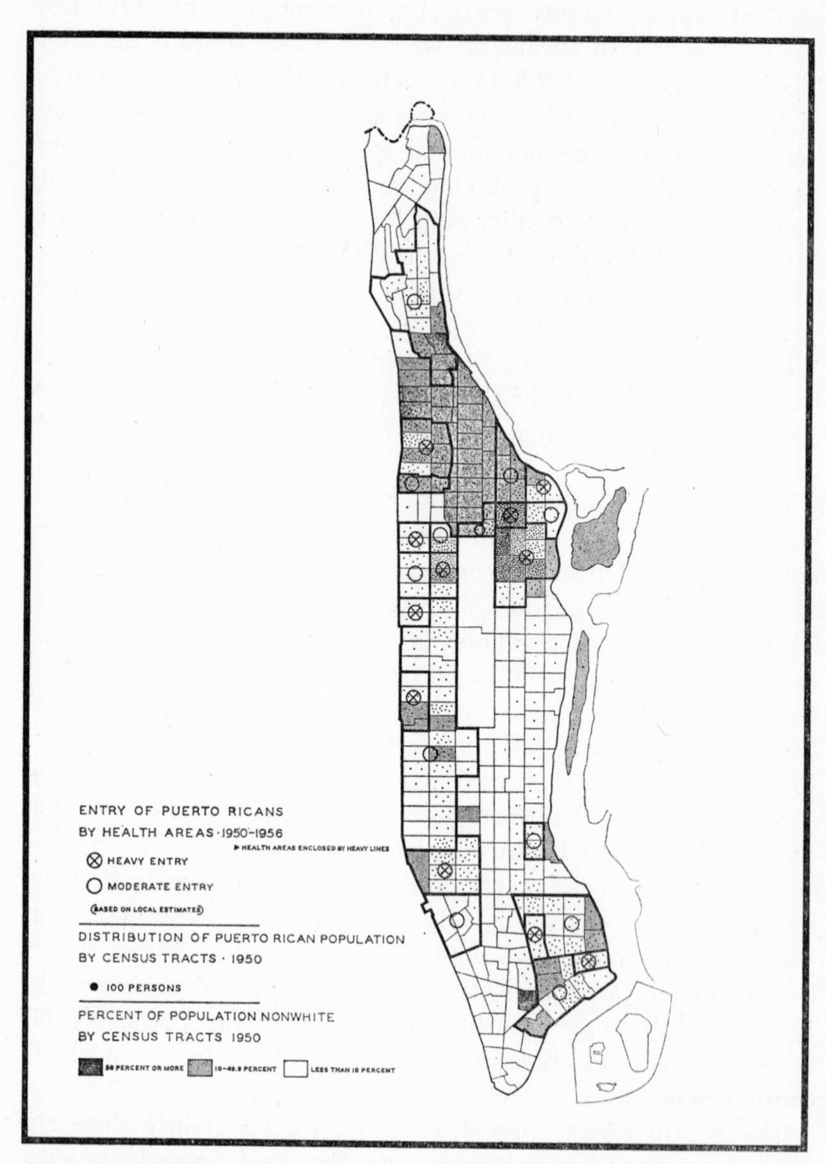

Map 5. Borough of Manhattan, New York City, entry of Puerto Ricans by health areas, 1950–1956, distribution of Puerto Rican population by census tracts, 1950, percent of population nonwhite by census tracts, 1950.

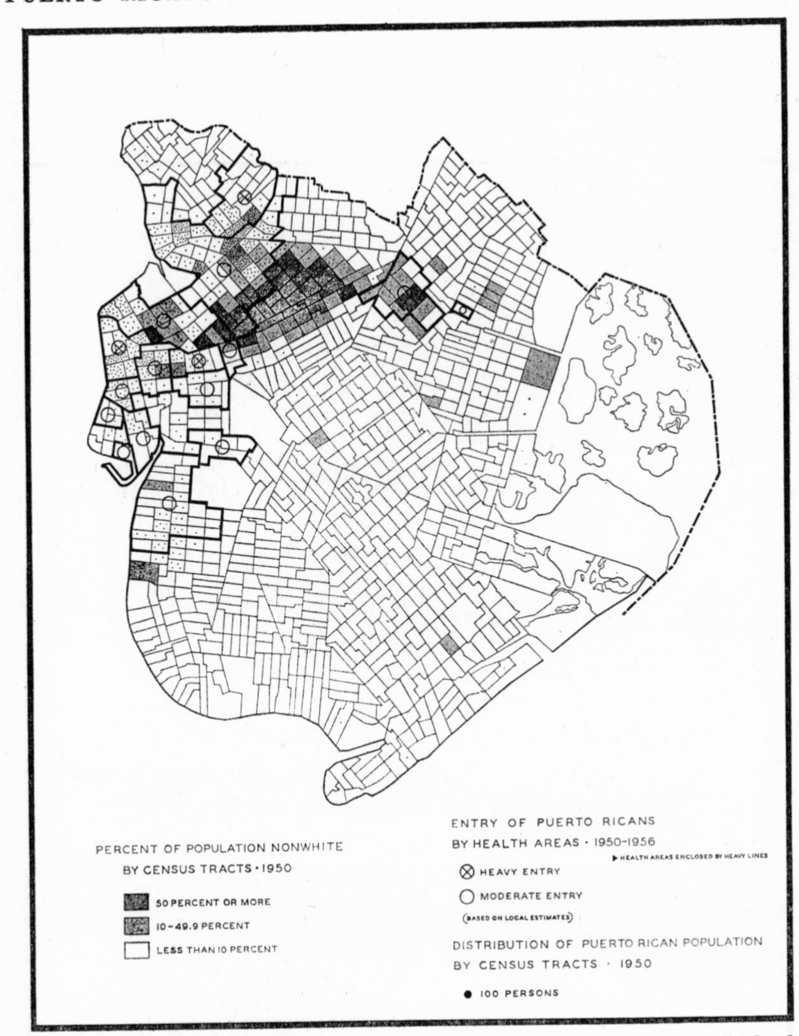

Map 6. Borough of Brooklyn, New York City, entry of Puetro Ricans by health areas, 1950–1956, distribution of Puerto Rican population by census tracts, 1950, percent of population nonwhite by census tracts, 1950.

new areas of concentration on the Lower East Side and the West Mid-City area (from 25th to 86th Street, between Eighth and Tenth Avenues, and between Columbus and Amsterdam Ave-

---

by Bertha Leviton (February, 1956). The report published by the Board of Education provides data on Puerto Rican pupil population for large units only (e.g., school district). Material on Puerto Rican student population for specific schools was taken from unpublished data made available by the Board of Education.

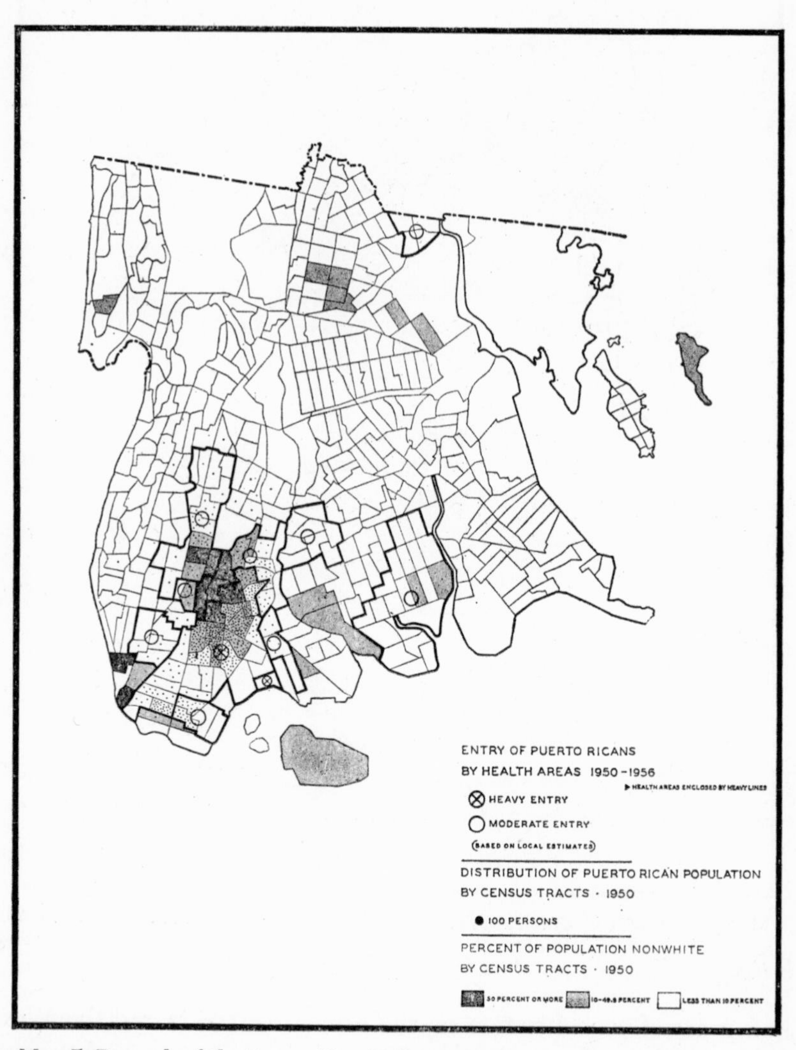

Map 7. Borough of the Bronx, New York City, entry of Puerto Ricans by health areas, 1950–1956, distribution of Puerto Rican population by census tracts, 1950, percent of population nonwhite by census tracts, 1950.

nues), and shows too that the older areas have spread. The study found about two-thirds of all Puerto Rican school children attending one-sixth (115) of the 712 New York elementary and junior high schools. The distribution of Puerto Ricans in 1950 and 1956 is pictured in the accompanying maps.

Within the large areas of relative concentration—and outside them too—the pattern of Puerto Rican settlement has been that of concentration in small areas—a block may be Puerto Rican, surrounded by blocks of non-Puerto Ricans, and even more typically, a single apartment house or adjoining group of houses may have only Puerto Ricans, with the neighboring houses having very few. While there are some solidly Puerto Rican areas, they are remarkably limited in size, in view of the total of the Puerto Rican population. This pattern of dispersal, it is clear, is related to the housing shortage at the time of Puerto Rican migration: one might say they had to squeeze in wherever they found an opening, and openings were found all over the city. Many had to give up the comfort of living near their own and surrounded by their own institutions to accept any space they could find. And, again because of the housing situation (as well as because of the indifference of many New Yorkers to their immediate neighbors), there was no strong pattern of flight before the invasion and there were thus no large empty areas to occupy.

We may get, as suggested, some idea of Puerto Rican housing conditions by examining the housing in those census tracts where Puerto Ricans are relatively concentrated. In 1950 there were 38 tracts containing populations that were 20 percent or more Puerto Rican. The comparisons in the tabulation below are indicative of the situation.[11]

Many more of the dwellings in these "Puerto Rican" tracts are dilapidated or without private toilet or bath as compared with those occupied by New York whites (although the situation is better as compared with nonwhites); the degree of overcrowding is much greater than for New York whites and about the same as that for nonwhites; a very high proportion, as compared with the city in general, are located in old buildings.

The comparative incidence of substandard housing in areas

---

[11] Calculated from the 1950 Census by New York City Planning Commission, *Tenant Relocation Report* (1954), tables 12 and 32.

Characteristic	All occupied dwelling units in New York City		Dwelling units in 38 "Puerto Rican" tracts (percent)
	White occupied (percent)	Nonwhite occupied (percent)	
Dilapidated or lacking private toilet or bath	10.0	29.0	22.0
Severely crowded (1.5 or more persons per room)	4.0	10.0	10.0
Structures built before 1920	49.1		82.6

extensively entered by Puerto Ricans since 1950 is shown in table 19. In general, the picture is the same as for census tracts that had substantial Puerto Rican populations in 1950. Significantly, however, there are two areas of post-1950 Puerto Rican settlement in

TABLE 19

NEW YORK CITY AREAS OF MAJOR PUERTO RICAN SETTLEMENT, 1950–1956: PERCENT OF DWELLING UNITS DILAPIDATED OR LACKING PRIVATE BATH OR RUNNING WATER IN 1950

Area	Percent
New York City, total	9.6
Manhattan, total	18.5
Lower East Side[a]	30.0
Chelsea[b]	27.0
Mid-West Side[c]	16.2
Brooklyn, total	8.4
Gowanus area[d]	5.9
Williamsburg[e]	10.1
Pacific Street area[f]	31.0
Bushwick Ave.[g]	25.8
Bronx, total	4.7
Morrisania[h]	17.4

SOURCE: Identification of areas: New York City Board of Education, *Census of Puerto Rican and Foreign-Born Pupils*, 1955, and present survey. Housing data from *U. S. Census of Population: 1950*, vol. III, *Census Tract Statistics*, chap. 37, "New York."

[a] Census tracts 2, 4, 6, 8, 10, 12, 14, 16, 18, 20, and 22.
[b] Tracts 83, 89, 93, 97, 103, 127, 133, 139, and 145.
[c] Tracts 149, 151, 153, 155, 157, 159, 161, 163, 165, 167, 169, and 171.
[d] Tracts 6, 12, and 14.
[e] Tracts 521, 523, 525, 527, 529, 539, and 545.
[f] Tracts 14, 27, 31, 37, 181, and 183.
[g] Tracts 389, 391, 455, 483, and 485.
[h] Tracts 27.1, 33, 37, 39, 41, 43, 45, 47, 49, 51, 61, 63, 65, 67, 69, 71, and 139.

which the quality of the housing is respectively better and about the same as in the city as a whole, and an additional area in Manhattan which compares favorably with Manhattan as a whole. The circumstances of Puerto Rican entry into these areas of comparatively good housing are discussed further below.

More significant, perhaps, is the great number of hotels and rooming houses in the Puerto Rican areas. According to a recent report of the New York Temporary State Housing Rent Commission, no less than one-fourth of all rent-controlled dwellings in Manhattan are now rooming houses, the bulk of them inhabited by families.[12] Persons living in rooming houses are distinguishable in the 1950 Census as residents of noninstitutional "quasi-households"—that is, living accommodations which did not meet the census definition of a "dwelling unit." A close correlation may be observed between the distribution of this quasi-household population and the Puerto Rican population. In New York City in general, the quasi-household population averaged 124 per census tract; in the tracts with 20 percent or more Puerto Rican, which we have been considering, this population averaged 536 persons per tract.

Supporting this indirect evidence at least nine studies conducted since 1950 (not including our own) provide direct information concerning the residential distribution and living conditions of Puerto Ricans in New York City.[13] These nine studies

[12] New York Temporary State Housing Rent Commission, Methods and Procedure Section, mimeographed sheet on total registrations and rooming house registrations for Manhattan.

[13] Special studies dealing with living conditions of Puerto Ricans in New York City, 1950–1955, are the following: (1) Rhetta M. Arter, *Living in Chelsea* (The Center for Human Relations Studies, New York University, 1954). (2) Rhetta M. Arter, *Mid-City, A Study of Human Relations in the Area of Manhattan Served by the Christ Church House* (The Center for Human Relations Studies, New York University, 1953). (3) Women's City Club of New York, *Tenant Relocation at West Park* (1954). (4) Mannay Diaz, *et al.*, "What Makes a Slum?" (unpublished Master's thesis, The New York School of Social Work, Columbia University, June, 1953). (5) Samuel Goodman, L. Goodman, and David Fox, *Who Are the Puerto Rican Pupils in the New York Public Schools?* (The Puerto Rican Study, Board of Education, New York City, 1955). (6) Leonora Hoppenfeld, *et al.*, "Attitudes of Puerto Ricans in New York City Toward Various Aspects of Their Environment" (unpublished Master's thesis, The New York School of Social Work, Columbia University, 1953). (7) E. Virginia Massimine, *Challenges of a Changing Population* (The Center for Human Relations Studies, New York University, 1954). (8) Unpublished Housing Survey, New York City Department of Welfare, 1955. (9) Sara Wacker, *Home and School Relations in New York City as Seen by Puerto Rican Children and Parents* (The Puerto Rican Study, Board of Education, New York City, June, 1955).

cover seven different neighborhoods, a 10 percent sample of public assistance families in the entire city, and Puerto Rican children in the public schools. The studies are of limited scope, but they draw a consistent picture. From them, and the indirect evidence as well, emerge the following outstanding characteristics of Puerto Rican housing:

1. A very high proportion of families live in furnished rooms and apartments.
2. Families have insufficient space.
3. They live mainly but not entirely in the more deteriorated areas.
4. They live in old buildings in poor condition.
5. They have inadequate service and facilities.
6. They pay high rents, as compared with those paid by comparable groups.

These conclusions are supported and extended by our own survey of Puerto Rican housing conditions.

THE SURVEY

This survey was undertaken to gain comprehensive data on how Puerto Ricans in New York live, but, more than that, to find out, as far as we could from a survey, why they lived that way. We wanted to discover the role of discrimination, of real estate rental practice, of subjective attitudes. While we may find out a good deal from census data, and the scattered studies we have referred to are consistent in the picture they show, the survey which forms the basis for the remaining part of this report provides us with the largest direct body of evidence on these problems.

The survey, conducted in the summer of 1956, covered 800 Puerto Rican households. Using the Board of Education 1955 Census, we selected twenty school areas in the three boroughs of Manhattan, Brooklyn, and the Bronx (half of the districts were in Manhattan and one-fourth in each of the other two boroughs). These areas were equally divided between old and new areas of Puerto Rican settlement. ("Old" areas are those showing high Puerto Rican concentration in the 1950 Census; "new" areas those into which the Puerto Rican population has come since 1950.) The areas we selected were those with the highest proportion of

Puerto Rican school children, within the limits imposed by our desire to distribute the areas between boroughs roughly in the proportion in which they contained Puerto Ricans, and to sample new and old areas.

All blocks (that is, groups of houses on one side of a street, bounded by cross streets at either end) were assigned numbers from a table of random numbers. From four to six blocks per area were randomly selected. A block was rejected if it had less than 20 percent Puerto Ricans or if it contained primarily commercial buildings, and the next block was chosen. In all, there were 102 blocks in the sample.

For each of these blocks, every dwelling unit was listed and every Nth Puerto Rican apartment was selected for interviewing. The respondents were thus all preselected. The interviewers were all bilingual and all had had previous interviewing experience. Almost all the interviews were conducted in Spanish. The number of refusals was remarkably low.

In addition to this survey, we interviewed representatives of nine real estate firms, through the good offices of the Real Estate Board of New York and the Greater New York Taxpayers Association. We also tried to interview a cross section of landlords who owned buildings in the areas in which our field study was conducted. We interviewed twelve landlords of unfurnished dwellings—six who rent to Puerto Ricans and six who do not—and eight landlords of furnished dwellings—again divided between those who rent to Puerto Ricans and those who do not. The writer and two associates conducted these interviews.

We should point out that, owing to our emphasis on areas of high concentration, we describe conditions that characterize only part of the Puerto Rican population, although a very large part. Perhaps those living in the more scattered locations have somewhat better conditions; however, common observation reveals that even in those areas where only one or a few buildings are occupied by Puerto Ricans, these buildings are overcrowded, dilapidated, and undermaintained. We would not, consequently, admit without further investigation that the conditions we describe exaggerate the circumstances under which Puerto Ricans live in New York.

Table 20 describes some salient conditions under which our

sample of Puerto Ricans live. We see that only two-thirds of these families have toilets for their private use; only slightly more have baths for private use; and almost one-tenth share their cooking facilities with other families. And this sharing is characteristically not with one or two families, but with three or more.

TABLE 20

PERCENT OF PUERTO RICAN FAMILIES WITH PRIVATE AND SHARED COOKING, BATH, AND TOILET FACILITIES

Category	Cooking facilities	Bath facilities	Toilet facilities
Private facilities	91.5	70.6	67.3
Share with one or two other families	0.5	3.2	6.5
Share with three or more families	8.0	26.2	26.2
Total	100.0	100.0	100.0

Almost one-third of our sample lived in furnished rooms or apartments. Actually, the term "furnished" is more a legal definition than a practical one, for the furniture generally consists of a bed, a table, a few chairs, a few other odds and ends, all usually in poor condition. To label a dwelling "furnished," under prevailing conditions in New York City, is generally a means of increasing maximum rent under the rent control laws; and this is true of almost all the furnished dwellings in our sample. It is the high proportion of Puerto Rican families in furnished dwellings that largely explains the poor housing conditions described above. Thus, all the sharing of cooking facilities and almost all the sharing of bath and toilet facilities is to be found in the furnished rooms. Of those who live in unfurnished apartments, only 3.8 percent share bath facilities and 6.4 percent toilet facilities.

Almost three out of five Puerto Rican dwellings surveyed contained more persons than rooms—a commonly used measure of crowding. Nearly 40 percent were severely crowded according to the criterion of a persons-per-room ratio of 1.5 or more. The crowding, too, is concentrated in the furnished rooms, as we may see from table 21. Using the criterion of more persons than rooms, approximately two-fifths of unfurnished dwellings are crowded, compared with more than four-fifths of the furnished dwellings.

TABLE 21

PERCENT OF PUERTO RICAN FAMILIES CROWDED, BY TYPE OF HOUSING

Persons per room	Unfurnished rooms and apartments	Furnished rooms and apartments
1.01 or more	43.4	81.6
1.51 or more	18.7	73.3
2.01 or more	5.5	46.9
2.51 or more	2.4	43.8

As would be expected, those who live in furnished dwellings pay higher rents even though the furnishings are of small value, as we may see from table 22. We may point out that the Puerto Rican population, for housing that is inferior to that of other New Yorkers, pays roughly the same amount of rent. In 1950, the median gross rent for New York City was $48.88.[14] If one adds to this the estimated 10 percent increases since 1950,[15] we reach a figure of $53.76, little higher than the $52.80 gross monthly median rental for our sample in 1956. It is thus clearly not only the low incomes that condemn the Puerto Rican population to poor housing, for on the average, Puerto Ricans pay almost as much as New Yorkers in general.

TABLE 22

MEDIAN RENT PAID BY PUERTO RICAN FAMILIES, BY TYPE OF HOUSING

Type of housing	Gross monthly rent	Gross monthly rent per room
Unfurnished	$48.53	$12.67
Furnished	63.07	17.00
All dwellings	52.80	15.40

The proportion living in furnished dwellings is not only the part of the Puerto Rican population that has the worst living conditions, it also pays the highest rents. It would seem that Puerto Ricans do not accept furnished dwellings as a matter of choice but because they find nothing else available.

[14] *U. S. Census of Housing: 1950,* vol. I, *General Characteristics,* chap. 32, "New York," table 21.

[15] Estimate by Dr. Morton Schussheim, Chief, Program Analysis Division, New York Temporary State Housing Rent Commission.

The same pattern we have described here was found in a study conducted in January, 1955, by the New York City Department of Welfare of families on relief.[16] Dependent Puerto Rican families pay more rent than either white or nonwhite families on relief. This difference is explained by the fact that a much higher proportion of the Puerto Ricans live in furnished rooms and apartments—52 percent, as against 41 percent of the nonwhite and 13 percent of the white relief families. The rents Puerto Rican families pay for unfurnished apartments—if they can find them—is the same as that paid by nonwhite and white families. But many fewer have such apartments, and consequently the average rent is much greater (table 23).

TABLE 23

MEDIAN MONTHLY RENT PAID BY NEW YORK CITY FAMILIES RECEIVING PUBLIC ASSISTANCE, BY TYPE OF HOUSING AND ETHNIC GROUP, 1954

Type of housing	Puerto Rican	White	Nonwhite
All types	$49	$37	$43
All types except public housing	55	37	46
Furnished rooms	63	60	61
Percent of families	(36.0)	(6.8)	(30.6)
Furnished apartments	66	63	63
Percent of families	(16.2)	(6.5)	(11.0)
Unfurnished apartments	35	35	35
Percent of families	(35.3)	(71.7)	(40.7)

SOURCE: New York City Department of Welfare, unpublished housing survey based on a 10 percent sample of the January, 1954, caseload of families with two or more persons receiving public assistance (1955).

But why do such a high proportion of Puerto Rican families live in furnished dwellings? One answer to this question is given when we examine how long each group of families has been in New York:

Length of time in New York	*Percent living in unfurnished dwellings*
Three years or less	43.2
Three to ten years	61.5
Ten years or more	76.7

[16] New York City Department of Welfare, unpublished housing survey based on a 10 percent sample of the January, 1954, caseload of families with two or more persons receiving public assistance (1955).

Arriving in New York, the Puerto Rican migrant is generally forced to take a furnished room; the turnover here is rapid and the rooms are available, he is surrounded by his countrymen, and he does not have to take the time to look for and furnish an unfurnished apartment. In time, as he learns more about the city and about the different ways in which one can live in it, he will look for and have a better chance to find an unfurnished apartment, which will give him more space and better facilities, and at less rent.

This is part of the explanation of this pattern; another part is that the earlier migrants arrived at a time when there were relatively fewer furnished rooms and apartments and more unfurnished. The pressure on these facilities has increased with time, for migration has continued, many apartments have been converted into furnished units, and there has been little building in New York of housing within the rentals Puerto Ricans can pay, except for public housing.

Owing to this pattern, we find the paradoxical result that the more Puerto Rican families earn, the less they pay on rent. As they spend more time in America, they simultaneously improve their economic position somewhat and also move out of their first furnished lodgings into unfurnished apartments, which rent at lower figures. Table 24 shows the relation between income, length of time in New York, and rent paid.

TABLE 24

MEDIAN INCOME AND MEDIAN GROSS RENT OF PUERTO RICAN FAMILIES BY LENGTH OF TIME IN NEW YORK

Income and rent	3 years or less	3 to 10 years	10 years or more	Total group
Median income	$2,470.00	$2,562.00	$2,999.00	$2,691.00
Median gross rent	57.98	54.37	49.12	52.80

It is now apparent that furnished dwellings have played a significant role in the housing of Puerto Rican migrants, and particularly of the more recent migrants. The response of the housing market to the coming of the Puerto Ricans was not the building of new housing for them; what happened was that, in part, older elements moved out and, in part, the existing housing supply was subdivided and larger numbers were accommodated in the same space.

The extent of this process is suggested by certain housing statistics of the Bureau of the Census. During the period 1950–1956, the National Housing Inventory (1956) found an estimated 109,000 dwelling units created by conversions in the metropolitan area containing New York City.[17] This figure is dwarfed by the volume of new housing construction (737,000 units), but the latter, of course, occurred mainly in the suburbs while conversions were concentrated in the cities, chiefly New York. Almost all of the conversions were in buildings dating from 1929 or earlier.

For the decade 1940–1949, records of the New York City Department of Housing and Buildings and Department of City Planning showed a net increase of 113,300 dwelling units,[18] but the Bureau of the Census reported an increase of 215,100 units in the city over substantially the same period. With generous allowance for differences in definitions and procedures, it seems probable that some considerable part of the large discrepancy resulted from the creation of dwelling units by conversions not reported to the municipal authorities. In a single section of Manhattan—the Middle West Side—the City Planning Department estimated, on the basis of census data, that 11,600 additional dwelling units were created during the 1940–1950 period by subdivision of space within buildings erected prior to 1920.[19]

The West Side contains two of the major concentrations of Puerto Ricans in Manhattan, and since 1950 the Puerto Rican population of this area has increased greatly. All of these statistics—of dwelling units—undoubtedly fail to reveal the full extent of subdivision of dwelling space, because living quarters that are merely rooms without cooking facilities or a separate entrance are not included in the census count of dwelling units. Many conversions have been to quarters of this type.

A good part of the West Side was originally built up with three-

[17] U. S. Bureau of the Census, *1956 National Housing Inventory*, vol. I, *Components of Change, 1950–1956*, part 8, "New York-Northeastern New Jersey Standard Metropolitan Area."

[18] New York City Planning Commission, *Tenant Relocation Report* (1954), pp. 56–57.

[19] Special tabulations supplied by courtesy of the New York City Planning Commission in a communication to the Commission on Race and Housing, March 13, 1959.

and four-story "brownstones" intended to house a single family or no more than three or four families. As subdivided into furnished rooms, they now house fifteen to twenty families. There is generally only one bathroom to a floor in these houses, which explains why three or more families have to share bath and toilet facilities.

The same thing has occurred in much larger multiple dwellings, which were often quite elegant, containing large apartments of six or more rooms. In these cases the apartments have been subdivided into furnished rooms with the kitchen now communal, or hotplates in each room. Thus, half a dozen families may now occupy the space originally designed for one.

The Adjustment of Puerto Rican Families

We have pointed out that, with the passage of time, more and more Puerto Ricans escape from furnished rooms and find better living quarters. With the movement out of furnished rooms, crowding declines and the percentage of families with private cooking facilities, bath, and toilet increases. We have also pointed out that with the passage of time there is an increase in the family's earnings. However, this index of improvement is more ambiguous, for it seems to be owing to the fact that the families settled here longer tend to have more wage earners: 26 percent of those families here three years or less have more than one wage earner, whereas 38 percent of those here ten years or more have more than one wage earner. Perhaps the woman goes to work as the children grow up; perhaps the children begin to work and contribute to the family income too. With time, there is also a decline in the proportion unemployed.

With the change in living quarters, satisfaction increases. Thus, while 42 percent of the furnished-room apartment dwellers said they were satisfied with their living quarters, of those with unfurnished dwellings, nearly 60 percent were satisfied. There is also a small improvement in satisfaction with neighborhood: two-thirds of those in furnished rooms and apartments are satisfied with their neighborhood as compared with three-fourths of those in unfurnished units. Satisfaction with New York is quite high and general: only 6 percent of our sample said they were dissatisfied with the city.

Also with time, there is a slight tendency for Puerto Ricans to live in somewhat more concentrated Puerto Rican neighborhoods; thus, those who have been here three years or less live in blocks where the median proportion of Puerto Ricans is 55 percent; for those who have been here three to ten years the median percentage is 52.5; while those who have been in New York ten years or more live in blocks with a median percentage of 62.

Does this indicate a higher degree of "segregation" with time? It does, of course, but it does not necessarily indicate a hitch in the assimilation process. It is characteristic of immigrant ethnic groups to further the process of assimilation while living in their own communities; they will read newspapers in their own languages which nevertheless are American newspapers; they will join organizations for their own groups which are nevertheless American political or religious or fraternal organizations. By these means their assimilation is speeded even while they seem to have withdrawn into their group. Then too, in the present situation, it is characteristic that the rooming houses in which Puerto Ricans first settle are of relatively recent origin, and the block in which they are located is often in a state of transition. The rooming house may often be the only house where Puerto Ricans live in the block. Eventually, as the non-Puerto Ricans in this transitional block find new housing, more and more houses "turn" to Puerto Rican occupancy. Hence, if we return after a few years to this block where there are now some new migrants among a largely non-Puerto Rican population, we will probably find a higher concentration of Puerto Ricans, even though they will have been here longer—which is what our statistics show. Perhaps if we returned to this block quite a few years later, we would witness the breakup of this high Puerto Rican concentration as they move up the socioeconomic ladder. But now, and for some time to come, it is safe to say we are witnessing the building up, not the breaking down, of Puerto Rican ghettos.

The relatively low degree of segregation for those here earlier reflects not integration but the disorganization of recent migration. If we ask the more meaningful question, "Do you have any good friends who are *not* Puerto Ricans?" we discover that in the most recently arrived group (under three years), about 79 percent do not have non-Puerto Rican friends, while this is true of only 51 percent of those who have been here ten years or more.

We may already detect small but meaningful changes in attitudes on housing among those here longer, which suggest the beginning of an "Americanizing" process which is leading to the adoption of more "middle-class" attitudes by Puerto Ricans. We asked respondents about the things they liked and disliked about their apartments and neighborhoods. There is a consistent tendency for the group here longest to attribute greater relative importance to a better neighborhood and a more adequately maintained building—qualities of a more "middle-class" nature which one generally becomes concerned with only after more basic problems, such as shelter and simple necessities, have been solved. It is interesting, too, that with time the "things liked about the neighborhood" are more frequently the items "facilities close by" and "quiet," and, less frequently, "people close by." Perhaps with time the Puerto Rican feels less dependent on a close, supportive, ethnic community, even though he lives in one. A somewhat less positive interpretation might be that with time the life centered in personal relations becomes less important than facilities and convenience, and this may reflect one of the less fortunate aspects of middle-class Americanization.

The problem of discrimination.—Despite the fact that considerable dissatisfaction is expressed with living quarters (47 percent dissatisfied) and somewhat less, although still a sizable amount of, dissatisfaction with neighborhood (26 percent)—and here the respondents cite such things as noise, crowded conditions, fights, and crimes—very few intend to return to Puerto Rico, and there is a high satisfaction with New York itself. Eighty-two percent of the respondents plan to stay in New York, and the percentage increases among those who have been here longest. Only 6 percent are dissatisfied with New York City; they cite most frequently, as reasons for liking it, its employment opportunities and higher salaries. But then what of the common belief—and more than belief—that Puerto Ricans are discriminated against, in housing and jobs?

One of the surprising results of our survey is that whatever the extent of this discrimination—and we shall present some independent evidence of that—Puerto Ricans do not on the whole *feel* they have received discriminatory treatment. We asked,

"Do you think Puerto Ricans can live anywhere they want to if they can afford the rent?" Eighty-seven percent said yes. We asked if they knew anyone who had been refused housing because he was a Puerto Rican; only 6 percent knew of such incidents. We asked if they personally had ever experienced discrimination on account of being Puerto Rican; only 5 percent said yes. We asked if they thought their families had been treated fairly in New York; 98 percent said yes. It is hard to know what these responses mean. In talks with Puerto Rican leaders, a number of possible reasons for this low evaluation of discrimination have been suggested.

For one thing, there is little ethnic or racial discrimination in Puerto Rico. The migrants, consequently, have little experience or education regarding discrimination and may sometimes interpret what is in fact discrimination on ethnic or racial grounds in some other way. A second possibility relates to the strong feeling of pride among Puerto Ricans, which may perhaps lead them to refuse to admit to themselves or others that they have been subjects of discrimination.

A third factor is that the migrants have relatively little contact with non-Puerto Ricans, and consequently do not have much occasion to experience discrimination. On arrival in New York, the migrant seeks the security that derives from familiarity and will move to buildings and areas of high Puerto Rican concentration without bothering to look elsewhere. He probably goes to a house where relatives are already living. Obviously, he will not meet discrimination here, since the landlord is already renting to Puerto Ricans. It is those who try to rent in non-Puerto Rican neighborhoods who probably run into discrimination, and very likely, if our sample had included Puerto Ricans in areas of low concentration, we would have found more awareness of discrimination.

Finally, we may point out that most recent migrants are so concerned with economic problems that they pay relatively little attention to discrimination unless it confronts them directly. It is only when the most pressing economic problems are met that a group becomes concerned with discrimination. It then begins to face the problem of moving into good neighborhoods, of getting jobs in areas where personal relations are important, of achieving social equality both for its own sake and as a means to better jobs. A certain movement upward is necessary before the awareness of discrimination becomes acute.

Thus, we see in our survey that with the passage of time there is greater awareness of discrimination: of those who have been here three years or less, only 3 percent mention discrimination as one of the things they dislike about living in New York, while of those who have been here ten years or more, fully 10 percent refer to discrimination as something they dislike about New York.

Certainly, the awareness of discrimination will rise as time passes, as Puerto Ricans develop a greater fund of experience in New York, as they attempt to penetrate new residential areas, and as they try to get into new fields of employment.

Real Estate Agents and Landlords

It is not within the province of this study to consider discrimination in areas other than housing, even though discrimination in employment, to the extent that it exists, will keep down money income and limit the Puerto Ricans in their efforts to get better housing. We are interested in the question of the extent to which discrimination is responsible for present housing conditions, and for this purpose we conducted interviews with representatives of real estate firms who had special knowledge of and interest in Puerto Rican housing, and landlords, some of whom do and some of whom do not rent to Puerto Ricans.

What factors, we wanted to know, affect the decision to rent or refuse to rent to Puerto Ricans? The emphasis of our respondents was primarily on economic considerations, whether real or fancied. Real estate agents and landlords gave the following picture:

First of all, they began with what they feel is an essential distinction. On the one hand is the "Puerto Rican," who is a relative newcomer to this country, who is without dependable and steady income, who is not able to speak English, who is often dark-skinned, who is not accustomed to apartment living and is therefore not trained to be careful in maintaining others' property. On the other hand, there is the man who comes from Puerto Rico but who is prosperous, English-speaking, and presentable; to the landlord, this man is not a "Puerto Rican," he is "Mr. Fernandez," and agents and landlords insist he is treated just as any other prospective tenant.[20]

The landlord who considers "turning" his building (a term frequently used to describe ethnic change in occupancy) does so in order to increase his profits. By "turning" he reduces his maintenance and service costs and increases his return from rents. While under rent control he must maintain the same level of services, but if his tenants are Puerto Rican, they will be less demanding and less likely to know their rights. As one landlord said, "Renting to Puerto Ricans is very profitable; they don't know about rent control." As for rents, even under rent control (maybe especially under rent control), the subdivision of apartments or a shift from unfurnished to furnished units does make possible a sizable increase in rents. As one landlord described the matter: "Rising building and maintenance costs, plus rent control has them [the landlords] in such a squeeze that they are forced to convert to furnished rooms for Puerto Ricans in order to make a profit." Another landlord, who did not rent to Puerto Ricans ("I have good tenants who appreciate this building") but who owned a building on a "Puerto Rican block," described the matter as follows: "There are always some landlords who let their buildings deteriorate. They don't give any services. In these buildings you get Puerto Ricans because whites won't rent. Then the other houses on the block are affected. And soon the whole block becomes a slum. Why should the landlord service the building? He can rent to Puerto Ricans, collect rents, and sit and do nothing but paper work."

The assumption in this response is that Puerto Rican tenants do not demand a high level of service. The basis of this is difficult to determine. Is it ignorance of their rights, is it that they can get nothing else and must take what they can get, or is it that even a low level of maintenance is more than they have been used to?

We see here another interesting assumption: the deterioration in service progresses so far that the landlord cannot get "white" tenants. We may interpret this to mean he can't get "good"

---

[20] Even if one accepts this distinction as determinative, it is, of course, very likely that the stereotyped notion of a Puerto Rican affects one's ability to perceive a Mr. Fernandez. One may therefore doubt whether landlords and agents can make such a distinction on objective grounds.

tenants, with steady jobs, high incomes, and good references, and he is consequently forced to take tenants—Puerto Ricans—without these qualities. In effect, the rental of an apartment in New York depends on more than the tenant's ability to pay rent. Differences in maintenance and service in apartment buildings charging the same rent (under rent control) are so great in New York that the "best buildings" impose all sorts of special requirements on tenants; landlords get their higher return for the better quality of their building not in the form of larger monthly rent payments but in the form of tenants who are highly dependable and responsible, who will probably stay a long time, who will give no trouble over rent collections, and who will not depreciate the value of the property. As one real estate agent said: "In renting to tenants, we want to know beforehand: (1) where the person has lived before, (2) reference from previous landlord, (3) reference from employer, and (4) credit rating. Any person or family who does not meet these requirements we don't rent to, regardless of race or nationality."

The agent might also have added that the better buildings require a two-year lease and a deposit of a month's rent as security for the fulfillment of the lease. It is a rare recent immigrant, Puerto Rican or otherwise, who can fulfill these demands. When a building begins to deteriorate and the landlord finds it difficult to find tenants who can fulfill these qualifications, he begins to lower them; and thus, even without conversion, it may gradually go over to Puerto Rican tenancy.

Under these circumstances, the only gain of the building owner initially is the saving on maintenance costs; he cannot increase the rents simply because he has Puerto Rican tenants. However, the real "killing" is in the conversion of his property to furnished rooms, and this process has been speeded, according to many of the real estate men interviewed, by rising maintenance costs and the fairly rigid ceilings of the state Rent Control Law. Since 1954 conversions from multiple dwellings to rooming houses have been illegal. Before that date, a permit was required, but many conversions took place without a permit.

The furnished-room operator is not looked upon in a very favorable light by the older, established owners or agents. They see him as someone who is interested in a "quick killing" and without interest in the long-term maintenance of property or neighborhood. "The slum-runner's business is to buy or lease brownstones and let them go to pot. If he's bought it, he'll sell it after he's made his killing for whatever he can get."

One real estate agent told us that on occasion a rooming-house operator will sell his building to an unsuspecting superintendent under such conditions that the superintendent pays almost all the rent money to keep up the mortgage payments. Then, if the building should fall in or someone get hurt, the superintendent is legally responsible, while the operator has been getting his return in the form of mortgage payments.

We have seen the processes whereby a building turns and the processes whereby it is maintained for non-Puerto Rican occupancy. Just what the role of discrimination is in all of this is hard to say. One agent said: "Landlords who refuse to rent to Puerto Ricans have usually invested quite a bit of money in their buildings and don't want to see them bursting at the seams. They usually have good tenancy with leases." This would seem to be rational economic motivation.

A landlord who owns a Puerto Rican building and others as well said: "I probably would not take Puerto Rican tenants into either of my other two houses because the other tenants would move out. It's not a nice attitude but I have to do it." This is a clear admission of discrimination, and without any suggestion that Puerto Ricans would differ from other tenants in any objective respects. Such action is declared illegal in the recently enacted local law forbidding discrimination in multiple-unit dwellings on account of race, religion, or ethnic origin. But concern for tenants' attitudes is unquestionably an important factor in leading landlords to discriminate.

Finally, one more quote in which we see the ghost of Mr. Fernandez again: "You must rent to people who have the same objectives. [This would certainly be a surprise to most New York tenants.] People must mix. But they must mix with people who have the same objectives and outlook. It doesn't matter if they're colored or Spanish."

The Puerto Rican as Tenant

One real estate agent quoted above spoke of seeing his building "bursting at the seams" if he took in Puerto Rican tenants. Most of our respondents seem to take it for granted that Puerto Rican tenants would lower the value of their buildings, and not for symbolic reasons. They pictured Puerto Ricans as ill-mannered, noisy, and destructive. Here are some typical quotations:

They're loudly dressed, rowdy, noisy, make noise all night, play music all day, get into fights, damage the property, have ill-mannered, dirty children.

Puerto Ricans make no effort to keep up standard conditions. They live very overcrowded.

They're very abusive for lack of education. They tear up everything. They don't know how to live in a metropolis. You, as social investigators, know more about this than we do. We tried to do some educating, but it's too big a problem. We're not social planners.

Most of them are unclean. Paint today or tomorrow and you won't know whether it's painted—they're destructive.

They're nice people. I have nothing against them. But they tend to break up the place. Quite a few of the young men are not able to find jobs. They hang around most of the day and get into trouble. If they had more to do, they'd get into less trouble. Also, they have no experience in urban living—they crowd a lot of people into one room.

Go over to East 107th Street and you wouldn't believe what can be done to a building. They tear the plaster down. I don't know why they do it.

Thus, we see a dual effect on property in the mind of the landlord: for the short run, greater profit, through less maintenance and bigger rents, but in the longer run, the destruction of one's property.

These views were not universal. Other landlords gave Puerto Ricans better marks as tenants:

You've got good and bad in all—some good, some bad. We've got some [Puerto Ricans] on Madison Avenue. You couldn't ask for better tenants.

The new crowd is terrible. Those who have been here a long time are often very fine people.

Those who have been here some time and have their feet on the ground are O. K.

To disentangle the effects of Puerto Rican occupancy per se from other factors involved in the deterioration of buildings or neighborhoods is extremely difficult. As previously noted, Puerto Ricans have settled most heavily in the older sections of New York City and in buildings already well advanced in decay. Thus, to a considerable extent, the deterioration observed in many Puerto Rican neighborhoods was already present when the Puerto Ricans moved in. Another factor, also previously dwelt upon and which our respondents made clear to us, is the tendency of many landlords, upon "turning" their buildings to Puerto Rican occupancy, to decrease maintenance and subdivide the space.

Puerto Ricans and Slum Formation

There is no question that *association,* in the minds of landlords, agents, and tenants, of Puerto Ricans with all those things that mean "slum" and "blight" is not an illusion. But it is true that the *real* association is a complex one, in which the personal habits of Puerto Ricans are inextricably mixed with other slum-generating influences. Let us consider for a moment the concrete situation of landlord and tenant in an area which is turning.

On the West Side of New York, which has a very large concentration of good apartment houses, in the area of such famous institutions as Columbia University, Union Theological Seminary, the American Museum of Natural History, and the Cathedral of St. John the Divine it is very common to see on a block containing brownstones and apartment houses a house suddenly going over to Puerto Rican occupancy. The curtains go from the windows, and one may see, in passing, dingy rooms with bare overhead bulbs, crowded with children. People of all ages are to be seen lingering around the stoop most of the day. The garbage containers are filled to overflowing and their contents spill onto the street. If there is a tree in front of the house, it is killed by the vigorous play of the children. There is no question that the block has "declined." The residents begin to wonder about the effect on the public school of the introduction of large numbers of children from such houses. The building becomes an eyesore (although its exterior remains exactly the same), and the tenants and landlords on the block are concerned with its future and the future of the neighborhood. Why did this happen?

On the basis of information from this study, it is clear that many factors are involved. First, the large migration of Puerto

Ricans into the city, looking for housing. Second, the scarcity of housing at rents they can afford. Third, the pressure of rising maintenance costs and rent control on landlords to find ways of increasing income. Fourth, the fact that some landlords are less interested in long-term investment than in immediate gain. Fifth, the fact that building code provisions in the City of New York have not been strictly enforced since World War II, for with the shortage of housing there would have been no way to house people if they had been. Sixth, the poverty of the new migrants, who are forced to crowd a family into a room: increase the population of a building sixfold, and of course there will be people seeking escape on the stoop and street, and there must inevitably be a great increase in the garbage produced.

The spreading blight on the West Side is only one aspect of the relation between Puerto Ricans and slums, although a striking one—New York seems peculiar in its ability to juxtapose the most vivid contrasts. Because this house on a West Side block is a newly created rooming house and its occupants probably among the newer and poorer and less well-adjusted migrants, middle-class New Yorkers are brought into contact with just that element of the Puerto Rican population which must create the most serious social problems. In time, as we have demonstrated, the families in this house will move off to other areas, have their own apartments, get more space and facilities, and become better adapted to New York life. Their adaptation often occurs, however, under the eyes of the middle class and under circumstances which have a devastating effect on residential neighborhoods.

But the West Side, prominent as it is, is not typical. It is more typical for Puerto Ricans, like all immigrant groups, to live in areas which have housed other immigrant groups before them—Spanish Harlem and the Lower East Side in Manhattan, Morrisania in the Bronx, Williamsburg in Brooklyn, and other areas—where they replace upwardly mobile Jews, Italians, Irish, and other immigrant groups. In this situation, the Puerto Ricans do not create slums—they merely move into existing slums. Certainly, had there been more housing available at the time of their immigration, these areas would have been more attractive to them than furnished rooms because of greater facilities and lower rents, and the radical change in certain residential quarters of Manhattan would not have occurred, or would have been delayed until a further migration. On the whole, the areas into which Puerto Rican migrants are moving are already slum areas. They have a higher proportion of dilapidated dwellings or dwellings with no private bath than the city in general and a higher proportion of old buildings. But some of these areas into which Puerto Ricans are moving, like the West Side, are superior in quality of dwellings to the city or borough average.

PROSPECTS FOR THE FUTURE—BY THE EDITORS

The long-run prospects for improvement in the living conditions of Puerto Rican migrants are certainly as good if not better than those of any white immigrant group in the past. The conditions of abundant employment opportunity and rising wages and incomes under which the Puerto Rican migration is occurring favor the economic progress of the newcomers. Their educational level low as it is, still is higher than that of many previous immigrant groups. Their status as American citizens is another factor favoring their rapid assimilation. As the Puerto Ricans improve their economic position and become socially assimilated, the supply of middle- to high-value housing will come within their reach and they will move to take advantage of it. As our survey data reveal, this process is already at work. Puerto Ricans who have lived in New York for a period of years have distinctly bette housing than the recent arrivals. It would be extraordinary indee if this were not true.

The question arises whether anything can be done to accelerate the assimilation of the newcomers. One rather obvious step would be to encourage their dispersal to cities other than New York The Migration Office of the Puerto Rican Commonwealth, operating on the Mainland, is in a strong position to take the lead fo this purpose through its program of job placement. Other helpfu measures would include instruction in English, vocational training for a variety of occupations, and encouragement of youth to pursue their formal education at least through high school. The development of effective programs along these lines is a challeng to social welfare agencies.

Possibilities for immediate betterment of existing condition appear to be contained in three approaches, namely (1) buildin new housing available to Puerto Ricans, (2) rehabilitating existing substandard dwellings, and (3) reducing discrimination in the housing market.

New housing construction for occupancy by low-income groups, under present cost conditions, must evidently be publicly subsidized. It is obvious that Puerto Rican and other low-income slum dwellers could be rehoused at public expense, but the extent to which public funds may be expanded for this purpose depends on political factors outside the scope of our study. The political climate of recent years has not favored expansion of low-rent public housing. Unless a major shift of emphasis should occur in national housing policy, publicly subsidized housing is unlikely to provide for more than a small part of the housing needs of low-income groups, Puerto Ricans included.

It is important to notice, in this connection, that low-rent public housing, as it has operated in New York City and elsewhere, does not increase but tends instead to reduce the total supply of low-rent dwelling units. This occurs because of the location of public housing projects on slum sites, involving the demolition, frequently, of more low-rent units than are replaced. Urban-redevelopment projects also make large net subtractions from the low-cost housing stock. In order for public housing to increase the total supply of low-rent units, projects would have to be located, to a much greater extent than in the past, on open-land sites.

Although net additions to the housing supply in New York have been made only at higher cost levels, indirectly these benefit the low-income groups by easing the general scarcity of housing and facilitating mobility through the entire housing supply. A general housing supply sufficient to permit reasonable flexibility and mobility in the housing market is undoubtedly prerequisite to any large-scale improvement in the housing conditions of low-income groups by any means other than direct, public provision of dwellings for their occupancy.

The rehabilitation of existing substandard dwellings is, on the surface at least, a matter of law enforcement. To a large extent, as previously indicated, the subdivision of dwelling space during and after the war, for rental to Puerto Ricans, was contrary to the laws of New York City. The municipal housing and sanitary codes were substantially strengthened in 1956. If existing legal requirements with respect to space, occupancy, facilities, and physical condition were strictly enforced, slum housing conditions would be largely eliminated. But adequate enforcement of the law is extremely difficult. We have described the economic pressures and incentives leading many landlords to "turn" their buildings to Puerto Rican occupancy with reduced space, facilities, and maintenance. Conformity to legal standards is frequently expensive and not economically supportable at existing rents. In many cases, undoubtedly, the alternative, unavoidable or preferred, to compliance with legal standards would be the vacating of dwellings. The Subcommittee on Relocation of the Mayor's Committee for Better Housing estimated in 1955 that approximately 268,000 *families* would be displaced if current and then-proposed provisions of the multiple-dwelling code (proposals subsequently enacted, for the most part) were strictly enforced.

Enforcement procedures, moreover, are slow and complex and penalties for violations usually light. The tenants of substandard buildings are typically unprepared to report violations either because their own standards are low, or they are party to the violations (as in overcrowding), or they fear eviction or rent increases if changes are made.

Any large-scale rehabilitation of old buildings in New York and elimination of illegal living quarters appear to require a combination of more effective enforcement procedures, incentives to property owners to bring their buildings up to standard, and education of the tenants to appreciation of good housing conditions. The framework for such a three-sided approach may be available in the neighborhood rehabilitation provisions of the National Housing Act Urban Renewal Program. Possibilities under these provisions are just beginning (1958) to be tested in New York City.

There remains to be considered the role of antidiscrimination laws in enlarging the housing opportunities of Puerto Ricans. Under existing municipal legislation, it is illegal in New York City to refuse housing (with certain exceptions) to any person because of his race, color, national origin, ancestry, or creed. As our study shows, New York landlords and real estate agents do generally treat Puerto Ricans as a distinct group, renting to them only in areas or buildings designated for Puerto Rican occupancy. As we have also seen, and attempted to explain, few Puerto Ricans are aware of being subject to discrimination and, therefore, are not likely to invoke the antidiscrimination law to any large extent. This appears to be borne out by initial experience under the Municipal Fair Housing Practices Law. During the first three months after the law became effective (April-June, 1958), the administering agency reported receipt of seventy complaints of discrimination, of which only six were from Puerto Ricans.[21]

As Puerto Ricans rise in the socioeconomic scale and seek middle-class housing in nonethnic neighborhoods, they will doubtless become more aware of any discrimination against them and also more inclined to assert their legal rights. At this point, however, if we accept the testimony of the real estate agents, discrimination against the Puerto Rican is likely to be minimal. From all the evidence, sheer ethnic discrimination, unmixed with other considerations, is a relatively minor factor in restricting the housing opportunities of Puerto Ricans. Much more important are their poverty, their behavior, and their inability to meet the general requirements of landlords for access to the better apartment buildings. Laws against discrimination, therefore, would appear to be much less important for the Puerto Ricans than for nonwhite groups.

---

[21] New York City Commission on Intergroup Relations, *Quarterly Report on Housing Complaints,* July 21, 1958.

HARRY H. L. KITANO

VI

Housing of Japanese-Americans in the San Francisco Bay Area

The Japanese in California have had a unique history among American ethnic and racial groups. For three and a half years, from 1942 to 1945, this state, which had had a large, settled Japanese population, scattered through cities and small towns but concentrated in farming, was Japanese *rein* (Japanese-free): there were fewer Japanese in wartime California than Jews in Hitler's Germany. Then many of them returned to California and it again became the chief center of the Japanese population in America. But this time the "Japanese problem" that loomed so large in that state's affairs before the war seems to have almost disappeared.

There is still prejudice and discrimination, but the reduction in both from before the war is striking. The area that is perhaps of more concern to Japanese than any other is housing. As a *New York Times* reporter wrote from Los Angeles: "The only conspicuous barrier, a Japanese-American leader said, . . . is in housing." [1] This is not to say there is no discrimination in jobs and elsewhere, but in the experience and thinking of Japanese-Americans, housing looms as the single most important area of discrimination. The purpose of this study, based on an interview survey of Japanese-Americans in the Bay Area, is to examine the extent of this barrier, to find out what kind of housing the Japanese have, the extent of their satisfaction or dissatisfaction with it, their aspirations for housing in the future, and the conditions—

---

[1] Gladwin Hill, "Japanese in U. S. Gaining Equality," *New York Times,* August 12, 1956, p. 38.

including prejudice and discrimination—which affect their chances for the housing they want.

The Japanese community of the United States dates only from about the turn of the century. The early immigration, as is characteristic of many immigrant groups, consisted largely of single men. In 1907 a "gentlemen's agreement" between President Theodore Roosevelt and the Government of Japan led to a severe restriction of this immigration. The reduced immigration became predominantly female, as the early male arrivals set up families. After the Immigration Exclusion Act of 1924 immigration was cut off almost completely.[2] And, except for Japanese war brides, it has never been resumed.

The overwhelming majority of the immigrants—90 percent or more—were from the peasant class of southern Japan.[3] Initially, they became farm laborers, then rapidly progressed to farming their own land, as tenants or owners. There was extensive and great hostility toward them in California, and various legislative acts were aimed against them, culminating in the California Alien Land Law of 1920, which prohibited Japanese and other aliens ineligible to citizenship from acquiring any agricultural land, directly or indirectly.

Despite the great prejudice, and the legal and extralegal discrimination, the Japanese in California before the First World War were able to improve their position. By various means, they achieved an important place in California agriculture, and the growing number of American-born Japanese, or nisei, who were citizens and consequently free of the legal restrictions on their parents gave promise of greater improvement in the economic status of the group.

The Japanese population of California grew from 72,000 in 1920 to 97,000 in 1930. It then declined to 94,000 in 1940, as many Japanese returned to Japan—including young Japanese born here who despaired of finding work adapted to their capabilities.

Pearl Harbor and the evacuation of the entire Japanese population to the interior wiped the slate clean. Houses and property were sold, savings were wiped out, and normal economic activities

---

[2] Elliot Grinnel Mears, *Resident Orientals on the American Pacific Coast* (Chicago: University of Chicago Press, 1928), p. 409.

[3] *Ibid.*, p. 14.

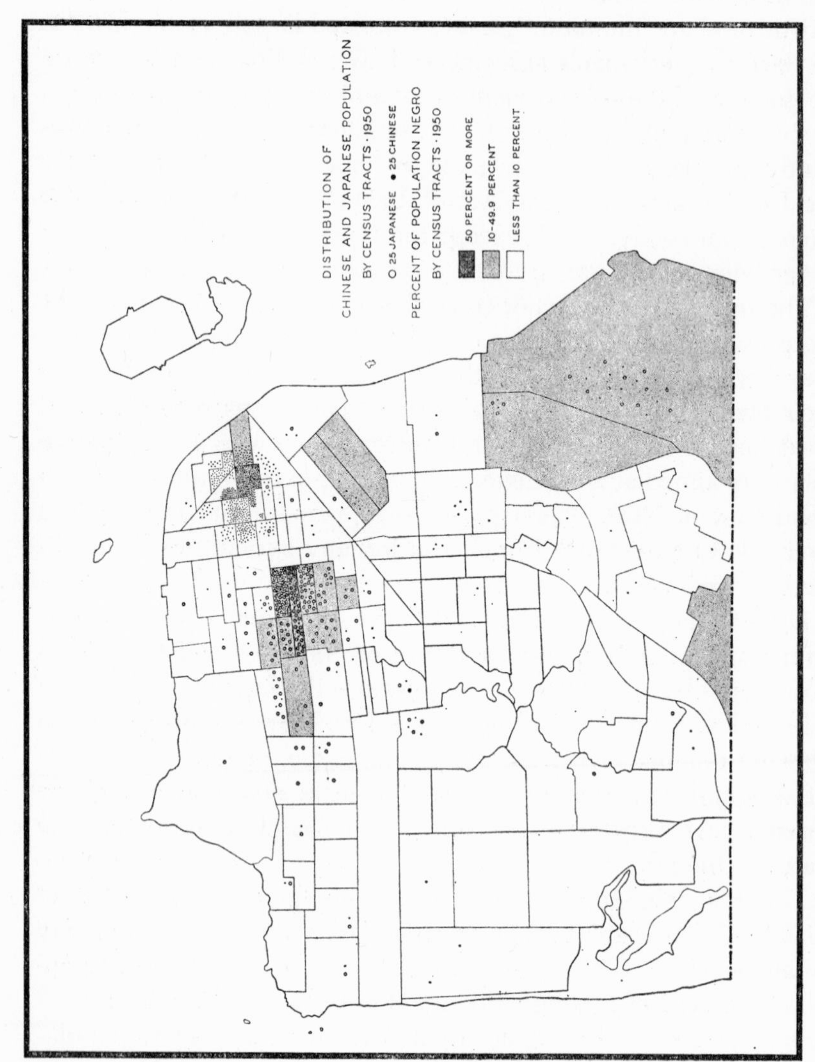

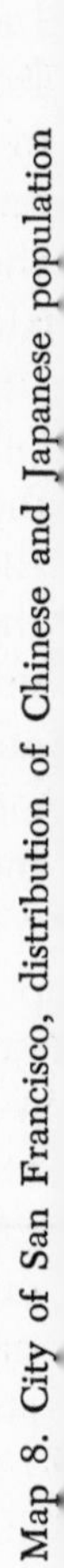
Map 8. City of San Francisco, distribution of Chinese and Japanese population

were ended. After the war, most of the evacuees returned to California, and by 1950, the Japanese population of the state had reached 85,000. But substantial numbers remained in midwestern and eastern cities where they had settled during the war. Chicago had become the principal Japanese center away from the Pacific Coast, with a population of 17,000 in 1950. Within California itself, the Japanese, while making a considerable comeback in agriculture (where now they are free of restrictive laws), are somewhat more concentrated in the cities. Los Angeles is the chief center, with 26,000 Japanese in 1950; at the same time San Francisco had 6,000, Sacramento 3,000, and Berkeley 2,000.

A smaller number of California Japanese now reside in a much larger total population: whereas they made up 1.4 percent of the population of California in 1940, they constituted only 0.8 percent in 1950.

Aside from the excess of single males in the oldest age groups, the Japanese of California are a relatively normal population in regard to sex and age distribution. In 1950, there were still 116 males to each 100 females, but in the age classes up to fifty years, there were approximately the same number of each sex.[4]

Among all the diverse groups which make up the American population, the Japanese are outstanding in their drive for education and economic advancement. While the Japanese-born parents, the issei, are not highly educated as a group, they place tremendous emphasis on having their children acquire as much education as possible and this at the cost of considerable self-sacrifice. Education is seen as the "great leveler" and the means whereby their children will achieve the comfort, security, and position the parents could not have. In 1950, well over half of all Japanese in California twenty-five years of age or older had graduated from high school. In the adult population of the state as a whole, only 44 percent had achieved this level of education.[5] This is remarkable, especially if we take into account the still large number of issei who have had little or no schooling.

The significance of this pattern of education cannot be overestimated. It meant, and means, that the Japanese population is

---

[4] Warren S. Thompson, *Growth and Changes in California's Population* (Los Angeles: The Haynes Foundation, 1955), p. 81.

[5] *Ibid.*, pp. 100 and 105.

potentially capable of very rapid upward changes in economic status. Even before the First World War, when severe depression and discrimination radically limited jobs for educated Japanese, they still insisted upon achieving the highest possible educational levels. This was at a time when the well-meaning employment bureau of the University of California questioned the advisability of higher training for nisei because of the difficulty of occupational placement.[6] Because of this reservoir of training, the nisei were in a position to move up rapidly after the war, when opportunities presented themselves. Their experience is a significant one for other minority groups and for those who may see a danger in educating or training people beyond "realistic levels." Conceivably, as has been argued, to do so results in frustration and is damaging to mental health, but this must be set against the objective possibilities for the achievement of a more satisfactory economic position and against the frustrations of those who can never achieve such a position because they have not been educated for it.

Together with this emphasis on education go certain attitudes toward work and saving that have aided the Japanese in their economic advance. These attitudes are not to be measured easily, and their sources probably lie deep in Japanese culture and in the ways in which it has changed in America. But the whole complex of striving for advancement, which we can see in the statistics of educational and occupational achievement, has played an important role in shaping the contemporary Japanese-American and cannot be ignored when we consider what he wishes for himself in housing, what he has achieved, and what his future course may be.[7]

In the summer of 1956, the writer directed a survey of the nisei population of San Francisco and Berkeley, designed to discover the objective facts of their housing situation: where they lived, the cost and age of their houses, and the like; their subjective feelings as to their housing, the degree of satisfaction or dissatisfac-

---

[6] Yamato Ichihashi, *Japanese in the United States* (Stanford: Stanford University Press, 1932), p. 357.

[7] See, for a fascinating and suggestive discussion of this question, William Caudill and George De Vos, "Achievement, Culture and Personality: The Case of the Japanese Americans," *American Anthropologist*, 58 (1956), 1102–1126.

tion; and the role of discrimination in limiting their housing choices. A less extensive investigation was conducted in Los Angeles. The rest of this paper is devoted to a report and analysis of the findings of this survey.

San Francisco and Berkeley, together with Oakland, which was not included in our questionnaire survey, form the second largest urban concentration of Japanese in the State of California. The 1950 Census gave the Japanese population of Los Angeles as 25,502; of San Francisco as 5,579; of Berkeley as 2,147; and of Oakland as 1,250. By 1956, the Japanese population of Los Angeles had risen to probably at least 40,000 and that of San Francisco and Berkeley to close to 7,000 and 3,000 respectively.

Before the war, the Japanese of San Francisco and Berkeley, as indeed the Japanese of all the cities of the West Coast, were concentrated in distinct ethnic colonies. This is the characteristic pattern of all new immigrant groups, even those not subjected to prejudice and discrimination. In the case of the Japanese, both outward pressure and inner needs helped create and sustain this pattern.

To quote one writer:

> The rank and file [of the Japanese] have been forced and led into sections of the city where rents were low, but, as a rule, where houses were being vacated for better ones elsewhere. Once a group has been formed, common language, acquaintance, shops and amusement places cause other Japanese to join it. Available buildings then command high rents as far as the colony spreads. These high rents and prejudice, in turn, cause other races to move elsewhere.[8]

Thus, a "Little Tokyo" was formed in Los Angeles and a "Little Osaka" in San Francisco. Here there were self-sufficient communities with their own shops, grocers, business establishments, apartment houses, churches, and professional people. Very few Japanese ventured beyond these comfortable environs, except for a few operators of small businesses and some professional people.

These communities were located in the older, less desirable sections of the city. Thus, in San Francisco in 1941, the Japanese

---

[8] H. A. Millis, *The Japanese Problem in the United States* (New York: The Macmillan Company, 1915), p. 70.

were concentrated in a small section of the Western Addition, which since the war has been the primary target for urban renewal and slum clearance plans.

All these communities were emptied of Japanese by the wartime removal, and they did not remain static or empty during this period. In San Francisco, the returning Japanese found that most of their former places of residence had been filled by in-migrating war workers, mostly Negroes. The Japanese population of the Bay Area gradually built up to its prewar size, but there were important changes in the distribution of this population. Ethnic colonies of Japanese are gone or rapidly going. We have studied the changes in the areas in which Japanese live by examining the addresses of Japanese families as listed in directories published by two newspapers (*Hokubei Mainichi Year Book* and *Nichi Bei Times Year Book*) and comparing their distribution in 1956 with census data in 1940. The directories contain substantially complete listings of Japanese families in the Bay Area.

In San Francisco, three census tracts embracing the former "Little Osaka" contained more than two-thirds of the Japanese population in 1940; sixteen years later only 46 percent of the Japanese families in the city were to be found in them. In the city of Oakland, across the bay from San Francisco, the Japanese were relatively dispersed even in 1940. The principal Japanese areas (three census tracts) contained only 29 percent of the group. By 1956 the Japanese neighborhood, by now in a different location, included only 18 percent of the Japanese population. In Berkeley, before the war, 59 percent of the Japanese lived in three adjacent tracts, but the same area contained only 33 percent of the Berkeley Japanese in 1956.

Our survey was limited to nisei, the American-born children of Japanese immigrants; we imposed this limitation largely because it is the nisei who are now forming and supporting families and who are actively in the housing market. The two Japanese directories previously described listed 1,027 families with nisei heads in San Francisco and 479 in Berkeley. From the lists we selected randomly chosen samples of 300 from San Francisco and 200 from Berkeley. The latter city is, therefore, somewhat over-represented in our total sample. We permitted our interviewers—

all nisei—to make substitutions in the cases where a designated family was not at home or had moved away; substitutions for San Francisco came to 22 percent of the original sample, for Berkeley to 15 percent. Only twenty-one families refused to be interviewed.

The median income of these 500 families in 1955–1956 was $5,350. In 43 percent of the families more than one person contributed to income. Occupationally, the sample of household heads showed a high concentration in professional, proprietory-managerial, and clerical pursuits, compared with the Japanese employed male population in California and the San Francisco Bay Area in 1950 (table 25). The question thus arises whether

TABLE 25

OCCUPATIONS OF JAPANESE IN CALIFORNIA: COMPARATIVE PERCENT DISTRIBUTIONS OF EMPLOYED MALE WORKERS, URBAN AND IN SAN FRANCISCO-OAKLAND STANDARD METROPOLITAN AREA, 1950, AND SURVEY HOUSEHOLD HEADS, SAN FRANCISCO AND BERKELEY, 1956

Occupation group	Urban male workers, California 1950	Male workers, San Francisco-Oakland SMA, 1950	Survey household heads, San Francisco and Berkeley, 1956
Total	100.0	100.0[a]	100.0[a]
Professional, technical, and kindred	6	7	26
Farmers and farm managers	9	8	*
Managers, officials, and proprietors, except farm	12	8	16
Clerical, sales and kindred workers	12	10	22
Craftsmen, foremen, and kindred workers	7	5	9
Operatives, and kindred workers	9	10	6
Private household workers	5	15	*
Service workers except private household	8	8	6
Laborers	32	30	14

SOURCES: *U. S. Census of Population: 1950*, vol. IV, *Special Reports*, part 3, chap. B, "Nonwhite Population by Race," table 22; and San Francisco-Berkeley Sample Survey, 1956.

* Less than 0.5 percent.

[a] Error due to rounding.

such a high-income, high-occupational-status group as appeared in the sample is representative of the nisei of the Bay Area. Several considerations are relevant. (1) Our sample consists of nisei, while the 1950 Census includes all Japanese, native-born and foreign-born, and unquestionably nisei are more heavily concentrated in the professional and clerical occupations than are the issei. (2) Our sample is drawn from San Francisco and Berkeley, and the Japanese population of these two cities is undoubtedly more concentrated in professional and clerical occupations than Japanese in the state or the metropolitan area. (3) In these cities, relatively few Japanese are engaged in agriculture, although this is an important occupation in the state and area. (4) There has been a very rapid change in the occupational status of nisei since the end of the war, owing to their high educational achievement, the reduction of prejudice, and the process of readjustment, and it is very likely more of this group were in professional occupations in 1956 than in 1950. (5) Finally, while we have recorded the occupation of only the household head or chief earner, the closest comparable census category is that of all males, 14 years of age or older. Very likely one will find a higher proportion of persons in professional and other high-status occupations if one limits oneself to household heads or chief earners.

Despite all this, our sample probably overrepresents the professionals among nisei household heads in the Bay Area; the directories we used possibly cover the professional group best, and probably a higher percentage of our refusals and "not-ins" or "moved" came from lower occupational categories.

Our sample of household heads includes high proportions of self-employed and government workers: 26 percent and 17 percent in each category, respectively. This distribution might suggest that the nisei, sensing or expecting discrimination from private employers, tend to favor self-employment or public employers. One may note similar patterns among such a group as American Jews, who also combine high educational attainment with experience of discrimination.[9]

Our sample shows a very high educational level: 34 percent

[9] Nathan Glazer, "Social Characteristics of American Jews, 1654–1954," *American Jewish Year Book,* 56 (1956), 3–41.

are college graduates, 25 percent have had some college, and nearly all the rest are high school graduates. Thus, 93 percent are high school graduates or higher! Our sample thus overrepresents the better educated, for only 53 percent of California Japanese in 1950 had graduated from high school. The same factors which explain why our sample has a high proportion of professional workers would explain the educational bias. In particular, the educational difference between issei and nisei is very great, greater even than the occupational differences.

We may sum up the salient findings of the survey in the form of a series of generalizations.

First: *The Japanese of the Bay Area have adequate dwelling units, using the criteria of space, physical condition, and plumbing facilities.*

If we consider any dwelling having more occupants than rooms to be crowded, there is little crowding among the Japanese families of San Francisco and Berkeley. The 1950 Census reported 9 percent of all dwelling units in the Bay Area with more persons than rooms and 30 percent of nonwhite households in that condition.[10] Only 11 percent of the households in our sample show this degree of crowding.

Ninety-five percent of our households had dwellings with private toilet and bath, a higher percentage than prevailed in the Bay Area generally, according to the 1950 Census. With respect to the physical condition of the dwellings, the interviewers reported—although, of course, it is difficult to standardize such judgments—that only 12 percent of the exteriors and 6 percent of the interiors of the houses were shabby or neglected.

Second: *The Japanese are less favored in other aspects of housing; in particular, their houses are generally old, and for this reason and perhaps others, they do not get as liberal financing as other home-buying groups.*

Approximately one-half of our sample own their own homes. About one-quarter of those who live in San Francisco and three-quarters of those who live in Berkeley are in the home-owning group. One-half of the entire group, homeowners and renters, live in houses built before 1920. Of the home-owning group, 37 per-

---

[10] *U. S. Census of Housing: 1950,* vol. I, *General Characteristics,* chap. 5, "California."

cent live in houses built before 1920. Only 12 percent live in houses built during the 1940's; only 4 percent live in houses built during the 1950's.

When we consider that 91 percent of the homeowners have bought their homes since they returned to California, beginning in 1945, and that during this entire period there has been a tremendous amount of new home building in the Bay Area as elsewhere, with favorable financing conditions, we can only wonder at this small proportion of new homes bought by nisei and conclude—with them—that they have been excluded from much of the new housing of the Bay Area. As our data clearly demonstrate, the desire for homeownership is at least as strong among the Japanese as in the general population. In fact, considering the financial sacrifices which many have made to acquire homes (further described below) it would appear that the Japanese have outstanding motivation to become homeowners. Wanting their own homes, larger homes, and desirable neighborhoods, they have nevertheless largely settled for older houses in built-up neighborhoods. It is for this reason that there has been in San Francisco a movement to the Richmond District, an area of older housing in the northwest part of the city, close to, but not adjoining, the area of former Japanese concentration.

In itself, an older house in an older neighborhood is not necessarily undesirable, and, indeed, perhaps offers more advantages in some respects than new tract houses, but special financing problems do arise when one buys an old house. In particular, we find in our sample high down payments and an extensive recourse to secondary financing.

Thus, 30 percent of the Japanese homeowners carried a second or third mortgage. Even so, half of the home buyers in our sample had made down payments greater than $3,882 (the median figure). Comparing this figure with the median family income of $5,330 suggests how strong must be the saving pattern among the nisei. They could only have begun working and saving money after the war, and yet they were capable of producing sums typically around three-quarters of a year's income for down payments.

Table 26 relates down payments and monthly amortization payments to family income. Neither the down payments nor monthly payments appear to vary greatly with income. And the cost of the house does not bear any strong relationship to present income; thus, those who live in houses that cost between $9,500 and $11,500 have about the same income as those who paid from $15,000 to $20,000 for their houses. It is not easy to determine the significance of these facts. One might suggest that the nisei have a certain minimum demand for housing, and even though income may be low, they will not accept less, but rather devote a higher proportion of income to it, while, on the other hand, when income goes up, the savings pattern comes into effect to induce them to remain in or accept cheaper houses than they could afford. But there is another factor that may be relevant: conceivably, they cannot find more expensive homes, even when they can afford them, because of discrimination.

TABLE 26

MEDIAN DOWN PAYMENTS AND MEDIAN MONTHLY PAYMENTS ON HOMES PURCHASED BY NISEI HOUSEHOLDS, SAN FRANCISCO AND BERKELEY, BY INCOME CLASS

Family income 1955–1956 (dollars)	Number of families	Median down payment	Median monthly payment (principal, interest, taxes)	Median monthly payment as percent of median income
Under 2,500	3	$2,000	$85	$41
2,500–2,999	5	5,000	90	39
3,000–3,999	22	3,100	84	29
4,000–4,999	50	3,500	77	21
5,000–5,999	45	3,500	96	21
6,000–6,999	27	4,125	80	15
7,000–7,999	27	4,000	91	15
8,000–10,000	24	4,700	100+	13
Over 10,000	19	3,875	100+	12
No information	5	...	...	...

Another financial consequence of the high proportion of old houses purchased by the nisei is the relatively small number of purchases financed under FHA or VA arrangements. Fifteen percent have FHA-insured mortgages, 7 percent have VA mortgages, 4 percent have California Veteran mortgages, and 75 percent have conventional financing. As we might expect, the conventional mortgage terms tend to be short. About one-third of all mortgages were to be amortized over a period of ten to fifteen years; only one-quarter had terms of more than twenty years.

Our sample is almost evenly divided between renters and homeowners. In general, it is the younger, less well-established nisei who rent. As in the case of the home-buying group, we find a pattern whereby a relatively small proportion of income is used for rent. (See table 27.) We may assume that the young renters are saving to buy houses, and when they do, will be able to put down the large down payments that we saw were characteristic for the group.

TABLE 27

MEDIAN RENT BY INCOME CLASS, NISEI HOUSEHOLDS IN SAN FRANCISCO AND BERKELEY, 1956

Household income (dollars)	Number of households	Median rent	Percent of income spent on rent
Under 2,500	14	$50	undetermined
2,500–2,999	9	50	19
3,000–3,999	48	58	17
4,000–4,999	59	63	14
5,000–5,999	25	62	11
6,000–6,999	24	62	10
7,000–7,999	24	65	9
8,000–10,000	24	74	8
Over 10,000	8	73	undetermined
No information	16	...	...

Conceivably, another factor in keeping rents low is the extensive pattern of renting from Japanese landlords. Almost half of the renters rent from Japanese landlords: 58 percent of those in San Francisco, 20 percent of those in Berkeley. The median rental paid to Japanese landlords is $53; that paid to non-Japanese landlords is $62. Although the Japanese-owned rental units are somewhat older on the average and slightly smaller, this does not quite explain this differential. Perhaps the Japanese landlord gives the Japanese tenant a better deal; perhaps landlord and renter are often related.

Third: *Most Japanese are satisfied with their houses, but many are dissatisfied with their neighborhoods.*

In view of the fact that most nisei have houses with sufficient space and physical facilities, it is not surprising that they generally express satisfaction with their homes; however, since they are restricted as to the neighborhoods into which they can move, it is also not surprising that many express dissatisfaction with their neighborhoods. Over-all, 85 percent of our sample are satisfied with their housing, but only 78 percent are satisfied with their neighborhoods. If we analyze the sample according to where they live—in the old Japanese area of San Francisco or elsewhere in San Francisco, in the old Japanese section in Berkeley, or elsewhere in Berkeley—interesting differences emerge. These are shown in the following table.

Locality	Percent satisfied with house	Percent satisfied with neighborhood
San Francisco, old Japanese area	75	55
San Francisco, elsewhere	86	78
Berkeley, Japanese area	87	93
Berkeley, elsewhere	97	93

The Berkeley group is more satisfied than that in San Francisco. The lowest satisfaction with house and neighborhood is in the old Japanese area of San Francisco, where 22 percent of our sample still live; nearly half of our sample families living there expressed dissatisfaction with the neighborhood, although the large majority were satisfied with their dwellings.

Taking another approach to the question of satisfaction with housing, we also asked our respondents, "Would you like to move?" As shown below, well over a third of the Berkeley residents and nearly half of those living in the old Japanese area of San Francisco said they would like to move.

Response to question "Would you like to move?"	San Francisco, old Japanese area (percent)	San Francisco, other (percent)	Berkeley (percent)
Yes	55	35	35
Yes, but in the future	18	16	14
No	26	48	51
Total	99	99	100

In order to get a better picture of the factors involved in desires to move, as well as some insight into the priority of values determining housing choices, we asked respondents contemplating a new move to new housing to list the things they looked for, in rank order, in considering a new location. They were given a choice of six factors: "plenty of space," "new house," "nice neighborhood," "nearness to work, schools, shopping," low monthly payments," "Japanese neighbors." A "nice neighborhood" came first; then "nearness to schools, transportation, shopping"; then "plenty of space." Hardly anyone listed as a consideration "Japanese neighbors." It would appear that proximity to a concentrated ethnic community is not an important value for the nisei. When they say a "nice neighborhood," we may assume they mean what other Americans mean: good houses, pleasant streets, good schools; in short, the environment that middle-class Americans in general search for.

Fourth: *Discrimination is a real factor affecting the housing choices of nisei.*

In the course of this report we have referred to various objective facts about the housing of nisei which suggest or would support the view that discrimination limits their choice of housing. It is often very difficult to isolate the effects of discrimination as such. Very often, the minority group is so badly off economically that it cannot make the effort to rent or buy houses in areas where discrimination would occur; it may be so poorly educated that it does not develop high demands as to housing; its experiences may have been so uniformly unsatisfying and punishing that it does not have any great expectations as to housing and so has little awareness of discrimination in this area and expresses no great overt dissatisfaction. On the other hand, a group may develop such sensitivity to the possibility of discrimination that it avoids getting into situations where discrimination may be experienced. The nisei, as we have seen, are fairly well-off economically, and are well educated. Their experiences have not been so self-damaging as to affect their demands for and expectations of good living conditions. As a result, we might expect to find great consciousness of discrimination, and a good deal of experience of it, too—and our study shows that both expectations are correct. We asked, "Do you think nisei nowadays can pretty much live anywhere they want to if they can pay the cost?" Fully one-half of the sample answered "no," another 20 percent said "yes, but," and only 30 percent felt they could live anywhere within the limitations imposed by income.

We also asked, "Do you know anyone who was refused housing because he was nisei?" Two out of five respondents knew of such cases.

And finally, we asked, "Have you yourself ever experienced discrimination in looking for housing?" Thirty-nine percent had had such experiences; 5 percent had not looked. Of the 56 percent who had not experienced discrimination, probably many had "played it safe" by finding housing through friends or Japanese real estate agents. It is clear that there is consciousness of discrimination, and that it has affected the free choice of nisei in housing. [Editors' note: It is interesting to compare the awareness of discrimination among the nisei with the nonrecognition of discrimination by the vast majority of Puerto Ricans. See chapter v above.]

The renter is more convinced of the presence of discrimination than the homeowner: only 23 percent of the renters, as against 36 percent of the home-buyers, felt nisei could live pretty much where they wanted to.

We asked those who claimed personal experience of discrimination just who had discriminated against them. In 22 percent of the cases discrimination was attributed to the owner of a desired house; an equal number cited the neighbors; and in 57 percent of the cases, it was the real estate agent who had discriminated.

Various reactions are possible when one faces discrimination. We wanted to know what the nisei reactions were, so we asked, "Suppose you wanted to buy or rent in a certain district and someone told you the neighbors would not like to have a Japanese family in the neighborhood. What would you do?" The replies could be grouped in three categories. There were the "withdrawers," who gave such answers as, "It's not worth the trouble," or, "I don't want to be the cause of any unpleasantness." This was the great majority of our group: 61 percent fell into this category. There were the "fighters," who said they would move in at any cost: this was 23 percent of the group. The rest took some middle position, such as, they would take a poll of the neighbors and move in only if accepted. About 15 percent fell into this category, which we might call the "reasoners." There were striking differences in our sample depending on education. (See table 28.) Among those with some high school education very few would fight; among high school graduates only 15 percent; while among those who had gone to college, fully 30 percent would fight. We see here the effect of education in leading both to the raising of expectations and the development of an aggressive attitude in the search for one's rights and a better life.

TABLE 28

REACTION TO DISCRIMINATION AMONG NISEI, BY LEVEL OF EDUCATION

Reaction	Some high school		High school graduates		Some college		College graduates	
	Number	Percent	Number	Percent	Number	Percent	Number	Percent
Fighters	2	6	25	15	37	30	52	31
Reasoners	2	6	22	13	23	19	24	14
Withdrawers	28	88	123	72	64	51	93	15
Total	32	100	170	100	124	100	169	100

In view of their expectation and experience of discrimination, the nisei have developed to some extent their own pattern of seeking homes and apartments. When asked how they had found their house or apartment, 36 percent said through "friends"; 19 percent had used a Caucasian real estate broker; 15 percent a Japanese broker; 15 percent newspaper advertisements; and 8 percent had dealt with the owner directly. Those who had approached friends or Japanese real estate brokers were sure of avoiding unpleasant incidents, for if a friend (very likely Japanese) was the intermediary, one knew being Japanese would not be a factor.

The real estate brokers of San Francisco and Berkeley are in somewhat different positions. In San Francisco, Japanese real estate men belong to the local real estate board and therefore have access to the multiple listing service. However, this involves certain responsibilities, such as fulfilling the real estate ethic of checking with brokers who have listed properties to see if Japanese are acceptable. If they are not, the house will not be shown to a Japanese. In order to conform to the professional code, the

Japanese real estate man will be instrumental in restricting the areas in which Japanese may buy. As other studies have shown, real estate brokers usually disguise discriminatory practice under statements that a particular house, or houses in a given area are not available for one reason or another.[11] But as we have seen, the majority of nisei are convinced that real estate brokers treat them unfairly.

In Berkeley, Japanese real estate men do not belong to the local association. They cannot use the multiple listing service, but they need have no qualms about selling any house they can, in any area, to a Japanese purchaser, if the seller has no objection. We are unable to determine the differential effects of the contrasting situations on the actual home-buying picture.

We have summed up the major findings of our survey as we have proceeded: the nisei have adequate housing in terms of space and physical facilities; their houses are generally old, and often in old neighborhoods, and they consequently do not have favorable financing; they are more satisfied with their housing than with their neighborhoods, but hope to improve both; they have often experienced discrimination, and expect to find it when they go house- or apartment-hunting.

Discrimination against the Japanese in California has diminished greatly since the end of the war. Partly as a result of this decline in discrimination, the economic and occupational status of the nisei has risen. Paradoxically, this economic progress has intensified the discriminatory situation in housing. For, before the war, very few nisei had the money or the inclination to seek independent housing. Most of them lived in the Japanese communities and many with their parents. The increase in income and in status of occupants have led many of them to search actively for better housing in better neighborhoods. And there they have often encountered discrimination. An editorial in the *Pacific Citizen,* the official publication of the Japanese-American Citizens'

---

[11] See Davis McEntire, *Residence and Race: Final and Comprehensive Report to the Commission on Race and Housing* (Berkeley: University of California Press, 1960), chap, xiv, "Real Estate Brokers"; Luigi Laurenti, *Property Values and Race: Studies in Seven Cities* (Berkeley: University of California Press, 1960), chap. ii, "Theories of Race and Property Value."

League, stated on April 13, 1956: "The . . . pattern of racial discrimination in private housing is still very much in existence, particularly in the new tracts and subdivisions in Southern California. Nisei themselves are still victims of this vicious mode, regardless of their standing in the community, credit rating, employment, or financial ability."

Although our survey was confined to the Bay Area, inquiries in and analysis of census data for southern California, where the Japanese population is perhaps three to four times as large, show very much the same situation: as the *Pacific Citizen* asserts, it is even somewhat harder for nisei to get into new suburban tracts in southern California than in the Bay Area.

It is not easy to measure the extent of discrimination. We have pointed out how the actual effect of discrimination will depend on the economic potential of the minority group. It will also depend on the behavior of the minority group in the face of discrimination. The Japanese group is small, and it cannot have any great faith in its power to influence public opinion or politics; it is also very strongly averse to "making a fuss," as was demonstrated by its remarkable docility in the face of wartime relocation with its severe hardships. It is also aware of the existence of housing discrimination. Under these circumstances, it tends to keep out of situations where it might face discrimination. Here we see a paradoxical effect of publicity and knowledge about discrimination: it leads people to avoid potentially discriminatory areas, and thus leads to a decrease in the amount of overt discrimination. Thus, while their economic potential tends to increase the amount of discrimination nisei will experience, their tendency to avoid trouble tends to decrease it.

The Japanese-Americans of the Bay Area do not represent one of the more serious cases of discriminatory restriction of housing opportunity; but for an economically successful, highly educated, upwardly mobile group, the discrimination which exists is a constant source of irritation, unhappiness, and deprivation. As the nisei continue their upward movement to better jobs and higher incomes, ever larger numbers will move out of the concentrated and older neighborhoods in which so many of them now live. Hopefully, as their desires for higher status and better living lead them to new neighborhoods, the present level of discrimination, already considerably lower than before the war, and possibly lower than in the late forties, will permit them to choose freely the housing to which their earning power entitles them and their desires lead them.

ALBERT J. MAYER

VII

Russel Woods: Change Without Conflict

A Case Study of Neighborhood Racial Transition in Detroit

The inherent drama of conflict and violence often accompanying racial change in an urban neighborhood has drawn the attention of both the popular press and the serious scholar. However, in many instances racial change is a peaceful process, differing only slightly from the usual movement of families into and out of a neighborhood. Only the rapidity of the turnover of families distinguishes it from so-called "normal" neighborhood change. Yet the social consequences may be more far-reaching than the sensational eruption of violence. Russel Woods, a subdivision in Detroit, is characteristic of the peaceful type of changing neighborhood. This type of change has occurred in many cities since the mass migration of Negroes to the North during and after World War II. Detroit itself contains at least a dozen neighborhoods similar to Russel Woods. And undoubtedly the process of peaceful change will be many times repeated.

The author has lived in Russel Woods since 1952. Early in 1955, when a house was about to be sold to Negroes, the author and several colleagues decided that they had been given an ideal opportunity to study the process of neighborhood change. A questionnaire was constructed, and graduate student interviewers visited a randomly drawn sample of approximately every third house in Russel Woods. We present here no formal analysis of these interviews, but most of our observations are based on them as well as on informal conversations with other residents of Russel Woods. To supplement the interview data, public records,

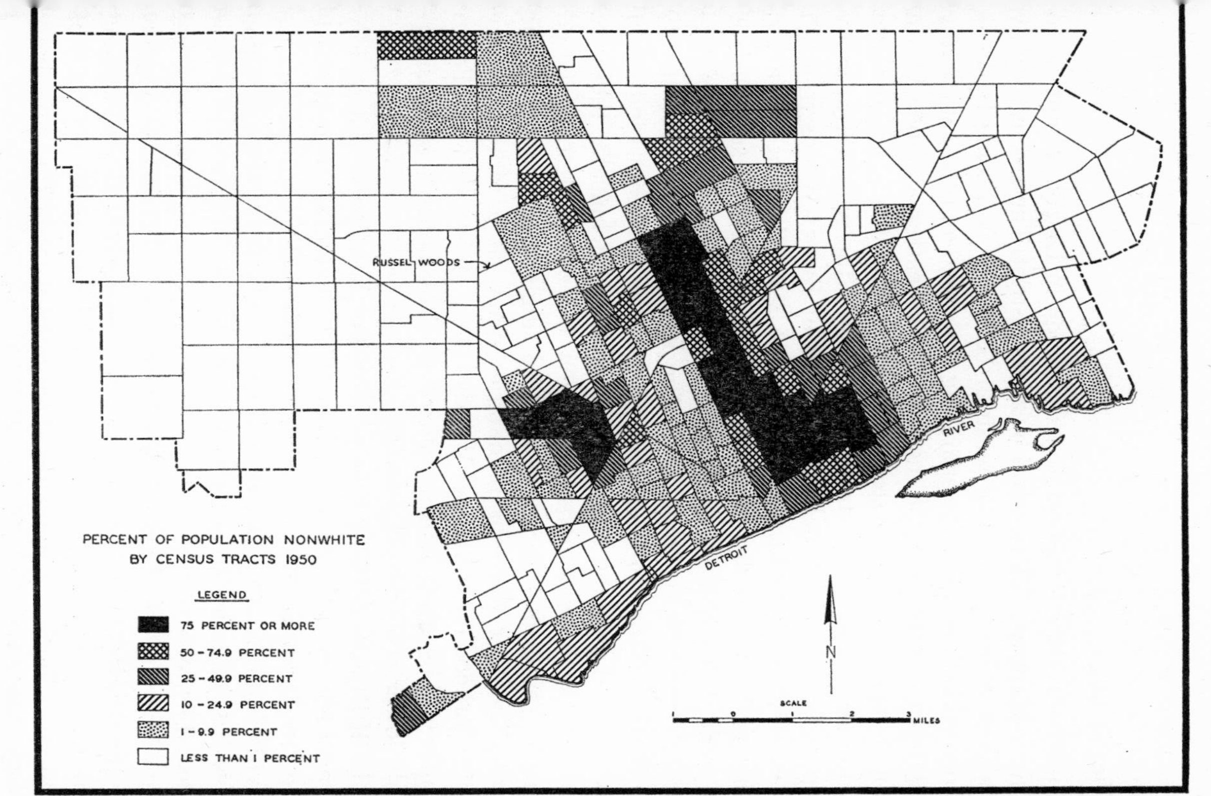

Map 9. City of Detroit, percent of population nonwhite by census tracts, 1950, and location of Russel Woods.

such as every deed transaction in Russel Woods from its platting in 1916 until the present, were studied.

THE FACTS

The Setting

Russel Woods is a real estate subdivision in Detroit, about seven miles northwest of the central business district. The area is roughly one half mile square. The western boundary is a wide business thoroughfare completely separating the area from the two-family flats on the other side of the street. The eastern boundary is a commercial street with stores for local shopping. The southern boundary is the most interesting, for only the width of an alley separates the substantial brick homes of Russel Woods from an area of cheaply constructed houses of a nondescript character. This sharp line of demarcation between real estate subdivisions of widely different socioeconomic levels is characteristic of Detroit. The northern boundary is the least marked. Three streets of "two-flats," or five- and six-room apartments, comprising about six hundred dwelling units, lie to the north. Technically, these are part of the Russel Woods subdivision, but our interest is focused on the approximately seven hundred single-family homes in the area. Together the four boundaries mark off a rather discrete neighborhood entity. Russel Woods is thus an island of middle- to upper-middle class housing, surrounded by housing of considerably lower economic character.

In 1919 Russel Wood was a forest on the edge of the rapidly expanding city. Its stately century-old trees marked it as a possible site for upper-income housing. Real estate developers subdivided the western half of the site and began the construction of substantial brick homes in the seven to ten thousand dollar class. The lot size was customarily 40 by 160—generous for that day. Many people bought double lots. By 1928 only a few lots in the subdivision were vacant. The area presented an imposing parklike appearance with its wide lawns, big trees, and rows of new brick homes. The houses themselves were of the same basic design: living room, dining room, kitchen, breakfast nook, and bath downstairs, and either three or four bedrooms and bath upstairs. The third floor or attic was usually furnished as maids' quarters. A few of the houses, particularly along one street, were even larger.

The eastern half of the area—technically another subdivision named Sullivan Woods, though the entire area is known as Russel Woods—stood almost vacant during the 1920's and the worst of the Depression and then was built up gradually until World War II. After 1945 the remaining lots were rapidly filled, and by 1955 only five or six houses were being constructed each year, with perhaps fifteen lots still remaining in 1956. The houses were much the same as those built earlier, although now priced in the range of fifteen to thirty-five thousand dollars. Neighborhood facilities are excellent. A grammar school containing grades one through six is located close to the southern boundary of the neighborhood. Public transportation, generally inadequate in Detroit, is good, with an express bus line running to the central business district. Churches, synagogues, YMCA's, community centers, and stores are all within easy walking distance.

In the beginning (1920) Russel Woods was considered a fashionable residential area—not "the top," but definitely upper-middle-class. The residents were almost all Protestants and Catholics of northwestern European ancestry. Professional men, executives of large businesses, and owners of small businesses predominated. A few Jewish families also lived there, but they were a small minority. During the 1920's the neighborhood remained stable. Some families moved, but they were replaced by others of the same type. During the Depression, a number of houses were lost on foreclosures, and then, as the Depression subsided, Jewish families began to move into Russel Woods. During this period the center of Jewish population in Detroit was moving northward and westward until in 1938 the eastern boundary of Russel Woods actually was the main street of Jewish life in the city. Synagogues and other Jewish institutions were located within easy walking distance of Russel Woods. Non-Jews began to leave. World War II slowed down almost all real estate activity, but when the war ended, Jews moved in increasing numbers to Russel Woods, and the vacant land in the eastern half was filled with new, expensive houses whose first owners were Jewish. By 1955 Jewish families made up about four-fifths of all families in Russel Woods.

The dominant Jewish population is a mixed group in many respects. Many are owners of small businesses. Most are financially successful. Many are foreign born, and most natives are children of the foreign born. The largest group is of the Conservative branch of American Judaism, but there are many Orthodox, some Reform, and some Jews without formal religious affiliation.

As might be expected, there is a civic association in Russel Woods. It was originally formed in the 1920's to oppose the intrusion of uses in violation of zoning regulations, for the area was rigorously zoned for single-family housing of a specified type. Since Russel Woods is bordered on two sides by business streets, occasionally someone would attempt to park a truck or conduct a business from his home. Several such instances occurred, and they were handled promptly and effectively by the association.

Some people say that the association board of directors was not happy when Jewish families began to move into the area in large numbers during the 1930's. However, no overt attempts were made to keep Jews out. At the time the first house was sold to Negroes the civic association's board of directors consisted of about a dozen elderly men, all old-time residents of the neighborhood. The president is a former local political figure now in his seventies.

Racial Change

It is hard to pinpoint a precise date when the possibility of Negroes' moving into the neighborhood became real. Some residents showed concern immediately after World War II—almost ten years before the first house was sold to Negroes. However, as early as 1952 it was apparent to even the casual observer that neighborhoods adjacent on three sides were becoming racially mixed. None of these neighborhoods was economically comparable to Russel Woods. The event which convinced almost everyone in Russel Woods that Negroes would soon buy in this neighborhood was the rapid change along Oakman Boulevard during 1953–1954. Oakman Boulevard lies about one quarter mile both north and west, curving around Russel Woods like a protecting arm. This street was developed at about the same time as the newer half of Russel Woods, and its single-family houses range in value from $20,000 to $60,000. Like Russel Woods, the homeowners are predominantly Jewish. Again like Russel Woods, Oakman Boulevard is on a much higher economic level than the blocks surrounding it, but there the contrast is even more marked. While Russel Woods forms a compact mass, Oakman Boulevard is a ribbon of one street with a broad middle parkway. It never has been a community in any sense. After the first Negroes bought on Oakman Boulevard it changed rapidly. This was particularly important for the people in Russel Woods, for it meant they were not only enclosed by racially mixed streets on all sides, but that an economically similar neighborhood had become mostly Negro very quickly.

In July, 1955, an army officer, who had bought a house three years before, was transferred to another post. Initially he had overpaid somewhat for the house, and during his three-year tenure had spent several thousand dollars more in home improvements. To avoid losing money, he needed far more than the house was worth. Moreover, there were very few potential white buyers. As the date of his transfer approached, his need to sell became desperate. Only a week before he was to leave the city he called upon a Negro real estate dealer to sell the house for him. A customer was quickly produced and the sale consummated. The instrument of sale was a land contract. The seller had made no attempt to conceal the facts from his neighbors.

The president of the Russel Woods Civic Association lived only two doors away from the army officer's house. Upon hearing of the sale he called a meeting of the board of directors of the civic association, and they agreed to buy back the house, if possible. The funds necessary to make the offer came from the past dues of the association (committed without the consent of the general membership) and from several of the board members. Accordingly, the new owners and the Negro real estate man were immediately approached and asked to sell the house to the association at a small profit. They agreed, especially since the buyer's wife was not convinced she wanted to live in an "all-white" neighborhood. The association had accomplished its purpose. The neighborhood remained "all-white."

But only for two weeks, when a second house was purchased by a Negro lawyer. The seller no longer lived in the city, and the house had been vacant for some time. Shortly afterwards a third house was sold to a Negro. This time the owner was living in the house and was subject to the criticism of his neighbors. He apparently was fearful of their reactions for he refused to talk to any of them and abruptly rejected attempts to make him reconsider. He did receive a few anonymous telephone calls berating him, but no threats were made. He moved within a month or so, and a Negro family replaced him.

The selling of the third house convinced everyone that the neighborhood was destined to become mixed. During the ensuing year (August, 1955, to August, 1956) about forty houses were sold to Negroes, with perhaps another hundred for sale. During this time about five white families also moved into the area. During the first year, sales to Negroes were confined to two streets. Not until August, 1956, were the first houses sold on two other streets in the neighborhood. Yet in 1956 practically all residents of Russel Woods defined the entire neighborhood as mixed. Opinions vary on whether Russel Woods will become a completely Negro neighborhood or not, with the weight of opinion tending to the view that it will.

The first forty Negro families to move into Russel Woods fell into several distinct groups. There were some with children of school age. This group consists mainly of business and professional people, with rather more professionals. These are the counterparts of the white families who are moving to the suburbs and also of the white families who moved into Russel Woods thirty years ago. If the housing market were completely open to Negroes, they probably would be moving to these same suburbs now. As it is, Russel Woods is their suburb, even though it is midcity. This is borne out by the local Negro press. In reporting the social news it refers to Russel Woods and like areas as "Northwest," a term frequently used by white persons to describe an area five to fifteen miles further northwest than Russel Woods.

The second group of Negroes might be called the "respectable couples." These families are childless—either they have had no children or their children are grown. Both husband and wife work, usually in white-collar or professional positions. Like the younger people, they are intensely middle-class. In social outlook, they differ little from the elderly white couples who live around them.

The third group of Negro homeowners in Russel Woods is

made up of families who have middle-class hopes and aspirations, although educationally and occupationally they are still working-class. From their responses to questions asked by an interviewer, it appears they have only a vague realization of the cost of owning and maintaining a house of the size they had bought. They are painfully earnest about the acquisition of middle-class values and respectability.

Panic selling is often a feature of neighborhood racial transition, but this has not occurred in Russel Woods. On the one hand the white sellers are not selling at any price just to get out, and on the other hand Negro buyers are not paying any price just to get in. The net effect approximates a normal real estate situation, with the exception that large numbers of houses are for sale. (This is an important "nonnormal" feature.) The situation is, of course, also abnormal from a market viewpoint in that sellers are all of one racial group and buyers nearly all of another. The writer knows of only one instance where unreasoning fear inspired the quick sale of a house. Most of the people who have now moved or are selling have a plausible objective reason: "The house is too big," "We want a one-story house," "children have married," etc. In some instances the given reason *is* the only reason; in others it is a rationalization and perhaps often an unconscious one at that. Some people experiment. As real estate men are always conveniently hovering in the background, it is tempting to "see what we can get"; so the house goes up for sale, sometimes with a sign on the lawn, sometimes with no sign. In one instance, at least, an owner found himself selling without really wanting to. He was made an offer within a few days after making a contract with an agent, and since the offer was quite good the owner agreed to sell and found himself committed to move within ninety days, even though he had no plans for another home. He moved into an apartment four blocks away, just outside the border of the single-family area, but in the same school district.

Information obtained on the selling prices of some twenty houses sold during the past year indicates little difference from sales prices in the neighborhood during the past five years. However, the recent sales have been mostly on land contracts, which require less than customary down payments, and in addition during this period the prices of similar houses in other areas have probably gone up. So it would appear there has been not an absolute but a relative decline in the value of houses in Russel Woods.

The Civic Association

Shortly after the first house was sold, several younger people in the neighborhood approached the president of the civic association and two or three key board members suggesting that its membership base be broadened and a mass meeting be held to explain the problems of a changing neighborhood. The association then had about 100 members. In September, 1955, the proposed meeting was held at the school. Attendance was excellent, with several hundred people present. Their motives were mixed. Some came hoping the association would take the lead in keeping the Negroes out, others came for directly opposite reasons—expecting that the association would suggest a plan for welcoming Negroes and for living in a biracial neighborhood. Still others attended out of curiosity. All were disappointed. Absolutely no mention was made of the racial issue. Instead, the speakers from several city agencies dwelt on the evils of unkempt alleys and garbage cans. None of this was applicable to Russel Woods. At the conclusion of the meeting new memberships were solicited. About sixty families joined, and in a membership drive during the next few weeks additional members were obtained. However, no more general membership meetings were held until the following spring. At this time another meeting was held, and again the race question was not mentioned. The meeting was a failure. No more general meetings have been held. The executive board has met occasionally. Several younger people have been elected to the board, but they are invited only when the old-timers have use for them.

The last meeting of the executive board in September, 1956, provided an opportunity to gauge the association's effectiveness. The president was asked whether he thought Negroes should be invited to join the association. He thought not. Someone inquired how a general meeting could be held without them. No one could suggest how to do this. The remainder of the board meeting was concerned with the problem of repaying those individuals who had loaned the civic association money to buy the first house sold to a Negro, which was later resold at a loss. The meeting ended with the question still not resolved.

The present civic association is for all practical purposes moribund. The old-timers in the neighborhood were not sufficiently active or aware to do anything constructive (or destructive either, for that matter), and not enough of the newer people in the neighborhood cared to take the association over purposefully. Perhaps the incoming Negroes will attach a value to the neighborhood and initiate a strong civic association aimed at supporting the zoning and property restrictions.

The Real Estate Brokers

It appears that the real estate firms in power positions in the local real estate board have worked out an agreement on changing neighborhoods. Whether this agreement is formal or informal is of no importance: it is generally observed. They rarely sell to nonwhites in an all-white block or neighborhood. They can afford to leave this function to the marginal real estate man (of both races) and to the individual who sells his home directly to the purchaser. In Russel Woods both the marginal real estate operator and the individual seller combined to sell the first house. Before this date the larger real estate firms had been active in the neighborhood with telephone calls, doorbell ringing, and post cards, but the racial question was not raised. However, soon after the sale of the first house, all real estate agents doing business in the vicinity increased their activity. Firms large and small, white and nonwhite, joined in the attempt to persuade homeowners to sell.

Since the neighborhood has become open to Negro occupancy, the actions of the real estate men have been steadily persistent rather than frantic. True, some of the marginal firms attempt to scare and pressure, and engage in dubious selling practices, but this is more a function of their struggle to survive than of the particular neighborhood situation. The great majority of homeowners are little impressed by pressure. Rather, the efforts of real estate salesmen have been accepted as a mild nuisance in the same category as magazine and storm window salesmen.

Financing

The function of finance in shaping the pattern of neighborhood change is of crucial importance. Most of the houses in Russel Woods are selling on land contracts. Under this type of financing, the seller holds the deed until the last payment is made. Almost any terms are theoretically possible. The seller assumes the risk. In practice, land contracts in Russel Woods demand from 10 to 20 percent of the purchase price as down payment. This compares with the customary conventional mortgage, which has a down payment of between 30 and 40 percent. Land contracts usually require ten to fifteen years for completion. In compensation for the higher risk taken on a land contract, the seller has recourse to a quicker and more expedient foreclosure procedure than the conventional mortgage holder. In Michigan, foreclosure of a mortgage takes at least eighteen months, whereas a land contract is usually foreclosed within six months. A typical Russel Woods "deal" is the sale of a house at $20,000 with $4,000 down and payments of $160 a month for eleven years and seven months. Only the shorter length of contract and a slightly higher interest rate distinguish this selling arrangement from a $20,000 suburban house sold on commercial mortgage terms. However, FHA-insured mortgages, which in the majority of cases are available in the newer neighborhoods only, are substantially cheaper to the buyer. This feature in itself makes a house in a new neighborhood a better buy.

The land contract arrangement has been described in detail here, as it plays an important role in the complex of social forces that produce results that have been observed in Russel Woods and in other similar areas.

The land contract has assumed such prominence in Russel Woods because Negro buyers have not had the large down payments that would be required by conventional mortgage financing for houses as old as those in Russel Woods, or demanded by banks in view of their uncertainty about the long-range prospects of Russel Woods, or because Negro buyers have not been able to obtain conventional financing altogether. In many cases, especially among lower income families, the mortgage is outside the cultural pattern, and the Negro buyer will not even inquire as to whether he could get a mortgage. A further factor in encouraging the use of land contracts is that the real estate agent's commission is payable upon sale, and a land-contract transaction may close within a few weeks, while a mortgage transaction may take months. Hence, the real estate agent "steers" both buyer and seller away from the mortgage arrangement and toward the land contract. The agent's commission is also higher on a land-contract transaction since the selling price is usually higher. Occasionally the land contract is chosen instead of the mortgage simply because the buyer or the seller or both want to settle matters quickly. Under these circumstances, the white buyer will accommodate the Negro purchaser with a land contract. This need not be disadvantageous to either party. The seller, to accept a land contract, must be willing to forego a large down payment and accept a good deal of financial risk. But as a matter of fact the Russel Woods seller is generally able to accommodate himself to both of these conditions. As businessmen they are used to accepting risk in a business situation, and the combination of a small down payment, a regular monthly payment, and an easy foreclosure procedure may seem to them an attractive arrangement. Also, as prosperous businessmen, they often are not chained to their property by the need for a high down payment to permit them to finance another house; they generally have resources to add to the down payment they receive for payment on a modern house, or, in many cases, they are old and without children and plan to move into an apartment. And then, too, the land-contract price is usually higher than the price would be for a straight sales transaction, and the seller can, if he chooses, resell his contract to a broker at a 10 to 30 percent discount. This probably means a loss for the seller, but the situation differs from transaction to transaction.

But not all sellers are in such fortunate circumstances, and many of them, required to sell on a land contract or not at all, see themselves without sufficient down payment for a new home, and feel quite hopeless.

THE DYNAMICS OF CHANGE

While there are perhaps common factors in racial change in neighborhoods at any income level, our special case is a middle-class neighborhood where single-family housing predominates, and what we say can only apply to such neighborhoods. There are a number of neighborhoods of roughly similar characteristics in Detroit, and counterparts of these neighborhoods can be found in other American cities as well. Some have gone through the process which was just beginning in Russel Woods in 1955–1956. Thus, the Boston-Edison neighborhood, closer to the center of the city, was in 1948 where Russel Woods was in 1955. It differed only in that the houses were larger and older. Correspondingly, the average income was and is somewhat higher. The present residents of the Boston-Edison area are proud that it is racially mixed after eight years. Its air of luxury and distinction is untouched. Nevertheless, each year sees fewer and fewer white families remaining. In this neighborhood, even before the first nonwhite family moved in, families with school-age children were uncommon, and in 1956 only a small minority of whites with children remained. As we shall see, the role of children is important in the process of change.

What, as we have been able to see them in our study, are the principal factors affecting the transition from white to Negro occupancy in Russel Woods? And can we, by the analysis of these factors, say anything as to the possibility that Russel Woods will be stabilized as a mixed white-Negro middle-class residential neighborhood? This is what we attempt to do in the remainder of this paper.

To begin with, we must point to a condition external to Russel Woods that is necessary for any racial change to take place at all, and that is the pressure of Negro population. More than 200,000 Negroes have moved to Detroit since 1940. All the old boundaries of Negro neighborhoods have been broken in an irrepressible search for additional housing. In 1950 Russel Woods was not far from the expanding area of Negro residence. In what way could it have prevented Negroes from moving in, in view of the expanding Negro population, the fact that this population was excluded from new suburban development, and that these in turn supplied places for a white population moving out?

Other neighborhoods have offered more than the nominal resistance of the civic association in Russel Woods. Conceivably the residents could have formed a strong property owners association with houses bought and sold through the association, as is the case in all-white Rosedale Park in Detroit. This would have been only a temporizing measure, for sooner or later a seller would rebel at the idea of others interfering with his right to sell. A second method, even less effective, would be to stone and threaten the first Negro family. The Detroit Police Department would have stepped in at that point. No matter what the feelings of the individual police officer may be, in this city the police power will enforce the right of a person to live where he wishes. Violence in Russel Woods probably would have delayed or slowed the process of change.

Thus, the stage for neighborhood change is set by large demographic and ecological changes. Russel Woods, as we saw, did not respond with either all-out resistance or panicky flight—two very common reactions to the advance of the area of Negro residence. Instead there was a rather slow beginning of the change-over of houses to Negro occupancy, with the future of the area still open. What then determined that neither resistance nor flight would be the Russel Woods pattern, and set the stage for the possibility—it is no more than the possibility—of an integrated neighborhood?

We must now point to a number of factors, some of which would be true of many middle-class neighborhoods in the path of the expansion of an area of Negro residence, others of them peculiar to Russel Woods, that tended to keep the outward movement moderate:

1. *Undervaluation of houses.*—Taking the structures as they now exist and the neighborhood as it is now constituted, houses in Russel Woods are a bargain compared with what can be obtained in the suburbs and newer parts of the city. A dwelling of the same standard of housing quality and with similar neighborhood facilities in the "Northwest," or the suburbs, costs at least twenty-five to forty thousand dollars. And in view of what one can get for a Russel Woods house, it is often the better part of economic wisdom to stay.

2. *Convenient location.*—For people who work in the central business district, Russel Woods is ideally located. It is still well served by public transportation, while newer areas are only poorly serviced. Nondrivers can live in Russel Woods and still

perform their daily tasks. This is particularly important for some of the older couples now living there. It will doubtless be one of the main reasons many of them will continue to live there.

3. *Religious persuasions.*—Of the 80 percent of the families in Russel Woods who are Jewish, about one-third are of strict Orthodox persuasion. Their demanding religious customs are the center of their world. In their eyes non-Orthodox neighbors, be they Negro or white, Protestant or Catholic, Reformed or Conservative Jews, all are members of the out-group and the differences between them are of no great consequence. Since they have little interest in or awareness of their neighbors, the Orthodox will remain in a neighborhood long after it has lost high social status in the eyes of the general community. Aside from this factor, Orthodox Jews must live within walking distance of a synagogue, for religious laws forbid them to drive to the synagogue on Saturdays and holidays. Russel Woods is within easy walking distance of many synagogues, and is thus an ideal area for the relatively well-to-do Orthodox Jew. Four or five Orthodox rabbis and a number of families have moved into the area within the past few years. However, even the Orthodox are beginning to respond to the same pressures as the other white groups. One of the most Orthodox organizations—a *yeshivah*—has purchased land in one of the "Northwest" Jewish neighborhoods.

4. *Liberal persuasions.*—The location, cost, and type of housing found in Russel Woods draws a small group of "intellectuals." This group consists of university faculty, labor union officials, social workers, and a sprinkling of other professionals. They have strong convictions on racial equality, and believe in integration in housing as in other fields. They have been slower to move out than other white elements.

At the same time, education is of great importance to them and the principal source of their social status. Therefore, they will be most sensitive to any reduction in the educational standards of the schools which their children attend. This is the one reason for moving which is acceptable to them.

Two of these factors—undervaluation of houses and convenience of location—are true of many neighborhoods in the path of expansion; the other two—the presence of a large number of Orthodox Jews and persons of liberal outlook—are more distinctive of Russel Woods and would by themselves explain its failure to resort to either massive resistance or panicky flight. But there are many other factors operating on the community as a whole, and some particularly significant for the liberal segment, that serve to influence people to leave. To this writer, these factors seem more potent in the present balance of forces than those influencing people to stay. We will now consider the factors leading people to leave:

1. *Loss of neighborhood prestige and the attraction of the new.* —Thirty years ago to live in Russel Woods was socially desirable. Even ten years ago the name carried status. Our interviews (they were made before Negroes moved in) show clearly the loss of status by the neighborhood. Almost without exception the informants were able to name more desirable places to move. Among the Jewish families, Huntington Woods, Oak Park, Franklin, Birmingham, and "Northwest" were mentioned. The smaller numbers of non-Jews were equally quick to mention Bloomfield Hills, Birmingham, and Grosse Pointe. At the same time, almost everyone agreed that new houses would be more expensive, and that living in new neighborhoods would become more expensive and complicated. Nevertheless, their friends lived there, although they were hard pressed to name individuals.

In American culture two conflicting ideas dominate our thinking about housing. One is a reverence for the stable, the old, the enduring. In housing this has its expression in the "old homestead," the focus of the family, where generations are born and die. Although this sentiment is losing ground in the urban milieu, it persists in some degree. The other idea, for which Detroit's automobile industry must take some responsibility, is the concept of the yearly "new model." Shiny, new, full of improvements, the new home is a testimony to the material success of the owner. Even a casual reading of the Friday home section of the paper reveals the nature of this appeal—"trade in your old home," "1957 model home," "Formica sink tops." The same advertisement more often than not says little or nothing of available schools, shopping, transportation, and the like. Not only is the dwelling unit itself "glorified" but the entire concept of "suburb" carries with it implications of well-being and success.

The net effect is a powerful pull out of a neighborhood of small prestige to one which signifies that its residents are achieving the American dream.

I would suggest that many of the residents of Russel Woods were not "pushed" out of the neighborhood by any feelings of prejudice against Negroes, but were "pulled" out by the American dream. For them the arrival of Negroes served as an excuse to invest in that stainless steel, formica, and plywood-paneled "dream house" and believe at the same time that they were acting wisely from an economic point of view.

2. *Race prejudice.*—We have said nothing in this report up to now about race prejudice. Is this playing a role in leading people to leave? Certainly it is: if there were no prejudice against Negroes in American society the reaction of Russel Woods residents would be very different. But its relationship to the outward movement is complex and indirect. Jews and liberals, the inhabitants of Russel Woods, have little prejudice themselves. They believe that Negroes and whites can live together, they are aware that the incoming Negroes are people much like themselves, who are well-to-do and well-educated, and who will be good neighbors, concerned with the quality of the school, with the character of the neighborhood, and so on.

And yet, despite this, there is the feeling that, regardless of what kind of Negroes are moving in, there will remain a wide gulf between them and the old residents: there is indeed a limited degree of shared experience in education, occupation, and religion, even though both groups are, generally speaking, "middle-class." This fear of being surrounded by people who are quite different is obviously stronger when the different people are low-status Negroes—but this is as far as the influence of anything that may be called race prejudice goes.

3. *Community institutions and facilities.*—More important than "race prejudice" in influencing the movement out of Russel Woods is its growing inability to support a complete set of servicing institutions and facilities. This is also true of Oakman Boulevard and the Boston-Edison area.

Dexter Boulevard, the shopping area closest to Russel Woods, is losing many stores as merchants follow customers to the suburbs. By leaving, a merchant catering to a middle-class clientele completes a circular reaction. Because there are fewer stores, more families leave. Then more merchants move and the trend is accelerated. On Dexter, empty stores are common today. When they are rented, it is for an establishment of lower prestige. The street is marred with unkempt stores, trash, tangled traffic, and garish signs. Actually, the street was never a first-class shopping center either in size or quality of stores. At least part of the decline of the street has resulted from the increased income and changing taste of the people in Russel Woods, which have led them to shop elsewhere. But part of it is owing to the feeling that the incoming Negro population will not have the income or the taste to lead them to patronize the old establishments.

Of all the neighborhood-influencing institutions, by far the most crucial is the school. Here, small and seemingly remote facts have an important bearing on the total situation. Almost half of the families in Russel Woods have children. The people who are the most "liberal" on the subject of living in mixed neighborhoods are precisely the ones who are most sensitive to the quality of the schools. All of Russel Woods is in the same grammar school district. The school district includes more than Russel Woods—perhaps half of the population of the school comes from areas immediately adjoining Russel Woods, all of distinctly lower economic character. Of this half, about one-third comes from the area immediately south of Russel Woods, a poor district now mostly Negro. At present the school is considered to be among the best in the city, but many of our respondents felt its days were numbered. Many of the Negroes who are moving into Russel Woods itself are childless. This means a decline in school enrollment of middle-class children. It is common for the residents to say "I'll stay until the school declines"—the assumption being that it will decline.

The decline of the school is important to these parents and their fears are not without foundation. In another middle-class changing neighborhood the school, which had been of excellent reputation, became markedly less desirable when, because of the small proportion of children among the new Negro residents, children were brought in by bus from several lower-class areas. Teachers asked for transfers and standards declined sharply. Russel Woods residents fear this will occur in their school. They may be right, but at present the school is well filled.

The intermediate and high school situation is more complicated. There are two possible intermediate schools and two possible high schools for families in the western portion of Russel Woods. One high school and one intermediate school are located together in a lower economic area about one mile to the east. In former years the majority of the student body was Jewish. The entire area from which these schools draw their students has become largely mixed, and so have the schools. In addition to the scholastic aspect, the parents express concern about the dating and social possibilities. Also, the "right kind" of people now attend another high school "northwest" (actually four miles to the northwest). This high school has replaced the older high school, and is now "the Jewish high school." Boys and girls from Russel Woods are not in this school district, but this can be solved by moving "northwest."

As mentioned before, there is actually another choice of both high school and intermediate school. These schools are located to the west. The students there are middle-class and lower-middle-class and are not Jewish. Although these schools are considered satisfactory from a scholastic point of view, the Jewish residents of Russel Woods are fearful of too many contacts with "gentiles." This introduces another important factor.

4. *The ethnic factor.*—The Orthodox Jews of whom we spoke earlier are in the minority in Russel Woods. Most Jews are either Conservative, Reform, or without formal attachment. The ethnic and cultural identification of these elements with the Jewish group remain powerful but they have little feeling for the Orthodox religious institutions clustered around Russel Woods. About 90 percent of Detroit Jewry live in a few areas within the city proper and only two suburbs, which are known as Jewish suburbs. Only about 30 percent of the families in these suburbs are Jewish but as time goes on the non-Jewish families tend to move out and be replaced by Jewish families.

Both suburbs have a powerful positive attraction for Jews. An important factor in this situation is the security Jews feel about an area which is "clearly Jewish" in character. There is also the strong desire to have the children meet other Jewish children. The same might be observed for other ethnic groups, but this self-segregation is probably particularly strong among Jews.

5. *Increasing prosperity.*—This is a rather obvious force tending to drive people to the newer, more expensive parts of the metropolitan area. Many of the present residents of Russel Woods are quite prosperous. Undoubtedly, if all other factors were held constant there still would be a number of families whose increased income and wealth would tend to influence them to seek more expensive housing in appropriate areas.

6. *Age problems.*—As against today's suburbs, with their high proportion of young parents and their growing children, Russel Woods shows a high proportion of elderly couples, and a comparatively low proportion of young children. The absence of large numbers of peers creates some difficulties for children and their parents, and the suburbs and newer parts of the city, where children and institutions catering to children abound, become attractive.

Then, too, the large houses are not really suitable for an elderly couple or a widow or a widower. About one-quarter of the houses in Russel Woods are now occupied by either one or two persons over fifty years of age. Many of the older people have lived there for a number of years and have a strong attachment to the neighborhood; hence, this is also a staying force. However, death or illness often brings an end to the household.

7. *Real estate and financing structure.*—Real estate agencies make money by selling houses. Naturally, they push a turnover in any neighborhood. Occasionally they are unethical, but even if not it is to their advantage to sell as much real estate as possible. The structure of financing for housing also acts as a strong force pulling families to new developments, by offering low down payments on easy terms, while at the same time it is a pushing force by classifying old neighborhoods as second-class financial risks. There is in effect an institutionalization of practices which favor new neighborhoods and new construction to the detriment of older parts of the city.

8. *Loss of property values.*—The fear of loss of property values as a factor in Russel Woods has been mentioned only in passing. Although it cannot be ignored, it appears to be but a minor element in the minds of the majority of persons. At the present writing, houses in Russel Woods are still selling at comfortable prices, roughly the same as or more than five years ago. Opinion

is divided as to whether there will be some drop. If the experience of other neighborhoods in the past is used as a guide, and it is, there has been no measurable drop in property values after Negroes have moved in. The drop, if any, occurred a number of years before, when the neighborhood lost its status with the real estate and financial sources and was classified as an undesirable area for liberal financing arrangements.

9. *New features in new housing.*—The more spacious home, typical of Russel Woods, has several serious disadvantages. Resident servants are now rare and costly and there is much housework to be done in this older type house. The heating bills run between $200 and $400 per year. The two- or three-story arrangement is less preferred today. The houses are drafty, as they are mostly uninsulated. Unless rebuilt at heavy cost (and many have been), the kitchens are hardly modern. Some residents, however, prefer older houses despite such drawbacks. Others have a strong desire to enjoy the technological improvements in new housing. It is not easy to tell just when this reason has a validity of its own apart from the prestige elements of new neighborhoods.

10. *Financial gain by quick sale.*—A few people in Russel Woods have put their houses on sale with the hope that Negroes would pay a premium price. Their efforts have not met with success because they misjudge today's housing market. Negroes at present have enough choices to be cautious in their housing buys. This does not preclude an occasional real estate man's finding or even seeking out a "policy hit" (gambling winner) who can be sold a house at rather more than careful homeseekers will pay. But with the relief of extreme housing pressure in Detroit, chances of quick sales at large premiums have just about vanished. This does not stop a few people from hoping, but it is a minor factor in the total picture.

CONCLUSION

We have described a changing neighborhood situation and attempted to explain why there was little or no conflict. We have evaluated the forces which might keep the former residents there and the forces leading them to move out. The latter forces, tending to make the neighborhood completely Negro, are the stronger, in our judgment. The presence of a strong liberal-minded element, we have suggested, will tend to reduce the tendency to either violent resistance or flight. But there are powerful forces that will lead even such groups to move away, and prevent the development of stable interracial neighborhoods. The analysis of some of these factors may suggest some social measures that may be helpful in encouraging the development of such neighborhoods.

EPILOGUE—RUSSEL WOODS, OCTOBER, 1958

Today I drove through Russel Woods. In the brilliant autumn sunshine the neighborhood looked more prosperous and better kept than when I first saw it in 1950. The only disturbing note was the ever-present moving van. It was standing in front of the door of a family who were one of the original residents of the neighborhood. This brought sharply to mind that the neighborhood is now more than 50 percent Negro. The social change which was anticipated in our earlier remarks has taken place more rapidly than expected. Russel Woods is now defined as a Negro neighborhood.

Practically everyone who relates himself closely to the American success ethic has moved away. A few who have highly individual reasons, such as a wife who does not drive, a business that is tantalizingly close to Russel Woods, or children completing school within a year or two, are not yet thinking of moving. While some of the Orthodox Jews have moved, some are staying because a complete set of their institutions still exists nearby. However, a new community is being prepared for them in a suburb to the northwest. Orthodox Jewish institutions are springing up in the suburban area, and shortly it will be possible for the transition to take place smoothly.

The "intellectuals," too, are leaving, even if with a certain amount of guilt. In many cases an important element in their decision to leave Russel Woods is the fact they have encountered this situation two or three or four times before, and they are emotionally exhausted. Some of them have leapfrogged intermediate areas to the middle-class and upper-middle-class suburbs where the possibility of invasion is remote.

The Negroes, to the best of my knowledge, have curiously mixed feelings. On one hand, although they have suspected this would happen, they feel hurt and chagrined. On the other hand, there is a certain relief in seeing a new Negro family move in. It automatically resolves a situation which must be psychologically as difficult for the Negro as it is for the white.

Summarizing the situation, a little more than three years after the first Negro family moved into Russel Woods, it can be said that there is little chance of its remaining a stable mixed neighborhood. It will become increasingly Negro. Meanwhile the Negroes who subscribe to the American success ethic will in turn have pulled up stakes. The ultimate end point of this process depends on ideals and values which have not yet been distilled out of the contrary and conflicting attitudes and opinions held individually and collectively in our present-day urban society.

Index